Going on the Turn

Also by Danny Baker

Going to Sea in a Sieve
Going Off Alarming

Going on the Turn

A MEMOIR

WEIDENFELD & NICOLSON

First published in Great Britain in 2017
by Weidenfeld & Nicolson

1 3 5 7 9 10 8 6 4 2

A CIP catalogue record for this book
is available from the British Library.

ISBN 978 0297 8701 3 5

Typeset by Input Data Services Ltd, Somerset

Printed and bound by CPI Group (UK) Ltd, Croydon, CR0 4YY

Weidenfeld & Nicolson

The Orion Publishing Group Ltd
Orion House
5 Upper Saint Martin's Lane
London, WC2H 9EA

www.orionbooks.co.uk

MIX
Paper from
responsible sources
FSC® C104740

This book is for Wendy, Bonnie, Sonny and Mancie.
Of course it is. Everything is.

Almighty thanks to Alan Samson at Weidenfeld & Nicolson whose
barely suppressed sighs and patient drumming of fingers as I offered
various phantom deadlines on this mighty work became as a
mother's heartbeat to me.

'It is impossible to enjoy idling thoroughly unless one has plenty
of work to do.' – Jerome K. Jerome

Frederick Joseph Baker (1928-2008)
Elizabeth Kathleen Baker (1931-2017)
Michael Edward Baker (1952-1982)

Contents

Prologue

In 1968 ITV broadcast an episode of the children's programme *Lost in Space* in which Will, the young boy of the family marooned on a faraway planet, discovered that the image he saw when he looked into a mirror was not simply a reflection of himself but another 'him' entirely, living a separate life on the other side of the glass. I cannot tell you how profound an effect this had on me. It struck me as not only entirely plausible, but just about the most mind-blowing thing I had learned since my brother explained to me that our parents were not related like the rest of us but simply a boy and girl who had got together by chance. That information pole-axed me for days afterwards and similarly, after the space show was over, I sat on the edge of our settee so mentally exploded that I could not quite conjure up the necessary impetus to lift my rear end fully away from the fabric of our three-piece suite. In truth, it always took extra effort to haul oneself away from the sort of deep, heavy sofas favoured by my parents; huge mauve monolithic structures that provided the furniture world's answer to Al Capone's bulletproof car.

So for about two minutes I hovered there, bum slightly raised and vacillating above the base cushion like a jockey entering the home stretch still with a chance of third place. My mind was whirling. How could I have gotten to fully ten years old without somebody alerting me to this parallel universe lurking just a veneer away, complete with a parallel me. A twin! I always suspected I was – that must be why so many of my contemporaries struck me as slightly backward misfits. But how to make contact with me/him?

I figured that in order to get this other self to break cover I would need to undertake an extended period of staring deep into my own reflection – and for this, absolute privacy would be paramount. The last thing I needed was my father catching me in the act as I ogled myself, trance-like, nose a half-inch from the full-length glass in his wardrobe door, murmuring, 'It's all right, you can come out now.' That would be as bad as the time he caught me kissing a photo of Dusty Springfield in, coincidentally, the *Daily Mirror*. On that occasion I had bluffed my way through the trauma by insisting I had dropped a piece of chewing gum on to the paper and was retrieving it, no-hands style. For about two hours afterwards I kept walking into his line of sight while theatrically over-chewing a non-existent Wrigley's so he would know how much that piece of gum meant to me. I thought I was carrying it off brilliantly until he said, 'You're fucking gone, you are! I hope there's room in the van when it comes round tonight.' (The 'van' was a vehicle the old man often referred to; according to him, lunatic asylums toured the streets looking for new inmates much in the way rag and bone men sought out broken-down gas cookers.)

Finally gathering enough wherewithal to escape the pull of our settee's mass, I hurried along the short passage that led to the downstairs toilet where a fair-sized mirror hung on the wall behind the cistern. Sliding the toilet door closed behind me, I leaned across the fixture itself and stared into the convex oval glass. And there I was. Or rather, there HE was. For quite some time we regarded each other, neither of us making the slightest move. I figured if I gave it long enough, 'he' would eventually crack and by dint of his flickering lip or the infinitesimal raising of an eyebrow, we could begin our secret relationship.

In the programme, Will had crossed into Mirror World right off the bat and gone off with his reflection to have an adventure. Though this was my ultimate aim, I was sensible enough to realize that it would probably require a few more trips to the toilet before we could embark on thrills like that. In fact, even though I tried to communicate telepathically so hard that my eyes were literally bulging out of my head, nothing happened – which was doubly disappointing, seeing as he appeared to be doing the exact same in trying to contact me. In the end I relaxed my stare and, in a soupy tone of voice that I hoped would indicate total empathy with his reticence, I said, 'I'll be here if ever you want me to come and play.'

As soon as I said it, I was jolted back into the here and now. All thoughts of a Mirror World shattered in an instant as I literally hauled in my neck and stood, hands clenched in horror. How loud had I said that? The prospect of having been overheard was all too real; not only did this toilet stand a mere two feet from our constantly occupied kitchen, but its frosted-glass window was all that separated any occupant from the communal council estate walkway outside. I often remarked on what a basic design flaw it was that, when we were playing football in the square, should one of the little net curtains on these 'smallest rooms' not be fully drawn, it was hard not to notice the fuzzy outline of, say, Lou Brimble at number 13 taking a thundering slash. Understandably, all the women who lived in our block, when seeking to take their ease, would usually wait until the upstairs bathrooms were vacant.

So any stray noises issuing from these frankly exposed fixtures had to be carefully guarded against – doubly so in the case of the wistful bilge I had just broadcast. In those unenlightened days, any passing police officer overhearing the phrase 'I'll be here if ever you want me to come and play' coyly emanating from an open lavatory window was good enough for a couple of years in Pentonville.

One such tragic case lived in a block called Moland Mead at the far end of our estate. A robust and popular part of my father's set that drank in the cavernous Jolly Gardeners pub on Rotherhithe New Road, he was nevertheless always known as 'Billy the Bummer'. Appalling, of course, and he had received this distressing epithet long before he was imprisoned merely for being gay. He was addressed thus, if you can imagine such a thing, with little intended malice. Recounting a previous night's card game at the pub, friends of my dad might say, 'You missed right out there, Spud. It was a busy table – fuckin' money going across it! There was George the Fish, Alfie Says, Long John, the Tumble brothers, Billy the Bummer . . .'

The point is, shocking though such casual oppression seems to us now, Billy wasn't ostracized by the community – only the law. After he was sentenced following a sting at some public toilets near London Bridge, the general reaction was, 'Silly fucker! How many times he been told he was going to come unstuck if he kept on with that?' In other words, much the same as it would have been had Billy been a kleptomaniac or an anarchist. When he was released, he came back to his chair in the card school with the usual tales of who he saw in the nick that the others might know and stories of the feuds, fights and fucking about that takes place on any B Wing. Who knows how it really was for him? Like every other aspect of those times and that culture, nobody made an open show of the personal. Besides, in the decades since, the lives and prejudices of the old working class have been so manipulated and inflated by an establishment that seeks to sow division via a guilt that springs chiefly from within, it seems almost irrelevant. Today the demonization is total: all poor people are thick, wicked and ignorant. And they're to blame.

Little of this fiery polemic was troubling me as I finally broadcast my exit from the downstairs chamber with a smart flush on the chain. I may even have added a superfluous puff on the air freshener to further cement the alibi. In the event, there was no need. Nobody had noted my stay in the bog – it would be many years before I heard anybody use the twee term 'loo' – and I slumped back into the reinforced settee cushions resigned to the idea that all portals to alien worlds were closed to me for the time being.

Now here's the thing. Following that doomed leap of faith in 1968, I found that I couldn't walk away from any mirror, anywhere, without taking a few seconds to smile broadly into it before making my exit. And when I say smile, I mean a real raised-eyebrow cartoon beam. Often accompanied by a sincere, 'How's it going with you?'

On the few occasions I have forgotten to do this, or even suspect I may have, I will go back and correct the oversight. Even in the middle of the night, if I get up and go to the bathroom I will go back immediately if I think I signed off from my reflection without a cheery grin.

On my eventual reappearance after this return trip, my wife will groggily say, 'Did you forget to smile at yourself?' When I confirm this, she will sigh. Then we will both lie there, now fully awake and turning over this pointless ritual from different ends of a spectrum that runs from infuriation to embarrassment. In truth, it's not a spectrum – those are the only two available emotions. I leave you to figure out which of us is feeling what.

I don't want you to think this is some sort of OCD tic or that I am still waiting for my invite to become the modern-day Alice. I do it chiefly because it's cheerful and harmless and, if you push me on it, I also think it may have helped shape my fortunes. Had I not smiled into every mirror I have passed since 1968, I genuinely think my life might have turned out very differently. Oh, I know what you're saying now. You're saying, 'Well, how do you like that? This old coot has left it till his third book before letting us in on the fact he's been as mad as Ajax all along.'

Not so fast! You'll be relieved to know I did stop grinning at myself in mirrors on 1 October 2010.

Why? Well, as I'll explain later, it was partly the fault of Spike Milligan. For now though, I think you'll agree what happened that day was a pretty unequivocal signal to put a stop to the whole vacuous ritual.

It was a few minutes after 1 p.m. on that Friday and I had just put our house phone down following a devastating exchange that had lasted barely thirty seconds. This is how it had played out:

'Hello!'

'Is that Mr Baker?'

'Yes it is . . .'

'Hello, this is Mr D'Souza's secretary at Blackheath Hospital.'

'Oh, right!'

'You came in this morning for some tests on your neck?'

'Yes, I did.'

'Mr D'Souza has asked if you could come back.'

'Back? Yes, sure. I mean, when's good?'

'Today. As soon as possible really.'

'Today?'

'Yes. And could you bring someone with you.'

'Right. OK. Sure. Right. Bye.'

Could you bring someone with you.

That was the phrase that condemned any hope that the call had been routine. I very slowly put the phone back in the cradle and then stood staring at myself in the circular white-wood framed mirror above it on the wall. I did not smile. I suddenly did not know how to. I didn't seem to know anything any more. I just stared into my own blank eyes in a way you never have to do in everyday life. Mirrors are for checking hair, make-up, shirt colours and whether your silly expression might pass for sober. Mirrors, it suddenly seemed to me, despite all those decades of my secret service, were there for everything else in your life's picture other than actually seeing yourself. But now there was nothing else to see. I became transfixed on the very centre of my jet-black pupils, trying to even see beyond them, trying to glimpse inside, trying to see if, whoever I now was, was still in there.

Then Wendy's voice called, surreally normal, from the kitchen downstairs.

'Who was that, Dan? Dan? Who was it?'

I didn't answer.

Could you bring someone with you.

Now I heard Wendy was making her way up to see me. She entered the front room and, like you can, immediately sensed something was not right.

Could you bring someone with you.

'Dan. Dan? Why you looking like that? Who was it?'

(I'm The) Urban Spaceman

By 1996 I wasn't a TV star any more. I am aware of course that the very phrase 'TV star' now has a wonderfully antiquated grandeur that ranks alongside such boasts as having been a noted pavement photographer or champion Charleston dancer in one's youth. Yet, may a million long-since recycled copies of *Radio* and *TV Times* show that a TV star is indeed what I was for about four years in the early nineties. The previous instalments of these memoirs will have explained how this unlikely sensation came to be and how quickly the general public realized what a horrible mistake they had made. Their panic passed relatively quickly, however, and by 1996, without question, my faded national celebrity had been returned to store. Unlike today when you can drop a water bomb out of any window and soak dozens of content creators making programmes for the Internet, twenty years ago, once your TV heat-index hit a temperature similar to that of the Piltdown Man, there was little else for you to do, nowhere else for you to go.

The truth was that I had become overexposed and old hat. Really old hat. A hat so old it made Clement Attlee's homburg look like a modern millinery breakthrough. Television was now entering its last great boom, one that would ultimately lead to its final bust, and the main catalyst for this combined revolution and suicide note was my great friend Chris Evans. Chris's shaking-the-medium-by-the-scruff-of-the-neck approach to live TV on both *The Big Breakfast* and *Don't Forget Your Toothbrush* had made most other mainstream TV look positively arthritic. His trademark copper-coloured coiffure shocked and illuminated the medium and came to signify all that

7

was new and daring. Me? I was literally and metaphorically going bald. Thankfully, I wasn't going broke, even when the big contracts dried up. The prudent financial system I had lived by since leaving school meant I could still live like a king – providing it was one of those long-exiled Balkan kings sometimes exposed by newspapers as they stand on the pavement in Earls Court selling shoelaces from a tray.

One of the last flickering embers of my onscreen celebrity prior to this time was being asked to deputize for Chris whenever he took a break from *The Big Breakfast*. I'd like to think this was because of some lingering public demand, but in reality several of the *Big Breakfast* production team had got their first break in TV a decade previously on the *Six O'Clock Show* on which I'd been the rising star and their clubbable pal. They knew I was a safe bet to bellow away on live TV for the six weeks until the wonder kid returned without needing any emotional wet-nursing, and I could be trusted not to indulge in some sly personal grandstanding in the hope that the gig would become permanent. I hadn't actually seen Chris since our days at Greater London Radio in the late eighties. We occasionally spoke on the phone and he had recorded a video message when I was the subject of *This Is Your Life*, thus avoiding a bullet on what might well be the most drawn-out night in television history.

Here's the thing about being the subject of *This Is Your Life*. It is magnificent. Every second of the programme is like supping from the elixir of life justification. Think about it. You sit in a comfortable chair while everyone you ever knew has to queue up to declare to the nation what a benevolent genius you are. Then they all stand and deliver you a standing ovation for minutes on end. This in itself would be a giddy enough experience, but the idea that at least 80 per cent of them – mainly your corralled legions of friends simply there for the free booze – are being FORCED to do this by the television people makes the experience so heightened you never want it to end. As you walk onstage from behind the sliding doors at the top of the show, accompanied by the famous four-note fanfare, all you can see are legions of clenched teeth protruding from the mouths

8

of everyone in your circle, each of them bowing to the orders of the floor manager who has instructed them to treat you like a Living God. *And they have no choice.* Similar body language can be seen in old footage of Communist Party rallies in the Soviet Union where, if you failed to applaud old Joe Stalin like he was Bruce Springsteen playing the opening bars of 'Thunder Road', you immediately had all your mail redirected to Mattress 7, The Gulag, Bleaksville. To make my own enforced 'Hallelujah Chorus' even sweeter, everybody had been hanging around waiting for me for over three hours, rounding off months of subterfuge, humbug and farce.

My wife had been the one who let slip that the show was planning to surprise me. One afternoon in our garden in Deptford, Wendy said, 'Oh, I forgot to tell you! While you were out yesterday I got a call asking me if I would meet up with the *This Is Your Life* team to talk about doing you on the show. I thought it was a joke, but it wasn't!'

Now the one thing I knew for sure about *TIYL* was that if the subject got a whiff of suspicion that they were being lined up for it, that particular episode would be abandoned immediately. Yet here was Wendy, casually deadheading roses, telling me that I better get a suit pressed because in a few weeks I was going to be given what was then still seen as the ultimate show business accolade. She would have known I am not a fan of surprises. This stems from when I was six years old and my mother picked me up from infant school one lunchtime saying that she had a 'really special surprise' for me indoors.

In my tiny fevered mind I had a good idea what this surprise was going to be. The previous Saturday, while out shopping with her in Southwark Park Road, I had made it clear that though my young life was, in the main, a full, rich and happy one, it had at its core a terrible sadness. A sadness that could only be assuaged by the purchase of a miniature knight on horseback that, by pure chance, Grant's Toy Shop had on display in its front window when we last passed it. And, why, wasn't that Grant's we were fast approaching now? If anything, Mum quickened her pace as we walked along that stretch of pavement and her rather terse pronouncement, 'You've got plenty of soldiers, you don't need any more,' clued me in that here was our old friend the pretend refusal. Plainly she'd either already bought it for me or was planning to return shortly to buy it, because . . . well, that's the sort of sweet and silly subterfuge mums like to indulge in when presenting gifts to their young ones. So I pretended to understand while inwardly becoming very excited by Sir Percival's imminent addition to the gleaming ranks of noblemen in the box beneath my bed. And now, barely forty-eight hours later, here it was: a 'special surprise' to accompany whatever it was she had knocked up for lunch in the forty-five minutes she had away from the factory floor. I prepared myself to feign the appropriate reaction so as not to spoil Mum's enjoyment of the big moment.

When we arrived indoors I acted as though I'd completely for-gotten her promise of a gift, nonchalantly wolfing down dinner – alphabet soup and buttered roll, as it turned out – and gaily laughing at *The Flower Pot Men* while using my peripheral vision to see if she was reaching into her bag to suddenly reveal Good Sir Knight.

'Come on – I better be getting you back to school,' she then declared. Oh, well played, I thought. If this was brinksmanship, she was taking it right to the wire. Lolling my arms into my anorak I stood distractedly while she knelt before me, attending to the zip. Now was the moment. 'Oh yes,' I drawled like Clifton Webb in one of his more distracted performances, 'didn't you say something about, what was it now . . . a surprise?'

Mum's face started in shock. 'Oh, good boy,' she said, rising to make her way down the short passage by our front door. 'Blimey, scatty cow I am, been looking forward to giving you this!'

While she was gone, I decided to change the knight's name from Sir Percival to Sir Lionheart. Already I was picturing him at the head of an army of fellow knights, leading our long-planned assault on Tommy Hodges' American Civil War soldiers at the earliest opportunity.

Mum rounded the corner from the kitchen holding what appeared to be a small box; *too* small a box for my liking. Indeed, it appeared to be a matchbox, and not even one of those that housed the then popular brand of toy cars under that name. This was an actual matchbox.

'There you are – open that!' she said.

As I fumbled with it, my mouth was dry, my hands shaking in confusion. What was happening? What had gone wrong? If there was what I hoped in here, then he would have to be the shortest knight of the year. Sir Pee Wee. Sir Lance-a-little.

Sliding the box open, I first saw a sliver of green leaf and then the minute shiny domed body of a sleeping ladybird.

'See it?' said Mum brightly. 'He was on a milk bottle outside this morning and look – it's black with red dots, not the other way round. You don't often see them, do ya? I thought, "I'll save him till Danny gets back."'

There was no preventing it; hot tears of crashing disappointment welled up behind my disbelieving eyes and, as I blinked to clear my vision, they erupted clear of the sockets, splashing down on to the dormant mini-beast. With reddened cheeks and by now having lost control of my facial muscles, I tried my best to mask the dreadful anticlimax of the moment. To make it worse, Mum began blaming herself.

'Oh no! Did I build it up too much? Oh, what a shame. Sorry, mate, I thought you'd like it.'

I thought you'd like it. Even now that breaks my heart. I did. I did like it and it was a lovely Mum-type thing to have done. Under any other circumstances a perfectly good ladybird, especially one with reversed markings, would have impressed the hell out of me. But I had allowed myself to get carried away with visions of medieval perfection and, with the best will in the world, you can't give even the most rugged ladybird a name like Sir Lionheart and expect it to vanquish Tommy Hodges' crack cavalry division in an ambush at the bomb site this coming Saturday. Then she made it even worse.

'Oh . . . I wish I hadn't done it now. What's the matter with me? Sorry, boy. Oh, I do feel a fool.'

Well that finished me off. I went from my barely contained Stan

Laurel-style upset to something that even Lucille Ball at her roaring broadest might have deemed OTT. And, next, wouldn't you know it, both of us were crying. There we sat, on the bottom of the stairs in the passage, holding each other and trying to articulate who was more sorry for the debacle.

So, as I say, don't talk to me about surprises.

Back in the garden in Deptford, as Wendy continued the slash-and-burn with her secateurs, it struck me that being 'surprised' by the bright lights, adoring fans and the Big Red Book might be just the thing to finally bring closure on the Great Ladybird Trauma of 1963.

'So when am I being done?' I asked, now relishing being in on the gag.

'Done?' she responded.

'*This Is Your Life*! Ha! You know you'll have to sit there on the night like the Good Wife, patting my hand and saying, "My hero!"'

Wendy blew a few blackfly from a stem. 'Oh well, it's not happening now, is it? I told them what you always said I should say: that it's a corny embarrassment of a programme that should have been buried along with Eamonn Andrews when he went.'

I bristled with rising alarm. '*I* said that?? When did I ever say that?'

'You say it every time it's on! You hate *This Is Your Life*. "How can anyone do that?" is what you say. You're as bad as your dad with it.'

There was something in this. I had, as the years passed, taken on my father's characteristic of getting tremendous pleasure in deriding certain popular programmes. Given that a lot of the nation probably did this to most of the vehicles I haunted their houses with, I felt it was fair game. And yes, *This Is Your Life* was one of the two shows my father particularly targeted. The other was Hughie Green's *Opportunity Knocks*.

'Who watches this? Who could like this?' was his constant mantra for the entire sixty-minute duration of that cheap and cheerful talent show. Hopeful singers barely got through the opening notes of their number before he was calling for them to 'Fuck off back to the pub!'

Ventriloquists never got a chance to deliver any repartee; before the dummy's mouth opened, Spud would be deriding the state of it.

'Fucking hell's he got on his arm? That's a disgrace to go on telly with; must have cost him about eight bob in a junk shop – look at it! He must reckon we're all backward.'

A troupe of dancing girls would be greeted with: 'Why have we got to sit through three minutes of this?' And the obligatory shot of Hughie benevolently looking on as they pranced would have him roaring, 'Look at him, that dirty old bastard – I know what he's thinking.'

But it was comedians that tried his – admittedly non-existent – patience the most. Comics didn't even have time to get to the microphone before Spud would be in full flow.

All acts on *Opportunity Knocks* had someone, usually a family member, who would be interviewed by Hughie before the turn they were sponsoring arrived onstage. If it was a comedian, here's how the exchange would be received. Let's say the sponsor is a woman in her seventies:

Hughie: Tell us who you are and where you're from, my darling.
Dad: Fucking "darling"!
Woman: I'm Joyce Bartlett from Esher.
Dad: Esher! She must have bundles.
Hughie: And how old are you, my lovely?
Joyce: I'm seventy-one. [Applause.]
Dad: Fuckin' looks about hundred and two, her.
Hughie: And who have you brought for us to meet tonight,
    Joyce?
Joyce: My son-in-law, Georgie.
Hughie: And I hear he's a very funny man, isn't he?
Dad: Oh no! NO! Oh please, not a comedian, we're only two acts
    in. Fuckin' hell, ain't there nothing on the other side?
Me: Terry Scott.
Dad: Oh that's it, we're trapped. Trapped!

Decades later, the show *Gogglebox* would become a hit by filming reactions such as this. Spud's running commentary was every bit as entertaining, giving a terrific vitality to otherwise dull programmes.

It was in the 1990s that British TV began its patronizing obsession with getting audiences 'more involved' in its piss-poor product, an abdication of responsibility that has now surely reached its zenith. Modern producers must believe their own lifelong desire to be part of the media is universal and that people really could give two fucks about being 'part of' their rotten shows. Dad's reaction was proof that working-class families had always felt themselves part of the TV theatre, catcalling from the stalls just as they had in music hall, deriding the products of an industry that seemed utterly removed from anything approaching hard graft.

Dad lived long enough to see the rise of today's pea-brained, deceitful phenomena of 'audience-led' shows and summed it up on first sight. As a glib voice-over banged on, 'We want to hear your voice. Be part of it! *You* decide! It's your show!' Spud growled, 'Well if it's *our* fucking show, how comes you're the only ponces getting paid for it?'

It perhaps would have startled the old man to learn that the only person I ever met who could out-swear him was, in fact, Hughie Green. To give him his due, Hughie Green is by some distance the foulest-mouthed person I have ever met – and scholars of these journals will know that that is quite some claim. He was also one of the strangest . . .

I know, I know. Do we need another diversion at this juncture to illustrate these facts, or shall we just press on with how I ended up on *This Is Your Life*? (After all, this is *your* book, I want *you* to be part of it.)

OK. The votes are in. Peculiar Hughie Green and his foul mouth it is.

So one day I'm indoors and the phone goes. This was during the period when I was on TV *a lot*. Immediately I recognize the nasal drawl of Canada's most divisive export.

'Danny Baker, I wanna introduce myself: my name is Hughie Green.'

I believe I actually said 'wow' in response.

'Now don't slam the phone down,' he continued. 'I know what you're thinking: What does this fucking washed-up old cunt want?'

I promise you, that's exactly what he said. You don't easily forget a sentence like that, particularly when it turns out Hughie Green has an uncanny ability to read exactly what is running through your mind.

'Let me get right to it – you're probably banging two whores at the same time right now, so I won't keep you from them for long. I'm kidding. Listen, I want ten minutes of your time, face to fuckin' face. Or ass-to-ass, if that's your thing. Can you do that for a broken-down old prick like me?'

Perhaps I should point out for any younger readers that Hughie Green was, for much of the fifties through to the eighties, the very personification of decent, upstanding family-values TV. His shows were homespun, sentimental and safe, while he himself was widely lampooned as an unctuous, sanctimonious old cornball whose catchphrase, 'And I mean that most sincerely', was mimicked by all and sundry. In short, no one ever mistook Hughie Green for what they now call 'the original gangsta'. Yet here he was, coming over as one who had verbally schooled Ozzy Osbourne.

After briefly wondering if I was the victim of a hoax call being taped for some zoo-format breakfast radio show, I shakily asked him if he could let me know what was on his mind over the phone.

'Jesus! If I could tell you over the fucking phone I wouldn't be asking to pull your dick in person, would I? Fucking Jesus and Mary! They let any cocksucker become a star these fucking days, I see! I'm only kidding again, Dan. Seriously, I have the TV idea of the fucking century for you, all ready to go. So, how about next week, you lucky little shitheel?'

Again, I am not laying this on for effect. I did flag him as the Champion Curser of my lifetime and, if anything, I am missing out a few expletives. His intimidating overtures continued for several minutes, until finally I agreed to meet him at his apartment near Baker Street the following Monday. Who wouldn't be intrigued by such an invite?

It turned out he lived in a large flat on the third floor of an impressive 1930s block. Hughie answered the door with his familiar grin and pop-eyed countenance that had pretty much been ever present on ITV until around a decade previously. His handshake was crushing. The place was expensively furnished, leaning toward the traditionally masculine with leather-studded sofas, high bookshelves and quite a bit of military paraphernalia. (He had served with great distinction in the Canadian Airforce.)

'I got in some Special Brew beer because I figured that's what a cockney son-of-a-bitch like you would drink!' he beamed.

He was already pulling a can open when I told him that I thought Special Brew tasted like the broth of curdled moose dung – a reference from his homeland that I thought he'd appreciate.

'Moose? Hey, don't throw me in with all those other backward maple-leaf motherfuckers, I been here a fuckin' long time. So whaddya want, you little fag – a glass of milk?'

All of this was being said with nothing but warmth and camaraderie, but I had never heard such relentless machismo outside of a few Jack Nicholson movies. He began pouring the Special Brew, a beer I genuinely dislike.

'Anyway, shut the fuck up with the whining, because you are going to need a goddamned good stiff drink one way or the other, my friend. This show I have got for you is going to knock you right on your ass – biggest fucking thing ever to hit TV.'

He handed me the vile glassful and sat in a chair directly opposite me, leaning forward until our foreheads were no more than three inches apart. He was smiling broadly yet inscrutably, his head nodding as though he had me exactly where he wanted me. For quite some time he never said a word. I must say I was inwardly wobbling a bit. Then he spoke, this time quieter, like it was a game.

'Look at you, your stupid fuckin' face right now. I know that look.

You know where I seen this fuckin' look you're fuckin' wearing?'

I barely stopped myself from saying, 'Was it the last guy you whacked and buried out in the weeds?'

'On me!' he giggled. 'I used to have that look all the time. The fucking hunger to get that next big hit under my belt, that GIVE ME look. And by God, I was ready to kill you, him, that asshole over there, Uncle Tom fucking Cobley and all their fucking mothers for that one fucking hit show. Well, I got it for you, you lucky cock-sucker. You'll remember this day a long fucking time.'

To be fair, he was bang on with that last point.

'But first, I want to show you something! Follow me, young master motherfucker – and put your beer back down, there are no drinks allowed where we're going . . . '

He began walking towards a large studded door in the far wall and before setting off after him I took a swig of Special Brew like it was the last swallow before the noose. He stopped outside the room.

'You know how many people I've allowed in here? None. Nobody. Nobody gets to come in this fucking room because their fucking world ends right where I'm standing and my fucking world starts on the other fucking side. But I need you to see this to appreciate where I'm coming from and what we're getting into. You little prick, come here!'

He was smiling so broadly, displaying such excitement I felt no threat as he put his arm tightly around my shoulder and pulled me to him.

'Shake my hand!'

I tried to but we were clamped so closely together it was little more than a bizarre arm-wrestle beneath our chins.

Releasing himself, he turned to the door and, without looking, punched a code into the number pad above the handle and swung back the door.

Overhead lights popped into life as he bade me enter. And there it was. Without doubt, still the most complicated, sprawling and com-plete train set I have seen in my life – and I've seen Rod Stewart's.

Naturally, I did what I always do when men show me their toy railways. I adopt a walk that hesitates between steps as if the very magnificence of what I am absorbing has robbed me of any motor skills. I widen the eyes, I open the jaw, I slowly raise my hands to the top of my head lest my blown mind fly straight out the cranium. I don't speak, because clearly I have forgotten how to, though I do attempt a few syllables that will fail to form words, so scrambled are my thoughts. Frankly, the shameful pantomime I employ at moments like this would make Lord Carnarvon's reaction to King Tut's burial chamber resemble a commuter regarding the men's room on Chislehurst station. The reality is that silently I am screaming, 'Oh no! A train set. Why have you still got a train set? I didn't particularly like train sets when I had a train set – and that was in 1968! Even a ladybird in a matchbox trumps a train set!'

For some reason men insist on showing you their train sets regardless of the fact that *you* don't have a train set. That really should tell them something. (Against this, the room in which I keep my collection of ten thousand vinyl albums from the 1970s is a thing of awe and wonder that I insist is visited even by blokes who've only come to read the gas meter.)

Hughie then began to flick various switches that caused the little trains to whizz around. This somehow made the exhibition more ridiculous.

'I know what you wanna do, you bastard,' he chuckled. 'You wanna put on the hat and stay here fucking around with this, don't you? Well we're not here for that, so fuckin' forget it!'

The hat?

Hands in his pockets, his eyes never leaving the miniature landscape he had created, Hughie now began to lovingly describe his greatest pleasure in life: imagining that the longest train on his track was a mobile studio and that every weekend a three-hour-long TV variety show would be broadcast live from its carriages, with guests being picked up at stops along the way. I've heard worse ideas, though I didn't want to deflate him by pointing out that several TV shows had already tried it, including both David Letterman and Jonathan Ross. He may have even known this because *Live from the Locomotive* turned out to be just the curtain raiser on his Big Vision for me.

'OK, show from a fuckin' train, cute idea, but today those cock-suckers out there will take your cute and tell you to stick it in your ass. It has to be something un-fuckin'-believable. Stu-fuckin'-pendous!'

(NB: This is Hughie talking, not me.)

'So I'm in here one night, moving the trains, scratching my balls, and JESUS! I get the idea of the fuckin' century. I look across to the far side and go, FUCK ME! THAT'S IT! Now what can you see on that far side? Beyond those cable cars – what's there?'

I looked and there appeared to be a sort of cove with a painted sea beyond, its horizon stretching on to the wall.

'The seaside,' I said.

'The *seaside*? The sea-fuckin'-side??' Hughie seemed outraged by my naïvety and for a few moments kept saying 'Oh, the seaside' in ever more silly-ass English tones.

'That's not the goddamned seaside, you half-witted prick! That is the Atlantic fucking Ocean!'

'Well, how am I supposed to know that?' I countered.

'Because you don't think big, Danny fuckin' Baker! Nobody does any more. You're used to TV pygmies yanking your dick. Not like Uncle Hughie here! That's why I've been in this business for forty-four fucking years and why you will go straight into the toilet unless you go into partnership with me on this. OK, don't say another fuck-ing word – here's what we're gonna do . . . '

I hope you're ready for this.

'So we do the first part of the show on a train and that's all well and good and Mr and Mrs Shit-for-Brains in Bum Fuck Lancashire are eating it up. They've had Shirley Bassey, some pop stars, magi-cians, fuck knows what else, but we haven't even started yet. We get OFF the train beside the River Thames, huge crowds, and – God this is so astounding, I'm shitting myself with excitement telling you. We get off the fucking train and A SUBMARINE SURFACES

OUTA THE FUCKING RIVER THAMES. We get on board this monster and the show continues, on the fucking sub! Then, as the sub goes under again, we say, "See you tomorrow, cocksuckers!" And the next night the show on the submarine carries on and on, climaxing when the whole fucking thing surfaces in New York harbour – bands playing, fireworks, six-gun-fucking-salutes the lot. The rest of TV may as well close down after that, because you can't follow a show on a submarine – that's it. Thank you, John Logie Baird, and now you can all just fuck off!'

I was dreading what was coming next.

'So what do you think?'

That.

Suddenly I was doing the 'Oh wow, what a train set' choreography again. Eventually I gathered myself and said the only possible thing a person could say.

'A submarine, Hughie?'

'You betcha. And not one of these fuckin' piss-ant things either. A nuke! Bigger than any fuckin' TV studio you've ever seen. Don't worry about it, I've already got permission.'

Now I have no idea whether Hughie Green really had the means or permission to present Shirley Bassey live from a nuclear submarine chugging towards the Hudson, but there was no doubting he believed he had. Why me, though?

'Well, I'll be honest with you, Danny boy, I would love to front up this thing, but I'm no fuckin' fool. My time's up. I don't know a single one of the sons o' bitches running the stations these days, but you do. I'll produce the whole thing but I need you to open a few doors. Do that, and you got the gig.'

What gig? What could I possibly do on a two-night, three-hour variety show running silent, running deep one mile beneath the restless spume of the Atlantic? Surely we'd have to leave the periscope up all the time just to get a signal out. And what if that signal went down? How would we know? Wouldn't it be a tad embarrassing to be thrashing away at hits of the day accompanied by elaborate dance routines down in Davy Jones' locker, only to be told when we surfaced that not a single person had seen any of it? I mean, what a waste of everyone's time.

We left the sacred railway room with Hughie going into more detail about the vessel and the route we might adopt on the night. Was he mad? I think not. His idea certainly was, but in those years before his death in 1997 I think anything that made him feel like he was back at the centre of the business again made his pulse race and, if you're going to indulge a crackpot phantom TV venture, well why *not* stage it on a nuclear submarine going around the world?

As for the maniacal swearing, it's possible he added all that extra salt to make me – someone he thought of as 'of the streets' – feel at home. Personally, I'd much rather believe he spoke like that all the time and that there are acres of outtakes lying in dusty vaults of Hughie turning to some sweet old man, who'd only come along to introduce his nephew, and saying, 'This ancient cocksucker is called Barney and he's here to introduce his prick of a juggling relative who's called Gary, for fuck's sake. And I mean that most sincerely.'

So, anyway, back in the garden in Deptford, thanks to Wendy thoughtlessly repeating exactly what I'd always told her to say, it seemed there would be zero chance now I could be further considered as a candidate for *This Is Your Life*. I even got my agent to call them up and plead that, if I promised to act extra specially shocked when they surprised me, would they reconsider? They said no. The credibility of the central idea of the programme – such as it was – was paramount.

But then some genius producer on the show had another thought. Apparently, he heard about me being scrubbed from the upcoming series' runners and riders and remarked that, now I was absolutely positively sure that I was never going to be featured, wouldn't that be the ultimate double bluff? What better cloak of ambush could there be than letting me know about it and then furiously withdrawing the offer? I must admit that as gags go it was a pip. Thus over the upcoming weeks, as I continued to tell the story of the great *This*

Is Your Life balls-up to everyone I knew, these same people were simultaneously receiving calls from the *TIYL* team saying, 'Let the bonkers old fat head rant and rave, we're all soon going to enjoy biting him right on the arse.'

And on the night that denture finally met buttock, I simply didn't have a clue.

I know I was not in the greatest of moods. There are many aspects of making television shows that I find dull to the point of infuriating. Chief among these is the time immediately after the programme has 'ended', where both cast and studio audience have to remain behind though drained, dry and miserable, while various moments are filmed again for editing purposes. God knows, anybody who has ever attended a television taping knows that these evenings are drawn out to the point where in more enlightened societies they would qualify as cruel and unusual punishment. But this unexpected extension never fails to raise an undertow of simmering violence. The audience, who have already endured being herded into their seats long before they needed to be, rightly resent being asked to laugh where they originally failed to laugh at all, applaud where they didn't applaud, and gaze lovingly toward someone that, as their hollow eyes betray, they would rather feed rat poison. It is a filthy, filthy business. Even much-loved fixtures of the TV schedules such as *QI* and *Have I Got News For You* will routinely record for two and a half hours in order to winkle out the necessary twenty-eight minutes to fill their spot. This will not be because the initial half hour was so weak that they must now bludgeon the crowd into submission but simply that this is how TV has evolved and atrophied. If the studio is booked for four hours they will keep you in it for four hours. If the show were live and had to be over in twenty-eight minutes, it would be over in twenty-eight minutes and be none the worse for that.

Of course, most of the vehicles I have delivered down the decades do not even remotely come under the heading 'much-loved fixtures', so the mood in the hot airless studio that night as I finished one of my failing chat shows was, as I recall it, spectacularly ugly. Four hundred people who had written in for tickets to *Noel's House Party* and instead received entry to this half-arsed festival of muddled hokum were now being commanded to artificially react to me as though I was a fantastic entertainer. It was always going to be a stretch for them. True, I was within a few feet of a bona fide star. Awaiting further instruction from the production gallery, I stood beneath a barely turning disco glitter ball that would soon be returned to its perch in the BBC prop store while to my left was Donna Summer – one of the better guests we had managed to get on to the programme during its run. She had just completed a second re-take of the song she was promoting at the time and now we were being told that, because of a technical problem, she would have to perform it once again. On hearing this, the audience – who had sat through thirty-five minutes of 'pick-ups', as they're called – let out a collective mournful sigh of disappointment. They HATED us now and even poor Donna muttered a quiet, 'I'm sorry,' as she saw any potential sales of her disc go flying up the chimney of a Big Flop furnace.

Sullenly we waited for the backing track to start. And we waited. Me in my sweltering velvet jacket, Donna in a dress whose haute couture had long since wilted under the onslaught of repeated per-formance. By rights, the warm-up man, who even at the best of times is little more than a rodeo clown, would have attempted to raise spirits, but even he knew not to antagonize the crowd further. The brooding silence in Studio One was only broken by the slow rhythmic squeak of that fucking disco ball rotating joylessly above our heads. After an interminable few minutes I began to address the production booth from the studio floor.

'Come on, everyone, eh? Can't we live with what we've got? Jesus, these poor people have got buses and trains to catch!'

I got a smattering of applause for that. Still the moments ticked on.

'Why can't the audience go! We can cut in any shots after!' Nothing. 'Can anybody hear me up there? This is beyond a joke now . . .'

I may have even stamped a frustrated foot. 'Be cool,' said Donna Summer. I wasn't cool.

'Tell you what, everybody,' I thundered, waving my arms like Mussolini, 'just get up and go. They're taking the piss out of you now, and—'

And at that point, behind me, Michael Aspel and his 'Big Red Book' entered the studio with another camera crew, causing the audience to suddenly understand all the hold-up and burst into spontaneous applause. I, naturally, thought the ovation was because I was siding with them and continued my showboating rabble-rousing for a few more embarrassing sentences until Donna Summer advised me I might like to turn around. The applause continued for some time as I lay spread out on the set trying to determine whether this was indeed happening and if my recent show of temperament had made me look as big an ass as I fancied. I fancy it had. The audience, meanwhile, were soon plunged back into bitterness when Michael Aspel announced that we were all leaving now to do the show over at Thames' studios at Teddington, 'where another audience is waiting'. And wait they did. It took around an hour to get over there, then there was a similar amount of time while everything was made ready.

Locked into a dressing room lest I stumble across any of the surprise guests lined up, I quickly guzzled down the bottle of champagne provided, smiled at myself in the mirror a good deal, and repeatedly ran through the various *This Is Your Life* clichés I was determined not to repeat. Chief among these was holding hands with Wendy or any other sort of show of overt affection. Amazed that she would even be there – you may recall that those teams of wild horses you often see outside TV centres are the ones that cannot get my wife to go in front of any cameras – I was acutely aware that whenever we watched the show we held to the theory that the more fuss the subject made over his/her partner the more likely they were to get divorced within the year. My dad had first identified this formula and its hit rate was phenomenally high. As he saw it, if a couple spent half the show gazing into each other's eyes, it was only to determine which one they would like to spit in first. Cynical maybe, but not without basis. Consequently, if you ever see my edition of *This Is Your Life* you may come away from it believing that the woman sitting next to me is a total stranger who had just wandered in for a sit down. Spud, in contrast, looked to be having the time of his life and delivered several good stories, only one of which made the air. When I first saw him on the set I instantly compiled a list of the Top 10 Things he would normally say while watching *This Is Your Life*. They were:

10. 'Never heard of him.'
9. 'Bet they don't mention how many times he's gone skint.'
8. 'She used to be a brass over Poplar way.'
7. 'He ain't got a clue who that is.'
6. 'Blimey, don't he look old now?'
5. 'Everyone knows he's a ginger beer.'
4. 'Them two obviously had it off at some point.'
3. 'He's only there for the piss-up afterwards.'
2. 'Fucking old liar, she's just made that story up.'
1. 'You can tell they hate each other.'

Certainly number three on that list held true for a good portion of the attendees, though 'the piss-up afterwards' didn't get underway until gone 2 a.m. It was still going at full tilt four hours later, which would have been fine, had it not been by then Saturday morning which meant I was due on the air at Radio 1 at nine. Nobody had thought to cancel the show lest it tip off some loose lips within the BBC, and so, drunk, reeling and still in my TV suit and make-up, I made my way into London's West End. In the words of Withnail (and I), I felt decidedly 'unusual'. Having been requested not to mention where I'd been all night, I subsequently delivered what, even by my standards, was a deranged and ragged broadcast.

Ironically it was on the radio show following the later airing of my *This Is Your Life* that I completely forgot where I was and, for the one and only time in my career, swore live on air. And a spectacular swear it was too, neither spoonerism nor slip of the tongue, featuring the ultimate four-letter word that even Hughie Green had used sparingly. Here's how it went.

After finally letting the radio audience in on the reason my show a few weeks previously may have sounded even more cross-eyed than usual, I looked across at my co-host Danny Kelly and announced that, all in all, I had been 'as drunk as a cunt'. Yep, that's what I said – on Wonderful Radio 1 on a Saturday lunchtime and straight into the microphone. So how come you never heard about it?

Well, firstly I suspect it's because listeners simply couldn't believe they'd heard it, and secondly because I swiftly confirmed that they shouldn't believe it because I hadn't actually said it. It was, in fact, their own warped and diseased minds that had *wanted* to hear such filth and the fault was entirely theirs. I was assisted in this Obi-Wan-like act of mind control by the constant background music that underscores all of my on-air dialogue even to this day, that had handily made the outrage not quite as clear cu(n)t as it might have been.

After a few moments' reflection on what I had just shared with Britain's pop kids, I allowed this backing track to play on unaccompanied for a bit then returned to the mic with the following, I feel rather brilliant, explanation:

'Ha! I have just been informed by my wretch of a producer that my last link may have sounded a tad salty, kids, certainly to the more base-minded of you low-lifes out there. Fact is, if you are going to leave the letter "s" off a word then it's possibly not advisable to do it with 'skunk' – as I apparently did with the phrase 'drunk as a skunk'. So relax! That is what I was as drunk as – now go and clean out your ears, minds and radio receivers, you degenerates . . . '

Voilà. Suddenly it became *their* fault and, though I say it myself, such magical quick-thinking is exactly why I have shelves full of radio awards . . . So if you were listening on that distant Saturday morning, I can now reveal that that phrase you heard while washing the car was not 'drunk as a kunk'. Easy mistake to make, though, what?

*

Anyway, we're getting nowhere here; the point is, my old friend Chris Evans couldn't be at my *TIYL* because he was busy elsewhere ripping up the TV rulebook. And yet, a couple of years later, both Megastar and Fallen Idol were to be reunited on a magnificent rock'n'roll juggernaut of a project where, coincidentally, I now see another major swear word was weekly left to the audience's imagination. It was called *TFI Friday*.

Get 'Em Out By Friday

*T*FI *Friday* was a hit from its very first episode. A breathless brew of live music, wild jokes and peerless immediacy, it would run for almost six years. I was paid an agreeable five grand a show to pile up its hellzapoppin' ideas and dizzying crazed dialogue. Given that it was on screen for forty weeks every year, I was once more riding a gravy train with biscuit wheels. It was in every way the perfect job, even better for me than it was for the host because I didn't have to go out and present it – not that anybody wanted that. Even Chris didn't want to present it. Originally, *TFI* had been designed as a vehicle for Jonathan Ross but that had fallen through and so Chris had stepped in with genuine reluctance to front it himself. One of our long-running backstage rituals was, after we had performed a final run-through of the script, he would wearily reach for his stage clothes as I'd say with a satisfied chuckle, 'And now YOU, my friend, have got to go and do all that.' His usual response was to wonder why we hadn't unearthed some hungry hot-shot kid to do the actual looning about while we watched it in the pub over the road. He would be deadly serious about it too.

Indeed, these final script 'meetings' usually took place in any one of the nearby pubs, sometimes only minutes before we were due live on air. Chris took a particular pleasure in never telling any of the production team which one it might be and on countless occasions the saloon bar door of, say, The Archers would bash open at five thirty – we were on air at six – and a fraught member of the crew, headphones around neck, script opened at the first link, eyes wild with panic, would bellow into a walkie-talkie, 'It's OK – I've found them!' More often than not Chris would invite them to sit and 'have one' with us because, 'We've got half an hour yet. Calm down.'

That said, the ensuing presenting would be a master class in late twentieth-century television. Famously chaotic and seemingly ad-libbed, *TFI Friday* was anything but. You simply cannot perform an hour of live TV with four bands, three guests, five sketches, four hundred audience members, eighty crew, ten cameras, VT to fly in and ad breaks to hit on time, on the hoof and as a bit of a lark. The rare skill is to make it appear so and *TFI Friday* – or more accurately Chris Evans – did that week in, week out. Like the Pied Piper, my work was done at the raging river's bank; it was Chris who then had to plunge into the maelstrom and get to the other side.

In the entire run of *TFI*, I only appeared on screen a handful of times – invariably when a sketch needed a cast of more than three. I can remember playing a rather good Herman Munster in a VT where, because Chris had decided there must be something better on TV than what we were offering, he 'changed channels' to watch what was on BBC2. I once played a member of the then very hot pop band Hanson. Another time, I was an outraged cinema audience member in a recurring segment called 'The Man Who Is Apparently Unaware His Hat Is On Fire'. The great Ronnie Fraser played the title role in that. A consequence of these infrequent cameos was that many people, unaware of my wider duties on the programme, thought I must be right down on my luck and now grabbing at any work available to me. This was most powerfully brought home to me in a wonderfully ignoble meeting with the broadcaster John Humphrys.

My agent had been for some weeks saying to me that *On the Ropes* were very keen to have me on. Now I don't know about you, but when someone mentions something by name that is clearly in the zeitgeist without any further information, I find I am very reluctant to admit I haven't got the faintest clue what they are on about. This includes anything from computer games to a happening new pastry and even the word 'zeitgeist', which I remember nodding along to whenever one of the writers at the *NME* would use it – *which was a lot*.

This *On the Ropes* sounded like a panel game to me and so I airily declined it. When I finally determined by roundabout means that it was a BBC Radio 4 show fronted by John Humphrys, I realized it must be some kind of distinguished interview format, the sort of thing that usually has Jonathan Miller or one of the Mitford sisters looking back over a long and eventful life. Yes, I could do that, I thought, but then I was told they only paid £250 and so I thanked them for their interest but declared I would be busy that day flicking playing cards into a top hat. They offered alternative dates. I still couldn't fit it in (for £250). Finally they offered to break precedent on the show and bring JH to me over at the *TFI* studios, if I could 'spare an hour'. My God, I thought, this Humphrys must be a big fan. Going further, I allowed myself to reason that poor old Radio 4 were probably tired of people like Jonathan Miller and the Mitford sisters always hogging their mikes and were now looking toward a more youthful roster. So, yes, I could spare *On the Ropes* an hour and the following week we found ourselves in one of the quieter rooms in our Factory of Dreams as John signalled to his producer to roll tape.

Well, ladies and gentlemen, ignoble was the word I advertised this hangdog pow-wow with and ignoble it very swiftly became. *On the Ropes*, it turned out, was a sort of anti *This Is Your Life* wherein some poor prune who once had the world at his feet explains how it all turned to ashes in his mouth. I literally had no idea there could be this perception of me, so John Humphrys and I were a good ten minutes into the exchanges before this ghastly penny dropped. Up until that point he had been running through a few of the things I'd done and headlines I'd garnered, but then the questions started to take on the distinct whiff of 'Where did it all go wrong?' and 'Do you mind if we just call you Icarus to save time?'

The next thing I know I'm overcompensating like crazy in my responses, dragging out names of people I was currently writing for and projects recently completed, which plainly gave the overall effect of a cashiered old general producing white fivers and forged IOUs in an effort to prove he's perfectly solvent. Then the ludicrousness of my position took hold and I got the most acute fit of the giggles.

'I'm so sorry,' I managed to spout, 'but I have just realized that at some point in the meetings for this your researchers must have used the phrase "broken-down old vaudeville performer".' To be fair, John Humphrys was by now laughing too and maybe starting to think this wasn't going to be the riches-to-rags cautionary tale his listeners loved to lap up. He kept at it though.

'I mean, look where we are,' he probed, 'at the studios of one of the biggest TV shows in the country and yet you have to watch Chris Evans go out there and take the applause. Surely that's got to hurt?'

I'm told I hooted so loud at this the digital recorder briefly switched itself off.

'Come on,' JH continued, like the top pro he is, 'don't you sit in the wings watching Chris front this big successful programme and think, "That should be me. I was at the top once."'

Protesting this bizarre image of myself, I think I invoked a scene from one of Sammy Davis Junior's deliciously hammy autobiographies where, after an early show of his that was poorly received, he sat in the window of his New York hotel room, looked out across the skyscrapers, and shaking his fist at the streets below, defiantly swearing, 'Big Town – I'll get you yet!'

I, of course, did try to explain about the little pre-show ritual that Chris and I went through each week, but all in all I don't think it washed. I never heard the finished programme but I must have sounded suitably pathetic because about a week later one of Wendy's friends told her, completely without malice, that she had heard me on the radio and I had been 'really struggling'. After tax, agent's commission and other deductions that £250 fee came down to about ninety-two quid, which has become my firm asking price should anyone else want to drum me through the streets with a stale loaf around my neck.

*

Undoubtedly I was resilient in the face of such indignities because the work on *TFI Friday* was so sumptuously rewarding. Actually, make that the work *and* play.

Picture this. It is eleven thirty on a Tuesday morning, the time we would usually congregate at one of Chris's places to start thinking about this week's programme, only we can't start any planning because Peter O'Toole hasn't arrived yet. Yes, Peter O'Toole. Let me just say, if you thought the first two books in this series were peppered with celebrity, this one chapter will now make them read like a Sidcup solicitor's client roster.

We were gathered in the basement of Chris's house in Notting Hill and upstairs the front door had been left ajar in case we didn't hear the Great Man at the buzzer. Arriving about twenty minutes late, Peter O'Toole made the sort of entrance you would have wanted Peter O'Toole to make. The first we knew of it was a distant soft closing of the front door, followed by the unhurried tread of expensive shoes upon the wooden floor above. We all looked at each other. Then there was a pause, for I fancy no other reason than dramatic effect, at the top of the stairs that led down to where we were. Next came the carefully measured descent. The stairs were at an angle to us, cut in half by the basement ceiling, so a person would have to be on the last few steps before being fully seen. It was almost as if he'd recce'd the place first.

Down he drifted, deliberate and theatrical, one ponderous stair at a time, slowly and deliberately, revealing shoes first, then the perfect amount of trouser, a long black overcoat loosely billowing below the knees, next a porcelain hand on the handrail, a multi-coloured silk scarf at the neck and finally, silver hair falling from beneath a brown fedora, smiling broadly and now at a complete stop: it's Peter O'Toole.

'Where the fucking hell have you been?' I said.

As opening gambits go, it was rather a gamble, but I figured a player like O'Toole would go for it. He did.

'Oh-ho! I like you, cocky,' he guffawed, wagging an admonishing finger, instantly dispersing the mood of the previous minute.

'Where the fucking hell have I been? Good title for a book that . . .'

O'Toole, you won't be staggered to hear, was rattling good company, everything you'd wish. A patient listener to all our jabbering yarns, he would let you reel out your story before drawing breath and then effortlessly make even your best tales of a Beatle or Michael Jackson seem like juvenile babble.

A couple of examples.

I had recently returned from a holiday in Florida (happily, a statement I can make most days you might bump into me). While there, I had purchased in one of the more reputable memorabilia stores a large doodle of the American flag drawn and then signed by Lenny Bruce, the doomed maverick comedian who had obsessed me for much of my early teenage life. The piece had cost me $400, a price that made it just about the cheapest item in the shop. In contrast, I remember there was a Macaulay Culkin signature nearby retailing at $1,750 that I'm betting is still there today, although now probably marked down to eight bucks, five for cash. Anyway, while getting O'Toole to sign his latest book – the reason he was appearing on the show – I told him about my purchase and what a steal it had been, as well as pointing Peter at a newish biography of Bruce that I had recently read and enjoyed. He let me finish going on about him then completed his own generously worded autograph before handing it back to me. Then he spoke.

'In nineteen sixty . . . let's see . . . *four*, I think . . . I was in the nick with Lenny Bruce.'

'In the nick?' I said, not a little startled.

'Yes, jail. Pokey,' he continued, his eyes now dancing at the memory. 'I had tried to keep some policemen from bundling him off the stage – I think this was in San Francisco – and subsequently ended up in the meat wagon and later the same jail cell as him. It was an all-nighter too. They kept asking us to call people about bail and what have you, very apologetic – at least towards me – but neither of us had anywhere special to go and so we stayed up all night talking. Nice guy. Naturally funny. Ronnie, you met Lenny Bruce didn't you?'

He looked across to Ronnie Fraser, his oldest chum, now a *TFI* regular and great friend of Chris.

Ronnie thought about whether he'd met Lenny Bruce but wasn't sure.

'Don't think so. Was that in Texas?'

O'Toole corrected him. 'No, no, definitely San Francisco. Lenny Bruce. You're thinking of when the police caught us supplying marijuana to Robert Mitchum.' And he broke into another rear-view chuckle.

I mean, what? I ask you. I've been about the show business block, but stories about Ernie Wise or Lulu start to look a touch green about the gills when you're dealing with this level of heavy-hitting. A little later he picked up the book I was reading at the time, about the last days of the Romanovs.

'This yours?' he asked. Again I, as I always do, over-answered and went rambling on about how the final year of czarist Russia is one of those subjects that I can repeatedly read and re-read. He flipped through the photos in the book then looked up at me.

'Many years ago I was in Moscow . . .'

Here we go.

'And I was taken to a small bar very late at night where myself and several other British actors all proceeded to get thoroughly pie-eyed on the best vodka and filthiest food imaginable. I wasn't allowed to pay a rouble towards any of this because the clutch of shady Muscovites peopling this den had spotted me and were convinced I had been in *Doctor* fucking *Zhivago*. Anyway, I was holding court as best I could around a large table when, at about 2 a.m., the door of the place opens and in comes this decrepit old geezer walking on two sticks and everyone suddenly jettisons me to attend to him. Not another drink is forthcoming, not another mangled word of Russian exchanged. A short while later, my company and I arise – unsteadily – and make to leave.

'Visiting the toilet before staggering back to our hotel, I find myself in there with one of the men who had, at least, a rudimentary grasp of English. "Who," I asked him, "is the old man?" Turns out he was the brother of Dimitri Kosorotov, the man who performed the autopsy on Rasputin and who claims to have the great mystic's huge heart and even bigger penis hidden in his apartment. Apparently, whenever he arrives, bidding begins to see if they can wrest one or the other, preferably both, from the old boy's grip. I mean, you have to accept second billing when that sort of history upstages you, don't you think?'

Quite.

'Extraordinarily, not long after that Ronnie and I found ourselves in a café in Paris and there was another old chap being feted and fawned over, and he eventually asked us over to join him. Do you remember, Ronnie?'

Ronnie cooed a gentle 'Of course, yes.'

'We didn't join him then, but we did stop by his table on the way out to get introduced, and it's Felix Yusupov – the man who *killed* Rasputin! I did shake his hand, but stopped short of dropping on him the bombshell that the mad monk is, in portion at least, still with us but that his dick is in private hands.'

Now THAT, my friends, is a story.

This momentous day ended with Chris, Will MacDonald, Peter O'Toole, Ronnie Fraser and I playing snooker, noisily and fantastically drunk, in Soho. There were probably tales told even more wondrous then those above as we sang and soldiered on, but you will have to forgive me if the memory of those is a little fogged.

O'Toole was one of the very few people who asked to meet with us prior to appearing on *TFI*. Another was John Cleese. Cleese's office, rather alarmingly, asked on the Monday whether John could be faxed the script for that Friday's show so he could then discuss it with 'the writers'. This would be tricky for us because the script didn't exist until the Thursday evening before broadcast and even then it would be liable to change. Suzi Aplin, the show's talent booker, made it clear to us that if JC didn't get a script in the next few hours he may pull out of the programme. We got away without producing a script on the Monday – some hopeless fudge and flannel about meetings and fine tuning – but on the Tuesday when we met down at Chris's country place in Kent, Suzi told us she'd already had five calls about seeing this script so we knew we had to do something.

Chris's first idea was a cracker. It was to go to the lane at the end of his drive and play a game called 'Who Will Wave Back?' This involved him standing on the pavement waving at any passing car to see how many drivers waved back. This would be filmed and a short video package of the results would then be played out on the programme. Oh, I know what you're thinking. Sounds like pretty thin gruel, doesn't it? How could this vacuous bastard froth come from the same TV nation that gave the world *The Ascent of Man*? Well, I have to tell you, 'Who Will Wave Back?' was a tense, unpredictable sensation and soon sat proudly alongside such other *TFI* fixtures as 'Live From Hammersmith Broadway! From Which Side of the Screen Will Next Come a Green Car?', 'One Fish, Three Arches', 'Baby Left, Baby Right (the Collapsing Toddler Game)', as well as another item that I would later revive to some success, 'Red Sauce, Brown Sauce, or No Sauce at All'. However, terrific though our commuter-waving game was, it probably wasn't enough in and of itself to fax out to John Cleese in New York with a note saying, 'More to follow'.

So there we sat in Chris's farmhouse lounge, wondering how on earth we could possibly get down to writing a show that wouldn't even be needed for another seventy-two hours. Why, the very idea lacked any zip to us. We just didn't – and couldn't – work like that. Suzi then took another call and a pretty fraught one it seemed. One of those where a minute into it the person on the receiving end gets up and takes it outside lest their own alarm should infect everyone else.

'Right,' she thundered, steaming back into our pit of lethargy. 'It's daybreak in New York and basically John Cleese has said if the script isn't there by this afternoon, we can forget it.'

Despite our goofiness, this was genuinely calamitous news. John Cleese was a huge star, hero to us all, and would undoubtedly play an enormous part throughout that week's show. Without John Cleese, we didn't know if we'd even have a show for that week. Thus, upon hearing this, everyone apart from Suzi, for whom this potentially had professional repercussions, now got the giggles.

'We can't write scripts on Tuesdays!' I protested. 'Nobody can. That's a mad thing to say. Tell him we're all exhausted from waving at cars.'

There were several minutes of such mania until Chris had one of the greatest brainwaves it has been my pleasure to witness. It came right after Suzi had suggested that he might ring Cleese personally and explain that the show didn't operate like other programmes. 'I think it will come better from you,' is what she said.

To which Chris replied, 'You're right. It will. Come on, let's go.'

Suzi wondered where we might go.

'To New York. Now. Let's go to New York, knock on his hotel room door and say, "Hello, Mr Cleese, we don't have a script but we would still like you to come on our show." We'll take a little video recorder and see what he says. It'll be a funny bit! Will, find out when the next plausible plane is. Come on, Dan, we're going to America. We'll write something on the way.'

And that, I promise you, is exactly what we did. There and then. I had to call home to Wendy and explain that instead of being home about four I was, in fact, going to New York with Chris for a while. A bike rider would be coming by to get my passport in about ten minutes. And so, barely two hours after waving at baffled motorists on a B road near Brands Hatch and with no further plans for the day, we found ourselves boarding a British Airways flight to JFK airport. First class too, because, apart from anything else, *TFI Friday* had what used to be called in televisual circles An Enormous Fucking Budget.

It was an irresistible idea, completely in keeping with the reckless nature of the programme, and surely John Cleese would be totally knocked out by its sheer audacity.

If only he'd got to hear about it. Because what happened when we got to New York rather took the shine off the whole swashbuckling adventure. See if you can spot the precise moment a sensible person might have flagged we were heading for the cliff face. I will place an asterisk where I feel we started to go wrong.

Coming through customs and taking a cab into town, Chris, show associate Johnny Revell and I knew exactly what hotel and what room John Cleese was staying in. It would take us approximately forty-five minutes to arrive at this destination and he had absolutely no idea we were in town and about to surprise him. By now it was late afternoon in New York and we had been tipped off he should be back in his suite by six. The timings were pretty perfect. In fact, we would have about half an hour to spare.

'Time enough for a little drink first!' said Chris.

*

Well, as it happened, we had almost an hour before John Cleese would arrive back at his pad and so I took us all off to a wonderful bar I know near Washington Square. This wasn't as handy for our target as it might be, but no matter; we could be back uptown in a rush-hour jiffy. Now then. I don't know if you've seen Washington Square in the autumn? It's a heart-stopping riot of greens, golds and deepening shades of red. The trees are yet to lose a leaf, the people still sit around playing chess, discussing art, skating for fun or becoming lost in a lover's eyes. The air is sweet and warm without any humidity and the sun's rays beam their long fingers down the avenues as yellow cabs glide across the blocks. Little welcoming establishments set their red-checked tables out on the pavements and a man can order hot clams and cold beer and watch New York City unfold its endless ballet of flow and movement.

Faced with such majesty, clearly, plainly, no single quick cold beer can ever do it justice. And so it proved for we happy trio of globetrotters. Draining that first delicious glass, it suddenly hit us that to keep gallivanting about after the taxing day we had just had – what with waving at cars and coming up with crackerjack ideas about going to America – might very well lead us to do something less than our very best work. There was obviously no point rushing into this thing. Also, we knew Cleese himself had been out filming all day and so he too might not be completely on top of his game when we ambushed him at the door. He wasn't checking out until the following afternoon, so what was all this ridiculous talk about going straight there to get this thing in the can? I think it was as several steaming plates of Veal Milanese and Spaghetti Vongole arrived with some Frascati so cold the instant condensation was causing the labels to slip from the bottles that we decided, unanimously, to visit 'Old Monty Python' first thing in the morning instead and leave the rest of the New York evening clear for getting ourselves in the best physical shape to deliver on such a brilliant plan.

I don't think I need detain you too long with what transpired as a result of this cleverly revised schedule. When Chris knocked on Cleese's hotel room door around lunchtime the following day, there was no reply. This was probably because at that moment, having checked out at 7 a.m., John Cleese was comfortably settled in on a flight to Paris. As goose chases go, it started to dawn on Chris and John that this one was getting toward the wilder end of the scale. Why didn't it dawn on me also? Because I was no longer with them. About the only thing Wendy had said when I told her I was suddenly going to New York was, 'If you have a chance, get me some of those coffee cups they sell at Dean & DeLuca.' Such a reaction can only come from a woman who is not easily fazed. Recalling this a couple of hours into that impromptu Hooray, We're in New York! celebration dinner, I rose from the table and, like Captain Oates, said I wouldn't be a moment. There was a large Dean & DeLuca store a few blocks away and my intention was to lighten their stock of coffee cups by at least six. Wouldn't Wendy be amazed I'd remembered such a detail? Well, I'll never know, because I never made it.

Immediately I left the bar, I stepped off the pavement to cross the street and my right foot buckled into a small excavation beneath the kerb. Now we've all done this undignified stumble and sometimes it results in a momentary snap of pain that, while sore, is more embarrassing than critical . . . But sometimes your ankle goes ominously numb as if to say, 'All right. This is a big one. You've done something bad here. I'll hold back the torrent of agony for as long as I can, but you better start aiming for Accident and Emergency right away.' This was one of those. This was a disaster. I stood there, still half in the road, taking stock and some very deep breaths while for the very first time asking myself what the fucking hell I was doing in Manhattan.

Wobbling back into the bar, I slumped down at the table and told my friends I had broken my ankle. Chris announced that red wine was a known cure for this. The fact I didn't even react to this untested theory in alternative medicine showed him that my claim, and my obvious shock, was real. I delicately peeled down my sock and already one side of my foot was three times the size it should be. Chris had a word with our waitress and she came back to us holding one of those large silver buckets from which champagne bottles usually protrude. She put it on the floor and I stuck my leg in it. Attempting to wiggle my foot through the ice cubes and into the bottom of the bucket it felt like a hacksaw was rasping away at every tendon in the area. Oh, this was BAD. Chris later told me that all I was saying was, 'I feel sick. I feel SO sick.'

'Why don't you go back to the hotel and lie down for an hour. We'll call you later,' suggested John, and soon they were helping me – slowly – into a cab.

'He's not drunk, he's injured,' said the waitress, noting the cabbie's worried face.

'Actually, he's injured AND he's drunk,' clarified Chris helpfully.

Back in my hotel room the pain was intense. I was sweating profusely and finding it impossible to settle in any position that would alleviate my growing sense of alarm. I knew nothing about the medical system in New York, other than fixing up an uninsured broken ankle was likely to cost many, many Dean & DeLuca coffee cups, and so I became fixated on one idea – I had to get home.

Plainly feeling a little guilty at cabbing me off, Chris and John arrived at my room less than twenty minutes later to see how I was doing. I had to hop to the door and then hop back to collapse on the bed – upon which I had neglected to move my chunky Nikon camera that now crunched into my spine. I screamed out in further distress. The actual words I said were, 'Oh Christ! I've landed on me camera. I think I've broke my back.'

This, quite naturally, caused both Chris and John to swiftly turn away from me lest I judge their sudden uncontrollable laughter unsympathetic.

John Revell then began making phone calls – something he excels at – and incredibly I made it out of New York to be decanted on to the 9.55 flight out of Newark. He'd even arranged for me to be met with a wheelchair at the other end. Turns out my ankle wasn't broken but shockingly ripped and torn. The insane irony was that, as I woozily made my way to Guy's Hospital less than twenty-four hours after the entire lunatic idea had been hatched, I was the one most likely to bump into John Cleese.

So how did the piece work on the show? Fantastically. Of course it did. Chris had been filming links throughout the whole jaunt and so when he finally was told JC wasn't in New York any more and looked blankly at the camera, it made the bit funnier than it would have been if it had gone to 'plan'. To keep the mania building, he and John Revell then themselves followed Cleese to Paris where, once again, they missed him. The film was a riot. An indulgent, expensive one, but Lord, what an experience.

I think I should park further *TFI* stories for the moment; they might come in handy later to lighten the mood. You see, that ill-fated trip culminating in my right foot being tightly bound up in Guy's casualty department marked the very first time in my entire life that I'd had the need to visit a hospital. Up until then, I'd never broken a bone, never had my tonsils out, never needed surgery and certainly never had anything approaching a serious illness. I was blessed! Bulletproof! Meanwhile, up in the heavens, the gods were quietly slipping a horseshoe into fate's boxing glove.

Look Out (Here Comes Tomorrow)

In March 1998 I was sitting in a Glasgow restaurant with Chris and Paul Gascoigne when one of those moments that, in a film, signify something of a major plot point is about to occur, actually happened. I didn't think maître d's really did discreetly tap you on the shoulder and whisper, 'Excuse me, sir, you are wanted on the telephone. I believe it's important.'

Ushered toward a landline in reception I stood there and heard Wendy's voice in London. Like any parent, my immediate thought was that something had happened to one of the kids. In this I was partially right. Except it wasn't 'the kids'. It was another kid.

'Dan,' she said. 'You know I said yesterday I haven't been feeling that great. Well, I'm having a baby.'

It is fair to say neither of us had seen that coming. By then our other children were aged fourteen (Bonnie) and eleven (Sonny). Whoever this new interloper was, was very much the hidden track on the CD. I am assured that when I came back to the table I looked suitably exploded. Looking across into one of the mirrors on the restaurant wall, I recall that my hair was standing straight up as if I had been fondling a Van der Graaf generator. Apparently, when I tried to get across the enormity of what I had just been told, about ten inches of tongue simply fell from my mouth, momentarily dangled there, before rapidly receding into my head again with a noise like a cash register displaying No Sale.

Mancie Mackenzie Hope Baker was born on 5 September 1998. Two weeks ago, as I write this, she played a solo set of her songs to an audience of thirty thousand people. Another reason why I wish we had stuck to my first choice of names for her: Pension Scheme.

The main discussions that Wendy and I had about this extraordinary bonus to life centred on moving house. Neither of us wanted to leave our home in Deptford, but having exploited every possible means of extension it finally looked like we had no choice. We thought back a few years to when we had flirted with living up the big hill to the south of the borough on well-to-do Blackheath. Blackheath was the area where, when I was a kid, most people on the council estates in South-East London imagined living if ever they won the pools. One evening we had walked past a beautiful, if enormous, property there that was for sale and stood at its gate marvelling. Seven bedrooms, huge garden, high ceilings, marble fireplaces, wrought-iron verandas, the asking price for this substantial drum: £350,000. We even viewed the place, all the while knowing it was only playacting. Finances aside, we just weren't the moving sort. Everyone and everything we knew was *down* the hill. Both Bonnie and Sonny would burst into tears if we ever spoke about friends who were moving. In Deptford, I could walk to Mum and Dad's in five minutes, on top of which our house was absolutely perfect. Well, perfect for four anyway. Now what? Reaching a shaky decision that moving immediately would be something that only maniacs would do, we decided to simply upgrade a few rooms and see how things went. First for overhaul would be the bathroom, a fixture that naturally would be crucial, come the baby's arrival. Feigning excitement at the prospect, deep down we knew that unless when we ripped out the old shower we were to discover three hitherto undiscovered rooms behind it, this wasn't going to be enough.

Now, if you've previously read the rather magical story of how we came to acquire our home in Scawen Road SE8, you'll understand why we were so reluctant to leave it. However, what happened next would match like a bookend that tale of an apparent guiding hand.

A few weeks after making our decision to stay put, we were in a local bathroom showroom hoping to see somebody about refreshing our tired old wet room. There was only one sales person available and two people ahead of us waiting for service. Impatient as ever, I suggested we come back another time.

'There's no point,' Wendy insisted. 'It's always busy in here and we've got to get this underway.'

We may have even quietly started arguing about it. Then the woman in front of us turned and said:

'Excuse me, I thought it was you. I don't know if you remember me, but I was the nanny in a house you looked at a couple of years ago. I hoped it would go to you – did you get somewhere else?'

Given that, other than our home, we had never looked at another property, this had to be the big place in Blackheath. Wendy explained to the woman that we'd simply decided to remain where we were.

'Oh,' the woman continued, 'only it's such a coincidence, because I was only talking about that house earlier on. Did you know it's going to be up for sale again?'

Something else that only happens in films is where a couple who are stunned into silence do a syncopated turn to look at each other, give it a beat, then both turn back to a third party and say, 'What?' in unison. Well, now that happened.

'Yes,' she said, 'they can't have been in there two years, but I know they are definitely putting it on the market. It's a wonderful house. How strange we should run into each other – maybe it's still waiting for you!'

There was another extended pause where Wendy and I looked at each other once more, breathing now a little rapid, communicating only through our eyes.

We left the bathroom shop there and then and made our way to Blackheath. Eighteen years later, we're still here.

Not fantastical enough? Then let me now relate a tale that involves both those houses and, this time, should you ever be asked to swallow such a thing as this in a film or novel, you would cry foul and try to hunt down the author with a credibility blunderbuss. It concerns the only other thing that in my heart rivals the boundless affection I have for my family – and that is my record collection.

As stated, the house in Scawen Road was bursting at the seams.

One of the first casualties of this was the enormous amount of vinyl albums and singles I had amassed from a career being connected with the music business. When I say casualty, I don't mean that they had to go – I am not deranged – but rather Wendy felt that to have the complete back catalogue of every touring rock band of the last thirty years on open display in the front room somewhat sabotaged her vision of the tasteful interior. Sadly the battle between Clarice Cliff and Uriah Heep is a scrap that most couples have to thrash out once they have opted for cohabitation, and, in my experience, it is rare that the hairier and more riff-based of those camps ever triumphs. She also felt my horde didn't belong in the kitchen, or the bathroom, or in either of the kids' rooms, and furthermore if I thought our bedroom would be enhanced by rack upon rack of patchouli-reeking platters, then I had not been observing her too closely these last fifteen years. I did float the idea that the hall might be a neutral enough venue for them, but this was rejected on the grounds that a) If five thousand albums were to be the first things that visitors saw when we invited them over they would instantly form the opinion that we lived 'in a madhouse'; and b) The hall was narrow enough as it was. If I filled it floor to ceiling with twelve-inch LPs, everyone would have to slink into the house sideways 'like they were shuffling along a mountain pass'.

And so the two halves of my collection – singles and long players – were divided up and sent to dwell in the unseen and forgotten portions of the house. The 45s to the cellar and my albums painstakingly, back-breakingly, hauled up into the loft where they were carefully placed across supporting beams lest their weight might one night send them crashing through the ceiling of our bedroom below. (Personally, I would find that a fitting way to depart this earth but, again, though I've not canvassed her view, I find it unlikely that Wendy would welcome an end that involved being crushed by Emerson Lake *AND* Palmer.)

Then, very soon after the news I was to become a dad again, I did something quite bizarre. Before the baby bombshell, we had booked a mini-skip to carry off rubble and detritus from some previously planned garden work and, job now completed, that skip was due to be collected. Still kidding ourselves there would be plenty of room for dozens more offspring, I went down into the cellar to see if there was any other old shit to pile on to this skip before it went so we could free up a bit of space. Now readers of the previous books will know this cellar of ours was more of a crawl space than a store room, one in which it was impossible to stand upright. (See: *The Great Discarded Balloon Fiasco of 1988*.) There were no lights down there (ditto) and one of the first encumbrances I literally stumbled across were two huge old suitcases, their zips straining to contain their neglected contents. Ladies and gentlemen, therein rested my singles collection. This being the peak era of CDs, I hadn't even looked at them, much less played them, for many years. My fingers hovered near the handle to haul them upstairs and pore over them once more, sort them out and perhaps bring the two cases down into one. The rest I would simply dump on the skip where the sort of vampires who hover near these containers in search of booty would be welcome to them. But could I be trusted to do that? Frankly, if I could find as many as five records to discard from my fabulous seven-inch library I would astound myself, so I conceded the plan was a nonstarter. These suitcases weren't full of generic chart records amassed casually through years of shallow teenage tastes. These were 100 per cent classic 45s with many rarities, acetates and promotional giveaways. I looked down at the cases; in the gloom they looked like a sunken cargo forgotten by time, treasure once prized now useless. Inexplicably, in an exhilarating fit of misguided zeal, I decided I was going to throw the lot out, sight unseen.

Moments later I was hauling the first of the bulging cases up the cellar steps. Wend saw me.

'What's in there, dead body?' she laughed.

'Nope, my old singles,' I puffed. 'I'm chucking them all out.'

The startled expression on Wendy's face showed that she couldn't have been more shocked had her initial guess proved true.

'You're not!' she cried, suddenly overcome with a new and profound respect.

'Oh yes I am,' I boomed. 'If I stop to go through these, I'll never get anything else done. I've got most of them on CD now anyway. They're going.'

As I heaved the dead weight past her in the passage I felt absolutely heroic. I sensed awestruck eyes watching my every move as I lifted the leaden load skyward then heaved it into the filthy skip. I may have even dusted off my hands afterwards, like Wild West saloon owners do following the successful ejection of the town drunk. This was impressive stuff. A man has to know when to put away childish things and I was clearly a man. My eyes were set on the future – I had children to raise! Don't talk to me about promo-only copies of the Clash's 'White Riot'. That Danny Baker was now dead.

Approximately eleven hours later, at around two in the morning, I sat bolt upright in bed and bellowed, 'Oh Sweet Jesus, what have I done?'

I had thrown away two thousand rare singles. Thrown them away! Why hadn't somebody stopped me? Why hadn't I been wrestled to the floor, sedated, had a tongue suppressor jammed in my mouth and forced into a straitjacket? In God's name, who was responsible for this outrage? This stupid full estate of manhood garbage seemed as nothing when set beside the lost council flat of idiot youth. I felt as though I had chucked my children into that skip, along with a note saying, *Help Yourself.*

I got up and looked out of the bedroom window down into the road. Under the streetlights the space where the skip had been yawned vacant, just a few paint stains and remnants of crushed concrete evidence of its recent tenancy. Not a sign of my records. They were gone, gone, gone.

Now cut to nearly ten years later. We had been living in the 'new' house at Blackheath for most of that time and I was in my study writing the script for the upcoming Concert for Diana to be staged at Wembley Stadium. (There is, of course, a tremendous tale affixed to that shaky debacle too and I've made a mental note to bring that story to you as soon as we've concluded the one now under examination.) Anyway, I was thankful my study faced on to the garden because had it faced the street I would have been forced to acknowledge the monster twelve-yard skip that temporarily blocked our drive. Needless to say, I hadn't been able to stomach the sight of a skip, any skip, since that dreadful day when I threw away my musical brain, heart, liver and lungs in what I now refer to as the 'kamikaze brainstorm'. However this latest one was essential because of the major kitchen revamp taking place downstairs, although I had insisted Wendy deal with every aspect of its arrival and departure. My memories were just too raw.

Halfway through a particularly tricky link I was honing for Fergie, late of the Black Eyed Peas, the doorbell went. I did what I always do when the doorbell goes – ignored it in the hope someone else would go. After it had sounded for a second, then third time, I started calling out the names of other people in the house in a peevish tone designed to signal that my delicate joke constructions demanded I stay at my post.

Nobody responded and so, like Basil Fawlty, I sprang from my chair shouting, 'OK, great, fine, I'll write a nine-hour show for eighty thousand people and do everything else all day around here too, OK, no problem . . . '

Swinging the front door open perhaps a tad too dramatically I saw standing halfway up the steps a working man of about my own age, pointing a thumb over his shoulder.

'The skip, mate,' he began, 'I've come to take it, but you might need to move your car . . . '

Before I could answer, his expression changed and with narrowed eyes he said, 'Here, you're Danny Baker, ain't ya?'

I tersely confirmed this.

'Blimey, you had a skip off us years ago, didn't ya? Down in Deptford.'

I ask you! Could he have said a worse, more inflammatory thing? Was there no end to this torment? Desperately trying to internalize any explosions, I gravely nodded in a way I should imagine Dr Crippen nodded when confronted by the authorities on the SS *Montrose*.

'You threw out a load of old records. In suitcases.'

We were now entering the world of science fiction. But it wasn't done yet.

"'Ere, you'll laugh at this! I've still got 'em – all of 'em. Don't want 'em back, do ya?'

OK. When I was a child I occasionally used to get myself lost in a magazine called *Eerie Tales*. Like that episode of *Lost in Space* with the boy who lived on the other side of the mirror, its content was strange, fantastical and far-fetched. I also used to be addicted to a TV series called *The Liars* in which a table of dinner party guests, headed by the great William Mervyn, would compete each week to deliver the most outlandish and unlikely anecdote. I think it is safe to say that nothing I ever read or witnessed via those two productions ever came close to the utter freakishness of what this man, in all seriousness, was now saying to me.

As he continued talking the Wagnerian storm in my head gave way to a prolonged glissando played on a sweet heavenly harp.

'Yeah, I was always going to have a car boot sale with 'em or something. A right "way out" lot, weren't they? Not my sort of thing, I'm more Gerry & the Pacemakers era, me! Any rate, I still got 'em in my lockup if you got the space now – I know you're back on the radio!'

The saintly fellow told me he lived in Dartford, Kent. That evening I went to Dartford and I got my records back. Still in the suitcases. Of all the peculiar and wonderful things that have happened to me – including being a member of Led Zeppelin for twenty-five minutes, which is another thing I must tell you about later – the story of how my singles came back to me is, for my money, the most phantasmagorical. Apart from the sheer chance that I should open the door that day and he be the same man who took them away a decade previously, I think we all know that you can place anything on a skip, from old gas cookers to cow pats, and within seconds some unseen lurker will have helped themselves to it. There is a container ship that I understand constantly crosses and re-crosses the oceans of the world because no nation is willing to allow it to dock with its deadly cargo of spent nuclear waste. Somebody should write to the captain and tell him if he simply dumped his freight in a British skip the whole lot would be gone by lunchtime. And yet somehow my vast collection of 45s went untouched.

Over the years, a favourite greeting from my wife whenever I came back home from some street market with several carrier bags full of albums was 'Managed to find one or two bits then? Haven't you got enough records now, Dan?' *Enough* records! What a concept! As though records were something you could have 'enough' of, like hiking boots or paintings of stags at bay. On the evening I arrived back from Dartford with my itinerant 45s, she said nothing. She may have even been quite pleased for me. But as I once more struggled past her with those bastard suitcases, albeit this time in a different, more spacious hallway, I couldn't resist one small observation.

'You see, Wend,' I huffed, 'far from having too many records, it seems to me Almighty God has decreed that I don't have nearly enough.'

To this day I continue to collect records of all speeds and sizes, like a public statue collects bird poop.

The final deadline for the Concert for Diana script was due but a few days after the records' return and so I wisely spent the next forty-eight hours ignoring all royal commands and attending to the boomeranged vinyl. Besides, every time I did check my emails I'd see that another act for the big event had been added to the line-up or that a promised mega-star had dropped out, so it seemed only sensible to me that I didn't waste any effort banging out bespoke intros for turns whose participation was, at best, flighty. Checking the current market value of, say, Satan's Rats' first EP seemed smarter time management all round.

I suppose I was taking a *TFI* attitude to this imminent global extravaganza, though I was well aware that not everyone would be comfortable with such a relaxed schedule; the various people in Buckingham Palace nervously waiting for the script, for example. To secure the gig, I'd had to go to St James's Palace and be formally interviewed (vetted) by a royal equerry, a nice but rather stereo-typical old cove who was something vital in the near orbit of Prince Charles. This meeting was an interesting trip in itself, but fairly routine in substance. I could tell he was merely checking me out for any suspicious twitches or obvious soft spots for al-Qaeda. (I presumed they already had photocopies of my old Millwall season tickets on file.) They had nothing to worry about, I knew the exact amounts of pizzazz, old oil and faux-inspirational hot air a day like this would require. I intended to make everyone sound like a beatific cross between Mahatma Gandhi and Forrest Gump.

One part of the running order I knew wouldn't change was the welcoming address to be delivered by Diana's sons and our hosts for the day, Prince William and Prince Harry. I set about that straight away and wrote up an absolute belter of a speech. Completing it within about half an hour of getting the original instruction, I couldn't wait to ping it straight back to the Palace for both glowing approval and to impress the fuck out of them that I could turn such crackerjack prose round in so short a time. After forty-eight hours of silence from their end, I mailed once again for confirmation they had received and read it. The eventual polite but distant reply informed me that their highnesses would not require me to provide their words on the day, it would be done in-house (so to speak). Fair enough, but I couldn't resist then asking, just between us, if they could agree what I had sent was some pretty hot copy and a tonic for the troops. A few hours later a frankly droopy reply arrived stating, in essence, that while they thanked me for my effort the words were 'too expressive' for the princes. Too expressive? I'll say so – this thing was dynamite, *drenched* with emotion. It was an absolute pip of an address, and I'd pulled out all the stops, intentionally rooting this massive worldwide celebration of the greatest emotional icon of modern times in the image of these two semi-orphans now standing dwarfed on the Wembley stage. Why, there wouldn't be a dry eye on the planet, let alone the stadium. This was surely the bang people wanted from their Diana buck, wasn't it? Apparently not, but I feel they missed a huge moment there. One that for the very first time

I can now bring you exactly as I envisaged it. Grab a hanky people because here we go!

OK. It's midday at a packed Wembley Stadium on what would have been Princess Diana's forty-sixth birthday. After a moment of calm the enormous PA system rumbles into life and for the next five minutes, set against a suitably smart soundtrack, a montage showing the late, tragic heroine plays out on the giant video screens and across the world. The film climaxes when the love in the crowd is at its peak. Then a booming voice announces:

'Ladies and gentlemen, to officially open this Concert for Diana, please welcome to the stage, your hosts, their Royal Highnesses Prince William and Prince Harry.'

Huge ovation. The chaps walk to centre stage and bask in all the warmth and emotion washing over them. After some time it dies down. Dressed suitably casually for such a day, they step forward to speak. A pause. Then in the absolute silence, alternating the delivery – this:

She was our mother.

And while we wouldn't suggest that our mother was more precious to us, or more loved, than the mothers of every child watching this worldwide right now, today is her day.

And she was *our* mother.

But beyond that, she was, of course, to countless millions, Diana, Princess of Wales.

A woman we shared with the world. Truly the world.

From the humblest home in a South African settlement to the most resplendent palaces on Earth, they knew her. They knew her face. They knew her message. They knew her hope.

We are fully aware that terms and titles like 'prince' or 'princess' are questioned and derided in many quarters in this modern world, yet our mother somehow managed to wrest that language from dusty library books and fairy-tale legends to reinvent that word as a meaningful, powerful, vital role. One that could not only be symbolic but essential, historic yet utterly modern, boundless and benevolent.

She showed that while a modern princess might no longer need to be saved from dragons, the all too real demons of this modern world can be confronted by a modern woman ready to face down the many evils people everywhere truly need to overcome.

It is our honour, both personal and public, not only to launch this magnificent day, but also to invite you to take part in a celebration of the ideals that Diana, Princess of Wales, worked hard to keep uppermost on the world agenda. Ideals that surely peace-loving people everywhere still see as the only hope for this beautiful, troubled, chaotic Earth that we all of us call home.

Have a terrific day, everybody, feel very free to rejoice in the better angels of our human nature, in the memory of a unique and remarkable woman, and from two brothers, two sons, simply thrilled to be here and witness it all.

Oh and [both turn to Diana portrait on screen behind] Happy Birthday, Mum.

Applause, lights up, first band.

Slam! Pow! Whack! I mean, what? Talk about some spin on the ball there. Did I feel like that about the day? Of course not, and I confess to chuckling along at the florid verbiage even as it poured forth. However, that's not the point. I felt, and still do, that such lofty sentiment on such a specific event was pretty much A1 on the jukebox. And there was plenty more where that came from. How about this pint-pot metaphysical treatise I penned for the great Dennis Hopper, who, for some reason, was one of the big names booked to introduce the groups. Dennis Hopper! And, God love him, he said it word for word:

Princess Diana was a free spirit. A free spirit. Yeah, I've been called that. But you know there's no point setting the spirit free if it just runs and hides someplace once sprung from the box. Too many free spirits confuse freedom with mere chaos. Fact is, you can't lose focus. You can't avoid the real world. A truly free spirit seizes time and works like a field mule right around the clock to try and haul all those souls less free to a better place. Inspiration. This is the true job of the artist, the seer and, yes, even the princess. Temptation is just the voice that whispers, 'Don't bother.' Well here's the word: Bother. Do it. Reach.

Oh I know! I hear you. And I am currently bowing low to left and right in recognition of your awe-struck hosannas. Not all the links were so high-blown though, and Dennis Hopper was among the few stars who even bothered with the script. Most simply bounced on to the Wembley stage and immediately began screeching the only words they knew to say to a stadium full of people: 'Whoo! How you doing out there?' followed by a few more whoos and the occasional 'Come on, give it up for Lady Diana!' In front of them, I could see the autocue being desperately whizzed through in an attempt to find if I had actually written 'You guys look amazing!' fifteen times in a row.

It had been that sort of day. Working in a windowless room deep in the bowels of the venue, I had received an endless procession of managers, agents, publicists and stylists of the mainly American turns awaiting their half hour onstage. Without exception, they wo··ld say that their star wasn't happy with their introduction so could I write something else. Something along the lines of, 'Now welcome a totally unique and awesome genius who has sold more records than anyone, whose last tour played to over a hundred billion fans in Europe alone and whose new fragrance is so unbelievable everyone is losing their minds.' I promise you that is not exaggerating some of the empty-headed claptrap suggested to me that day by what Chris Evans and I termed 'the scribble'. (In general, on *TFI* we found even the biggest stars to be perfectly reasonable people, happy to muck in with a sketch or game if you asked them directly. Ask a member of the star's 'scribble' first and even the lightest of requests was treated as though the Fate of Nations depended on it and they couldn't possibly bother their Artist with such a difficult and exhausting enquiry.) The scribble from Kanye West, P. Diddy and Fergie all wanted to check exactly how many words other performers had in their introduction and, having tallied them, they would then request I make their act's intro longer. This I would do; they would then thank me in that sing-song oily LA way that drips insincerity, and as soon as they went I would delete it and paste my original back. It was all tremendous fun.

My chief concern was Wendy and the kids. They were not allowed backstage – the security was understandably intense – and they'd been allocated rotten seats. I felt sure they must be finding the long day starting to drag come nightfall, particularly during some of the more operatic offerings. I had mistakenly believed my duties on the actual day of the show would be relatively light, but, as it turned out, I was not allowed to unplug my laptop until the final act, Elton John, left the stage and the crowds were streaming for the exits. Stuffing everything hurriedly into my bag, I put on my coat and made for the corridor. I had last checked in with my family around five hours ago, when we'd agreed that if I couldn't get free again before this thing ended they should sit tight and I'd come and find them. Just as I was busting out of my anchorite's cell, however, the royal equerry appeared in the doorway.

'Danny, thank you so much for all your help today,' he began, then proceeded to tell me what a success he felt the day had been. I made a few polite responses but inwardly was picturing Wendy still up in the stands, fuming in the belief that I was now swigging champagne from the bottle while hanging with my new pal Kanye. I began to try and edge past my effusive guest, but as I did so he said:

'Anyway, look, we're keeping this very low key, but the two princes would like to personally thank some of the people involved today and so we're having a small reception upstairs in the suite. They have asked that you join them.'

Continuing to edge around him, I attempted to outline my predicament:

'Now? Oh, do you know what, that'd be great, but I've got to shoot off.'

He looked stunned. 'Shoot off?' I remember him saying.

'Yes, honestly, straight off. I'll get slaughtered if I hang about, so could you say I had to go.'

He managed to utter the words 'I see . . . ' before I squeezed out of the room and began a swift jog towards the main arena. As I did so, it hit me for the first time that his gentle invitation was probably nothing of the sort. I now realized it was more a subtle command of the type that probably influenced the way future MBEs got distributed. Most likely my name would have been on some carefully drawn-up list of those to be honoured with a personal meet-and-greet and, in turning it down like a bedspread, I may have thrown the whole machinery out of whack.

'I am so sorry, your highnesses,' I imagine he said to them as a string quartet played in the background, 'but Mr Baker, our writer, has had to, um, "shoot off". He did say, and I quote, "If I get a chance later, I'll put me nut around the door to see if anyone's still about." It was most irregular. So now allow me to introduce the next cab off the rank; the Grand Exalted High Macha of Raspur . . . '

When I managed to make it back to everyone, I found I could, in fact, have nipped up for a quick one.

'Oh,' said Wend, 'I thought you'd be ages yet!'

'I could have been,' I replied, 'but I just blew out the future king of England.'

To be fair, I have absolutely no strong feelings one way or the other about the royals. Certainly not the immediate family, anyway, though a cull of all the earls, dukes and viscounts – or as Spud always called them 'the lickers' – seems well overdue.

On the way back from Wembley, Wendy asked if I had done the right thing in legging it. I said absolutely and she then asked if there was a famous person that I would have abandoned them all for. I knew of only one: David Bowie. If Bowie had asked me to go for a few drinks that night, it's entirely likely that my wife and children would have still been sitting in row Z at Wembley Stadium as the crowd filed in for the first of the World Cup qualifiers two months later. Even though, as these books chronicle, I have met virtually every big name in show business over the last 40 years, from Tommy Cooper to Michael Jackson, from Bob Dylan to Kenneth Williams, I had to play the long game to meet finally Bowie. In truth, I never truly thought this particular sit-down would ever happen. Bowie, to me, was too mythical, too sensational, too much. However, one Friday afternoon in 1999, while half lost in reverie in a deserted west London room, I finally found myself sitting smack bang opposite the eternal Dame.

The Low Spark Of High-Heeled Boys

By 1998, *TFI Friday* was such a hit fixture in the TV schedules that we no longer had to scramble to attract major guests. It was more a case of having to place anti-tank guns on our studio roof to keep them at bay. Everyone but everyone came through those doors during its stellar run until inevitably came the week when Suzi Aplin casually said during the Tuesday get-together that David Bowie had been confirmed for that coming Friday's broadcast. The meeting probably went on for another hour after that, but I didn't hear a word of it. Though seemingly listening attentively, in fact all I could hear was a voice, rather like when Gene Wilder goes nuts in *The Producers*, shouting: 'I'm going to meet David Bowie! I am going to meet DAVID BOWIE!' Up until that point, I had not met David Bowie – and spectacularly so. Let me explain.

My secondary school, West Greenwich Secondary Modern Boys, was a big old comprehensive close to Deptford High Street. Deptford High Street was, and to some extent remains, about as perfect an example of run-down inner-city life as even a location scout for the next Ray Winstone movie might dream about. Recently I came across a film made by the Children's Film Foundation called *Hide and Seek* that was shot almost entirely in and around Deptford High Street in 1972, even including some shots of the house in Scawen Road that was to become my own home ten years down the line. The film starred a young Gary Kemp and I emailed Gary to tell him how, for me, every frame of *Hide and Seek* made Proust's rotten madeleines suddenly seem such a piddling allusion. I explained that I was constantly pausing the gripping action – a thoroughly ripe yarn about local kids getting mixed up with some fake policeman and a missing twenty-pound note – to weep hot nostalgic tears at the vanished old street scene literally frozen in time. Did he know, for example, that the poorly painted swastika on the wall of the bomb site he got chased across was put there by a kid called Phillip Chapman who was in my class? (Swastikas were not uncommon graffiti in that pre-Banksy age. Invariably daubed by youngsters, they carried no intentional political message and were deceptively difficult to draw. Chapman's effort was typical in that he had bent the front of it up when it should have gone down and vice versa at the back. Consequently, the thing looked like a lopsided, angular number eight. He had compounded the howler by writing 'High Hitlar' underneath it.) I further told Gary that, in all probability, I would have been just around the corner in school while he and his scripted chums were bringing the burglars to justice.

Brother Kemp, as loyal to North London as I am to South, replied that, while happy I was getting so much pleasure from this early entry into his oeuvre, his overriding memory of the shoot was having to constantly duck bottles and half-bricks aimed at him and his fellow actors by 'hordes of local toughs'. 'Don't suppose you were among them, were you?' he added as a PS. Well, the answer to that is absolutely not. I assured Gary that, in 1972, had I seen a film crew in Deptford, far from aiming rubble at the players, I would have been in among them, greasing away, asking the director whether there might not be an impromptu part for a local lad with authentic accent and a strong line in meaningful pauses. All references could be provided by anyone who had seen my Mad Hatter in the Rotherhithe (Junior Mixed) production of *Alice in Wonderland* (1967).

Anyway, should you ever see this film, described in the BFI brochure as 'containing its fair share of fun', you will see that the area in which my school was located did not look like the sort of place that in 1972 David Bowie, in the guise of his brand-new alter ego Ziggy Stardust, was going to be hanging around in, queuing for sausage rolls or waiting for a bus. I use these examples because queuing for sausage rolls and waiting for a bus were two of the things that the non-music-obsessed boys in my year claimed to have seen David Bowie doing when they related the sightings to Bernard Sibley and me, who happened to be the biggest Bowie fans in the school. 'Oi, Baker,' they would shout as they returned from spending their school dinner money (and other kids' school dinner money) on fags and chips. 'That weirdo bloke you like, he was in the chemist just now.' Or maybe, 'Dan. You keep missing that queer geezer – he was lining up in Broomfield's the Baker's with some other dropouts.' Naturally, Bernard Sibley and I rose above such baiting and continued to pore over the lyrics to Bowie's 'The Bewlay Brothers' in an effort to discern what he might have meant when he said, 'Lay me place and bake me pie, I'm starving for me gravy.'

Quite often after school, Bernard and I would get the number 1 bus that, an hour later, decanted us into Charing Cross Road. From here we would go to Trident Recording Studios in Soho and stand outside in all weathers, hoping that this would be the night Bowie and his band would appear. They never did, although we once convinced ourselves we saw Rick Wakeman, who had been a long-time side man of David's, get some sort of beverage from a half-hidden vending machine. Even this low-wattage sighting was denied us when later 'Rick Wakeman' exited Trident and turned out to be a blonde woman in a green silk blouse.

In the meantime, our giggling classmates kept up with the Bowie sightings that, somehow, we always seemed to miss. He was 'sitting on the pavement by the chemist, strumming a guitar'. He was 'going through old singles in the junk shop up the road'. He was 'finishing some fish and chips down Greenwich High Road'. They always urged Bernard and me to move quickly lest we miss him. I am happy to say we never gave them the satisfaction and simply rewarded them with indulgent smiles.

So. Let us now fast-forward to 2010 and the publication of Kevin Cann's exhaustive *Any Day Now: David Bowie The London Years 1947–1974*, for my money one of the truly indispensable Bowie books. This definitive work chronicles day-by-day exactly what David

Bowie was doing and where David Bowie was for the first third of his life. It was when I arrived at the period during which Bowie was piecing together tours in support of *Hunky Dory* and *Ziggy Stardust* that the book fell from my hands and I began gasping for air like a stupefied skate just landed on the trawler. For I now know, thanks to Mr Cann's tireless research, that David Bowie spent a great deal of 1971–72 at Underhill Rehearsal Studios, 'beneath a chemist's shop on Greenwich High Road at the foot of Blackheath Hill'. Or, to give you another contemporary map reference, *about a hundred yards from West Greenwich Secondary Modern Boys School.*

Four decades on, I learned the astounding truth. My thug-life chums were not guying us, teasing us, winding us up, or having a laugh. David Bowie really was ligging about outside. He *was* having his fish and chips. He *was* smoking a fag. He *was* queuing for his sausage roll. He was doing all these things about forty seconds' walk away from where Bernard Sibley and I were freaking out in our moonage daydream, foppishly playing the homo superior to our tin-ear peers and refusing to fall for their 'pranks'. On top of this, we would then get that fucking bus *all that way* to idiotically stand in the pissing rain in Soho playing a pointless game of peek-a-boo with women who were not Rick Wakeman.

In 1973, Bowie played the Lewisham Odeon, my local cinema, and something of a homecoming for a man who had spent a good part of his creative life ten minutes up the road in Beckenham. Bernard and I failed to secure tickets for this. The reason for that involves the naked treachery of a black-hearted 'friend' of mine called Russell Watson who *to this day* swears it was all a misunderstanding. On the night of the concert we arrived ultra early to see if, as a consolation, we could simply glimpse Bowie arriving. As we approached the stage door of the Odeon we heard the muffled thump of music coming from within, though it was only late afternoon and the venue's doors weren't due to open till a few hours hence. Getting as close to the building as we could, we discerned that this thump-thump-thump was a vocal-free version of 'The Jean Genie'. It then stopped sharply. Now we could hear amplified voices going back and forth, though the conversation was not decipherable against the noise of the traffic at our backs. The song started up once more and a man emerged from some large metal gates about thirty yards away. He walked towards us.

'Excuse me, do you work in there?' I said, pointing directly at the Lewisham Odeon (there was an ice-cream van nearby and I didn't want there to be any confusion about such an important query). The man said he did work in there.

'Is that David Bowie we can hear?' asked Bernard with trembling breath.

'Yer, sound check,' said the fellow, now striding past us. To be honest, neither my pal Sibley nor I knew what a sound check was, but we both cooed, 'Oh sound check, right.' Then, this bizarre individual who seemed to think nothing of leaving a place with David Bowie in it, delivered the killer blow: 'If you'd been here ten minutes ago, you'd have seen him go in.'

Are you sensing a pattern here? Well, Bern and I remained where we were in the hope that Bowie would emerge. He didn't. The hours went by and the crowds started arriving and the gig began and we were joined outside the Odeon by a hundred or so other unfortunates like us who hadn't got tickets but couldn't stay away. We listened as best we could to the whole concert, muffled, thudding and distorted as it boomed through the brickwork. When it was over, the streets became chaotic as masses of wild-eyed and hysterical Bowie fans poured out into the night and gathered around any door that looked like it might be his escape route. We held our ground right at the front of the crowd by the big doors we had been camped outside for nearly six hours and even when a rumour went around that Bowie might be going out through another exit on the other side of the building, we decided to stand firm where we were. Guess what? Bowie went out through that exit on the other side of the building. Even we started to see the grimly funny side of it. Bowie and the band had probably been popping in and out of that portal all day, may even have played football in the street or invited the few stragglers over there inside to share their sausage rolls and sing along at the sound check. The gods had decided that my meeting David Bowie was simply not to be.

And then, twenty-six years after Lewisham, here he was, coming to me.

I had a particular, and largely successful, modus operandi whenever *TFI Friday* welcomed a performer of great magnitude. Shortly after they arrived I would greet them irreverently while trying to incorporate a reference that would indicate we knew more about them than the usual headline. For example, when Paul McCartney did the show, he arrived very early because he wanted to rehearse a technical effect he had planned. This involved six or seven old-fashioned TV screens behind him that, when synced together live, showed Paul being his own backing band. When I got to the Riverside Studios that Friday he was already onstage, running through the various cues and prompts necessary for the tricky performance. I watched this from the darkness of the studio floor for a bit until there was a suitable short break in the work, and bellowed, 'What's all this? You should have turned it in after "Besame Mucho".'

The mention of this obscure, cheesy number that the Beatles had discarded early on in their career and that had played some part in them getting famously turned down by Decca Records caused McCartney to throw back his head and laugh out loud.

Shielding his eyes against the spotlight, he peered at me. 'Oh, it's you!' he said. 'I've heard about you.'

This was another of those moments in my life when Gabriel could have floated down and gathered me to the Lord and I wouldn't have complained. Still smiling at the idea, Paul then proceeded to sing the notorious old ballroom standard pretty much in its entirety. It sounded fine. Finishing with it, he looked down at his guitar and said, 'That's a good song actually . . . '

Leaving it a beat, I said, 'No it's not.' He laughed again and I knew we'd be fine.

I employed this same device when Led Zeppelin came on. Barging into the dressing room in which both Jimmy Page and Robert Plant were billeted, I looked from one to the other and with great joy cried, 'Stone the crows – it's Miki and Griff!'

Now I don't know how old you are, good reader, but even contemporaries of mine would struggle to remember Miki and Griff, a moderately successful, entirely wholesome British country and western duo from the late 1950s. I figured Page and Plant would, though – this being the kind of obscure act that musicians love to recall. Sure enough, Jimmy P. pretty much spat his tea out all over the floor. 'God, man!' he bubbled. 'Miki and Griff! Wow!' And within moments the pair of them were trying to recall the names of their hits before striking up ramshackle versions of the same. With just the three of us in the room, I believe I am alone among Led Zep aficionados to have witnessed them performing M&G's immortal 'Deedle-Dum-Doo-Die-Day'.

When it came to Led Zeppelin, however, I wasn't cold-calling as much I had been with McCartney. As previously mentioned, I had been in the band for twenty-five minutes a few years earlier in the decade. I assure you this preposterous statement is nothing but the facts of the matter. In the very early nineties Led Zeppelin, who had not been a functioning unit for some considerable time, had agreed to reunite to receive the Lifetime Achievement award from *Q Magazine* in an era when such things did still carry some cachet. Even so, this was an enormous coup for *Q Magazine*, at that time being edited by my friend Danny Kelly. On the day of the awards everyone in the grand room of the Park Lane Hotel was abuzz with the fact that Led Zeppelin were going to be all in one place for the first time since Live Aid and, in the UK, for the first time since 1980.

In fact, even though the ceremony was delayed as long as possible, they still arrived late and the first anyone saw of them was a bunch of shuffling silhouettes making their way between the tables as up on stage some poor clod found their own acceptance speech irretrievably upstaged. A few moments later the lights in the room came up and it was announced that there would be an intermission while dinner was served, following which the conclusion of the giving out of gongs would commence. All heads in the room turned to get a look at Led Zeppelin. This was tricky because their table was now completely surrounded by people and camera crews all hoping to get their moment with the band.

I had had a good few glasses of the crisp-and-chilled by this point and decided that only the sort of watery chump who prized appearing cool above all else would let this moment pass. I resolved to do something other than simply get a handshake and a few wasted words, intent on marking my meeting with the mighty Led Zeppelin a little more indelibly. Calculating that within a five-minute jog was the enormous Tower Records shop at Piccadilly, I hit upon a plan. Checking with Danny K that this interval would last approximately forty-five minutes, I rose from my seat and began legging it toward the Tower Records store.

I'll concede that I had underestimated my fitness somewhat and was puffing a fair bit as I passed Green Park tube. By the time I got to Fortnum and Mason's, I had to wrench off my bow tie and lean heavily on the ex-army veteran playing his accordion outside. Eventually I arrived at Tower and made straight for a pile of the recently released Led Zeppelin 'Best Of' box set. Taking two of these large packages, I swiftly paid up and was soon on the journey back, this time only stopping briefly at Burlington Arcade, where I pretended to look at two-grand-a-pop handbags in a shop window while wheezing like my lungs had grown a fringe.

When I made it back to the grand hotel itself, the top-hatted doorman looked at me as though I had just emerged from the main sewer. My face was a vivid cerise, my hair matted with sweat, the once-crisp dress shirt was now hanging out from all points of the gut circumference, I was limping because of a blister on my heel the size of those gaseous orbs that kept the Prisoner incarcerated and, as was helpfully pointed out to me by an elderly woman as I staggered through reception, my discarded bow tie had somehow slipped from my trouser pocket and was now affixed to the heel of my shoe, trailing behind me like a dead rat on a leash. Against this, I had managed the whole trip in under fifteen minutes. I went to the toilets and shocked myself at how detonated I appeared.

After a quick smarten up, back into the awards room I went. Led Zeppelin's table was still swarming with media and well-wishers. Taking my place in this scrum, I had the box sets tucked under my arm, my plan being to get one signed for myself and the other autographed to give away on the Radio 5 breakfast show I was then hosting. After a few moments it dawned on me I would never get anything like the time and space allotted to me to get this done. Then something quite extraordinary happened: Robert Plant called out my name. Not only that, but he seemed absolutely thrilled to see me and started gesturing to come over to him. He was even telling someone to 'Get him a chair, get him a chair . . . '

I carried on as if this was entirely expected, even though my brain was already forming excuses for what to say when I found out these events were part of my post-exhaustion mania and even now security were on their way to thump the life out of me. But no. I took my place at Led Zeppelin's table with Page on one side and Plant on the other. Ignoring the barrage of questions being fired at them, Robert introduced me to both Jimmy and John Paul Jones, and then to Jason Bonham. A Spanish cameraman working for MTV Europe asked in broken English who I was. 'This is Danny Baker,' said Robert Plant. 'He's our latest drummer. Sorry, Jason,' he smiled, looking over at the son of the late John. 'Been meaning to tell you, but he's got the gig now.'

So what had caused this surreal rupture in the mesh of rationality? Football, my friends, football. Apart from the breakfast show on 5, I was also tearing up the airwaves on the football phone-in show 606. It turned out that the programme had no bigger devotee than Robert Anthony Plant, born in West Bromwich, but today a season-ticket holder of one of the better-positioned seats at Wolverhampton Wanderers. All he wanted to do was yak about not just the game, but such and such caller I'd had on weeks previously, and had I heard about this brewing scandal and what could we all do about that manager or England's club-footed midfield, pausing for breath only to take my box sets from me and say to the others, 'Come on. Sign these for Danny, please.' I hadn't even asked.

Soon a disembodied voice asked if we could kindly take our seats for the second half of the awards and Robert Plant did something even more mind-blowing. He wrote down his home phone number on a scrap of paper and shoved it in my hand. 'When your lot are next up at Molineux, give me a ring – we'll go together.' I agreed, though, on the few occasions both our teams have been in the same league, I've never taken him up on the invite. Trousering the phone number, I rose grandly from my seat and announced to the throng of media still circling us, 'I hereby resign from this band. Our ideas for the future of Led Zeppelin are too far apart. I quit.' And I shook their hands and walked away. However, may the record please now show that for about twenty-five minutes I was a member of just about the most astonishing rock group the world has ever seen.

So, that was my calling card when meeting any of the heroes of my youth: be bold, irreverent and, hopefully, funny. As I say, it usually works. It didn't work with David Bowie. This had less to do with the Dame's impervious aloofness than the fact that, when sitting face to face with Bowie, I found myself rendered absolutely speechless for the only time in my life.

As you can imagine, I had not expected this. I had worked out exactly what was going to happen when we two DBs finally shook hands. As far as I was concerned, within a few moments of this greeting David Bowie was going to realize that he had, in fact, wasted much of his life in not having me as his best mate. (I also believed I could get the same reaction if I ever met Bill Murray, but that has yet to be put to the test.)

The key to my winkling my way into Bowie's life was in the choice of item I had brought along for him to autograph for me. I knew that shoving a copy of *Hunky Dory* or *Station to Station* under his nose wouldn't grab his attention, and asking him to sign my arm so I could later have a tattooist go over it permanently might seem a bit creepy. So what to do? In the end I went out into the shed that abuts our house and began rummaging through the four hundred or so

LaserDiscs that I had stored out there in case that disastrous movie format ever came roaring back into style. There was about as much chance of this happening as a sedan chair revival or the sudden reappearance of telegram boys on our streets, but I had no idea what else to do with them. I had thrown in my lot with LaserDiscs on a quite stupendous scale. As with the VHS player, I had got in early and gone big.

LaserDiscs, for those of you who somehow resisted their allure, were expensive album-sized silver plates whose picture quality was a sensation right up until the advent of the DVD. Unfortunately, the advent of the DVD came about twenty minutes after LaserDiscs began wowing rubes like myself. Oh and, unlike DVDs, halfway through a film LaserDiscs would suddenly stop and have to be turned over like a pancake so the second part of your night's entertainment could continue. Longer films would often come on four separate sides.

Then there was the player itself. At a time when home video players were becoming slimline, in barged these behemoths to dominate your front room like the Enigma machine. Necessarily bulky, given that the discs themselves were twelve inches in circumference, they had the added bonus of making a noise like the shunting of the Flying Scotsman when loading, followed by a cartoonish UFO whine that increased in pitch as the thing thundered up to speed. I recall during one of these preparations, as my electronic folly desperately tried to locate the beginning of *Barton Fink*, Wendy said she could feel the whole house shake. Even as DVDs became the norm in British households I still continued to insist LaserDiscs were a superior experience, forking over an average of forty quid a time for such evergreen titles as *George of the Jungle*, Chevy Chase in *Cops and Robbersons* and the piss-poor *Super Mario Bros* movie that even my son, a games fanatic, said he felt sick after. The only advantage LaserDiscs might conceivably offer was in their packaging. Like LPs, they had the cover space to splash the artwork – no great bonus when it came to a stinker like *Mr Nanny* starring Hulk Hogan, but something rather beautiful when it's David Bowie in Nick Roeg's

The Man Who Fell to Earth. This then was what I would bring before The Man himself.

The plan fell down when, as I stood alone on the *TFI* set during first rehearsal watching the edit of a sketch called 'Famous Historical Characters React to This Week's Chart Positions' on a monitor, in walked David Bowie alone and completely unannounced. Slight, smaller than I'd anticipated and with a head a fraction too large for his narrow shoulders, he started taking a look around. Shocked into action, I rushed into conversation. 'David Bowie!' I said with some confidence. 'Thanks for coming, come and sit down.' I pointed to the two empty chairs either side of the large wooden desk that was all that comprised our basic bar-room set. Muttering a quiet, 'OK,' Bowie sat himself down. I took the chair opposite, the one Chris inhabited during all the show's interviews. And there we were. Me and David Bowie. He looked at me blankly and waited to see why I'd asked him to sit down and, I must confess, in this he rather had me. Alarmingly, I suddenly realized that I had no reason whatsoever to ask him to join me – none. Had I not been so surprised by his sudden appearance, I might have had the LaserDisc with me or at least been armed with one of my 'Besame Mucho' / 'Miki and Griff' zingers. Had I known then the story about the proximity of Underhill Studios to my old school, I reckon I could have had him slapping his thigh for a full half hour – but at that exact moment as I looked into his famously mismatched eyes I hadn't the foggiest idea why on earth I had so forcefully bearded him. An inner voice screamed at me, 'Speak, man, speak!'

'I'm Danny Baker, the writer on the show,' I heard myself saying.

Once again he flatly said, 'OK.'

Now what? That was all I had. Having made this bald opening statement, I began frantically searching all the rooms in my mind for some sort of signpost as to where this conversation could possibly go next. Meanwhile, David Bowie continued to look directly at me with expectation, right into my hopelessly conventional pupils, pupils that I hoped were not, at that very instant, twitching away, betraying my rising panic. Mentally I concocted then discarded a series of lame second sallies, including such hardcore tosh as 'I'm a huge fan of yours', 'Any trouble finding the place?' and 'I'm a South London boy too.' I mean, honestly, the paucity of those limp lines should indicate exactly how desperate I was. In the end, I plumped for the least weak of the thin options.

'Do you need anything?' were the words that fell burbling from my useless lips. Oh great, yes. That was certainly worth asking him to come and take a seat for.

'Such as?' he said.

'Such as?' Oh for the love of God, don't throw it back to me again! *I don't fucking know, mate!* was what I wanted to scream, *I've literally not a clue why I asked you to sit down, David – not a clue! I'm drowning here, throw me a bone, sing me a song, punch me in the face, just bring this torture to a close before I pass out or something.*

I eventually managed, after a silence of what might have been a hundred years, to come up with, 'A script? Would you like to see one of those?' *One of those!*

Clearing his throat, Bowie mercifully switched his gaze to look around the rest of the set. 'No, won't be needing that,' he chirped. 'I'm happy to be surprised if you are.'

If I was? Had he sensed my shock? Read my thoughts? He was David Bowie, he could probably do stuff like that.

'So you're . . . ' and I came *this close* to saying 'hunky dory'. I promise you, I nearly said that. Can you imagine? It wasn't an attempt at the world's clunkiest wordplay but born of sheer Freudian subconscious and a barely concealed flap.

' . . . all good then,' I somehow finished but, man, that had been a close call.

David confirmed he was fine and I rose relieved from the table, giving the impression of a man who had just had a bloody good meeting that, for him, had covered all the important points. It wasn't quite over though.

'Is that it?' he said with a slight smile.

I laughed and began to walk away, anywhere would do. I may have said something else in my retreating, I really don't recall. I only hoped I wasn't leaving behind a trail of steaming loser ooze in my wake.

He was terrific on the show and I was particularly pleased to see him enjoying a series of vignettes by the entertainer Joe Longthorne for whom I'd written 'Joe Longthorne Sings Just the Big Finish to Famous Songs'. (It's on YouTube, if you fancy it.) After the show I called at Bowie's dressing room, this time in my full-on mode, brandishing my LaserDisc of *The Man Who Fell to Earth*.

Now it was Bowie's turn to be taken aback. It appeared that, like most of the sane world, he had never seen such a thing before. Inspecting the cover back and front, and then removing the shiny silver disc from within it, he asked me what it was. I told him and he seemed to unearth a slight memory of the day some charlatan had tried to convince him that they were the future. 'And you've got one of the players, have you?' he gleefully asked. My confirmation seemed to tickle him. He turned to an assistant. 'It IS a lovely thing, though. Could you try and get me one of these? Don't bother about the player – he's got the only one left in the world, I should imagine.' Now was my chance to do my thing. 'Oh funny!' I barked as he signed it. 'You know you should have turned it in after "Ching-A-Ling".' The line got the required snort of recognition from him, but it was too little too late. My overriding memory of meeting David Bowie is of squirming like a worm as whatever genes usually govern my eloquence scrambled aboard a vacant torpedo and fired themselves out my ear.

In 2008 a large gaudily painted lorry turned up at our house and began carting away the collapsing contents of our shed that had by now become overrun with boxes, bags and old suitcases. All of these contained mountains of tumbling junk that, over the years, we had put away 'for the time being', but for which we subsequently had little use and only a fuzzy recollection of why we'd wanted to hang on to the stuff in the first place. Among the teeming detritus were my hundreds of LaserDiscs and I allowed the blokes to load them on the van without ever wanting to check through the boxes to look at the titles. This was not going to be a repeat of my singles-in-the-skip miracle and I knew the precious signed Bowie disc was safely stored with his albums inside the house. Besides, my appetite for hoarding the past had dimmed a little that year, directly leading to this latest purge.

The reason for that was, in the February of that year, my dad Fred, otherwise known as Spud, hitherto the hero of these books, had done the one thing I never actually believed he could be capable of.

He died.

It's All Over Now

In writing the previous chapters I've had the inescapable notion that many of you who have been with this story since *Going to Sea in a Sieve* were growing restless for more tales about my old man. Well, the truth of that is that from the late nineties onwards, even though his presence remained enormous, he seemed more than content to hand over the alpha-male reins in our family to me – not that I knew what to do with them – and to focus all his attention on our youngest daughter, Mancie. To say he doted on her might sound like a cliché, but there really is no other word for it. Whereas he would once come to the house and sit with me, reminiscing and rambling over expertly poured glasses of Guinness or deep draughts of red wine, now as he came through the front door he would immediately say, 'Where's my girl?' and proceed to read her picture books for as long as she wanted, play stooge for hours in her endless and unfocused games of shop or dollies, or just walk with her in his arms singing either 'A, You're Adorable' or 'A Pal Must Be a Pal Forever'.

A favourite gag I had, if ever I wanted to check that the Spud of my youth was still fully functioning, was to wait until he was hanging up his flat cap in our cupboard under the stairs and then say, 'On the way to school yesterday, Wendy says some bloke shouted at Mancie.'

He would jump as if stabbed by a cattle prod. 'What?!' he'd bellow, eyes aflame. 'Who did? Where?!' And his arms would tense, fists clenched, ready right there and then to scour the district and pole-axe this monster. Even when I assured him that it was only another of my wind-ups, he would be unable to shake off the red mist for at least a minute, continually growling, 'That's fucking right! Shout at her? I'll fucking sort 'em, straight out. Don't you worry about that. You let me fucking know and I'll fucking give 'em something to bastard shout about . . . '

About three weeks later I would indeed 'let him know' and he'd fall for it all over again. A fighter all his life, in every sense, he had seen his life in later years get flattened out with the need to duck and dive – or 'forage' as he always called it – growing less and less urgent. I looked after him financially and as the borough of Bermondsey finally succumbed to the numbing march of gentrification, a lot of his old haunts and boltholes began to disappear. Even the various moody businesses that operated out of the endless railway arches, and where he would often find the sort of casual work tinged with illegality that he relished, began to be forced out as areas like Deptford started to be rebranded by dull-eyed estate agents as 'Blackheath Approach'. On top of all this, the dozen upon dozen of local pubs by which working people navigated their movements, in which they met and consolidated, around which all social life revolved, started, at a staggering pace, to get boarded up and close down forever. More than any notice of eviction, it was the pogrom declared upon the pubs that told people who had populated these areas for hundreds of years that their time was up.

I can see my dad now, sitting in the big leather chair in our kitchen, saying with disbelief in his voice, 'You'll never guess what's gone? The Suffolk. The fuckin' Duke of Suffolk. The Jolly Caulkers is up for sale, the Victory closes next month . . . I've got to walk to the pissing Crystal now if I want a skimish before tea.' The next month it would be the Crystal Tavern too.

In 2001 it was announced that even Debnams Road, the once state-of-the-art council block, our family's home for decades, where my mum and dad had raised their children, was to be demolished to make way for private flats in line with the rest of the Silwood Estate, SE16. When I told the old man this news, he formed his mouth into a tight, joyless smile, sighed heavily and shrugged his shoulders. 'Well, there it is. That's how it's all going,' he said. He then put the leads on our dogs and, buttoning up his big Crombie overcoat, left the house in silence to walk them, one of the duties he performed early each morning no matter how bad the weather or how acute the pain in his hip. He took much longer than usual that day. I expect he sat on one of the benches in Greenwich Park that afford magnificent views of the River Thames and down into those areas of the city that were once the sole province of the working class. He would have seen, across the river, the giant banking towers of Canary Wharf where as a docker he worked, drank and played forty years before. Now, on the south, our side, he'd note the growing number of cranes appearing, the rising clouds of brick dust as another block of homes was pulverized into oblivion, and the gaps along the river where once were working wharves, packed pubs and thriving factories. That was how it was all going.

His personality did not shrink, however. Watching a football match on television with him was still as explosive an event as it always had been. He was of the unshakable belief that match commentators could hear him. If, for example, John Motson observed during a tight international that England had conceded late goals in each of their last three matches, he would say, 'Yeah, well, that's not going to happen in this one is it, so keep your trap shut.' If Ron Atkinson pointed out the ball from Paul Ince that led to a goal was 'a beautiful threaded pass', Dad would fume, 'Threaded? What you talking about, "threaded"? You're just pulling these words out your arse, Ron.'

Apart from these sort of comments, there was also a full-on raging that, as a child, made me worry he would next pull on his coat and charge over to wherever the match was being broadcast from to punch the reporter or 'upend them', as he put it. As in, 'If he says that once more, Bet, I'm getting the bus over there to upend him!' It was always the bus he was going to get to settle his grievances, even if the game onscreen was being beamed live from Kiev.

Possibly his greatest-ever eruption was, albeit understandably, after one of the most sickening goals in English football history. This was West Germany's equalizer with almost the last kick of the match that made it 2-2 in the 1966 World Cup Final. In the five minutes prior to the goal being scored, Spud had been constantly on his feet, screaming at the top of his lungs: 'How much longer is he gonna play? Blow the whistle! Blow that fucking whistle, you Swiss ponce!' The 'Swiss ponce' was referee Gottfried Dienst, and Dad was hoping that in standing right over our television set his voice might carry down the speaker into the stadium itself. The volume he was shouting at made me and my brother feel that this was not such an improbability. We had to wait for a suitable halt in the tirade to request he at least stand aside a shade so everyone else in the room could see what was happening. Apologizing, he'd back off, but within seconds he'd be back, blocking the view, hollering, 'Blow, you fucking twot! It's over!' Then, turning ostensibly to us but actually to what he felt was a global audience: 'The fucking Swiss, see? They love the Germans, love 'em! That old bollocks about 'em being neutral in the war – fuck off!'

Nobody dared point out that, by anyone's watch, there had only been eighty-seven minutes played. Then, in the eighty-ninth minute, Jack Charlton gave away a free kick right on the edge of the England penalty area. The fury Spud discharged at this decision rather impressively came with some historical qualification that I have since found is not without some truth. Following several more general tirades against the myth of Swiss impartiality in the Second World War, and while England's players formed their wall to fend off this one last threat, the old man started elaborating.

'Knew it! Soon as I saw he was a Swiss, I said we were fucked – didn't I, Bet? They've sorted all this out beforehand! They're like the fucking Swedes, the Swiss, supposed to be neutral but selling the Nazis iron ore and all the gold on the fucking side. Now this . . .'

Be fair, that's a pretty impressive diversion to work into your apoplectic ranting.

However, it wasn't Mr Dienst that provided the ultimate flame to Spud's blue touchpaper. As the watching world held its breath and the Germans jostled for position in the run-up to the free kick, BBC commentator Kenneth Wolstenholme took this moment to recap events:

'All England have to do is successfully defend this last-gasp danger and they will be crowned world champions!'

Well even I, at nine years old, thought that sounded a bit of a fate tempter and the 'SHUT. UP!' that Dad launched in the wake of these words literally blew the fruit bowl off the top of the telly.

I don't think I need to describe what happened next. The ball ping-ponged around the England goal for a bit before Wolfgang Weber fired home to take the match into extra time. As it went in, I was filled with horror both at what I saw and at the levels of wrath this would elevate Spud to – and beyond. I ran from the house. I literally ran away. I ran across the cobbled square out front, past the stone boat the flats had had gifted to them by the council, up on to the wire fence by the wall, over the wall and up Corbett's Lane to my best friend Tommy Hodges' house. All the while my legs were going like the Roadrunner's, I could hear the ear-splitting oaths, curses and threats bursting out of our front room.

'That's his fault! Fucking Kenneth fucking Wolsten-fucking-holme! Why would you say that unless you were fucking back-ward? What a no-good ponce! How thick have you got to be to do that?!'

Opening the bolt on to Tommy's yard – his family owned the local newsagent's – I rang the bell on his back door. Tom's father, Bill, who wasn't a sports fan, answered and was puzzled to see me. He knew my dad well though, so as soon as I said Spud was going so mad I'd had to get out, he gave a chuckle and bade me join his boys huddling around their set. So I was denied witnessing Dad's turnaround of emotions as England went on to score twice in extra time, and how he reacted when Bobby Moore lifted the trophy in tri-umph. I do know that England's controversial third goal, gifted to us by a Russian linesman, would have slotted right in with his Second World War still in flux by proxy theory. By the time I returned home about an hour later, Dad had already left for the Jolly Gardeners, there to thirstily join the rest of the country in toasting the glorious result.

*

Sky-high emotion wasn't Spud's only contribution to televised football. During every single game when he had some sort of investment in the result – so that would be roughly 100 per cent of all matches – he had one spectacular and unique offering that, as far as I know, he truly believed influenced the action. It was only ever employed late on in games where the team he needed to win would give away a corner kick. With a cry of 'Sorry, I'll have to go up for this,' he would raise his rear from whatever chair or sofa he was sitting in and perch himself on the armrest. Literally 'go up' and sit on the arm. Even if there were five corners in the last ten minutes, he would 'go up' every time until the danger was cleared. As soon as it was, he would settle back in his previous position on the main body of the settee and carry on as normal. Intently staring at the TV, he never cared what anyone thought of this peculiar move, and I have to tell you I never saw it fail to get his desired outcome. Should his preferred team concede from a corner early in the game, he would feel partially responsible: 'That's my fucking fault, that. I should have gone up for it.'

He hated getting old and looking back now, I can see he was never designed to be an old man in the accepted sense of the term. His temperament, his spirit and his appetites were never geared for a life of lesser responsibility and gentler days. Though he was an ideal granddad, it was his very robustness and irreverence that the kids enjoyed. When he would leave here after seeing Mancie, he would drop in at one of the dwindling number of pubs on the journey home to see if any of the old crowd were around but, if they were, they increasingly disappointed him.

'Shot into the Black Horse on the way back yesterday,' he'd tell me. 'Frankie Marks was in there. Fucking 'ell, he's got old. On a stick – and he's the same age as me. Johnny Donnelly, too. I only had one; the pair of 'em talk like a couple of old boys. Fucking boring, they've got.' There was truth in what he observed, given that whenever I later saw him in company in a pub you would not have believed he was a contemporary of the rest of the hesitant, stooping crowd. Though bald by the time he was twenty, his face remained unwrinkled and his body strong almost throughout his entire life.

But you can't escape entirely. Spud's eyesight was first to go. His response to this was entirely typical for someone who never visited hospitals and only went to see his GP to get bogus sick-notes or advice on what might be a believable injury to result from tripping on a discarded length of rope left on the quayside in the docks. Once he could no longer properly see the print in his beloved *Daily Mirror*, he got in touch with his sister to see if she knew what had happened to the drawerful of spectacles they had come across when cleaning out their mother's flat after her death. I remembered seeing these and asking why my nan needed so many – at least twenty pairs, all of them of the round National Health variety and all quite tiny for such a big woman as Alice Baker. Nobody knew how she had come to amass such a horde, particularly as she didn't routinely wear glasses in the first place. Anyway, as luck would have it, they hadn't been junked and once this cache had been located, Spud started using them indoors. The arms being too narrow to fit around his head, he used to hold them by the edge of the frame and, with the paper in the other hand, move them backwards and forwards like a lorgnette sans handle until he could make out the words. Time and again as I watched him squinting into the lenses of these possibly century-old spectacles, I would urge him to come to an optician's with me and get a proper pair. This was fiercely resisted. 'Leave off! These do me all right, you just got to get the distance right. Besides, I only use 'em for reading – what's the point of giving him bundles to make the same thing as I got here?'

The truth was, he didn't want to go public with this new, minor disability. He might run into another ex-docker in the waiting room and then the word would be all over town: Spud Baker's falling to bits. As it turned out, he managed to last with his mother's spectacle collection right up to the advent of prescription-free glasses being sold on carousels in Boots the Chemist. By that time he was down to her last few pairs, thanks to his growing habit of sitting, lying or stepping on all the others after falling asleep in the chair with them still in his hands.

His teeth were next, and here his attempts to conceal the evidence while fending off any professional help bordered on the insane. As far as I know, he hadn't visited a dentist since being in the army in 1945, yet he had strong straight white teeth that gave him no trouble. Their only flaw was a small chip out of the one that sat top centre right. This minor breakage had happened after he had left Debnams Road one winter's night to use the phone box at the bottom of Hawkstone Road about two minutes' walk away. Arriving at the classic red fixture he found it already in use. When the bloke inside failed to curtail his call after a couple of minutes, the old man started giving him a few taps on the window to gee him up. After a further few minutes, his knocks became more urgent and were accompanied by, 'You gonna be much longer? It's freezing out here!' This progressed to a more insistent 'Other people want to use the fucking phone, you know!' and finally, 'You got another minute, then I'm turfing you out!' The man in the booth not only ignored all this, when he finally did replace the receiver on the cradle he immediately picked it up again to make a further call.

Seeing this, Spud went off like a rocket. Seizing the recessed silver handle on the phone box door he yanked it open with tremendous force. Unfortunately, he got his sums all wrong and brought the door smack into contact with his face, knocking himself to the pavement and taking out a piece of his front tooth in the process. Dazed, he eventually managed to get up on to one knee – just in time to see his tormentor jump on a pushbike and pedal away into the night. Infuriated, the old man threw the old pennies he still had clutched in his right hand after the escaping stranger, missing him entirely, and now leaving him with no means of making his phone call. 'I only come out with enough to be on the phone for a few minutes,' I heard him telling my mum later as she shone a torch into his mouth. 'I couldn't see fuck all when I tried to find 'em again. We'll have to get our phone put back on again, we can't live like this.'

That small imperfection apart, his teeth remained sound and solid until one morning in the year 2000 when his front tooth, and not the one with the chip in it, simply fell out as he ran his toothbrush over it. Horrified, he made a grab for it before it disappeared down the plughole and, as he later told me, immediately tried to fix it back into the space it had occupied for the last sixty-odd years. But the tooth would not lodge in the gap.

Many people have dreams that their teeth are suddenly falling from their gums and I have read that this is bound up with anxiety about major life changes rooted (*sic*) in that often traumatic time when our milk teeth make way for the adult version. For Dad, however, this was no dream. He stood for some time looking in the bathroom mirror at the dreadful and very obvious absentee in what had been only last night his famous winning smile.

I did notice that he was much later than usual coming to fetch the dogs that morning, but when he eventually rang the doorbell I didn't spot anything wrong, though he didn't give much of an answer to my question about the local traffic. In fact, unusually for him, he didn't really speak at all. And he kept his back to me as he applied the leashes to Bingo and Sally's collars. As he went out with them, I thought it a little strange, but not overly so. I assumed he'd had a row at the barber's or a slanging match with another motorist, and it was still riling him. Full details would doubtless be supplied on his return.

About an hour later he was back at our door again, asking for a towel because the mutts were 'rotten', as he put it. And it was as he was putting it that I noticed his teeth or, to be precise, his tooth. The one at the top front appeared to be breaking rank and going it alone, protruding proud of its peers and framed, it seemed, by some sort of ghostly proscenium arch. Now my dad and I never had the sort of relationship where we had to dance around delicate subjects and so I came straight to it.

'Dad,' I said, 'what's the matter with your tooth?'

Looking frankly stunned that I had somehow detected his makeshift dentistry, he replied, 'Oh fuck – does it show?'

Did it show? It almost obscured his head. It was Frankentooth!

Sucking upon the slab, he attempted to reassure me.

'It's holding in there all right. It's not moving, but it looks funny, does it? Balls.'

I asked him to fill me in – an apposite choice of words, as it turned out.

'Fucking tooth fell out. Looks terrible, so I've stuck it back with a bit of putty.'

A bit of putty.

'It's all I had indoors. Fuck it, it looked all right when I left home. You sure it notices?'

'Dad,' I said, 'you look like Talfryn Thomas.'

By nature suspicious of public opinion and received wisdom, Spud stuck with the puttied tooth even after I had flagged the absurdity of it. The day after its first public appearance my mum rang me.

'Can't you tell him about that tooth?' she begged. 'He does look choice. It's only because he won't go to the dentist. Though when he does, Gawd knows what they'll say about using putty to keep it in. He won't even buy the proper denture stuff – it's just a bit left over from when the council did the window in the passage. I'm not going out with him while it's like that.'

This bizarre and farcical state of events was finally resolved after three days when, while downing a bottle of Guinness in the Blue Anchor, the incisor was finally washed from its moorings and nearly choked him to death.

I never saw Spud unwell. Without question, he must have contracted all the usual viruses and mild diseases that descend on us all, but no pox or contagion ever seemed to overwhelm him. If anything, they seemed to shock and annoy him. 'Bollocks! I've got a fucking cold! That's that bloke on the fucking bus the other day!' was a typical announcement, but we would then hear no more about it, apart from his regular explosive sneezes that, especially in later years, I've tried to match in volume and power but without success. The only way I knew he'd got the flu was when, after he'd returned from work, I might attempt to show him something in the newspaper and he'd say, 'Don't come near me, boy, I've got the poxy flu!'

And looking at his heavy eyes and dry lips, I could see this was true.

All ailments would be treated with either the trusted brands or home treatments handed down to him from his parents and therefore chiefly Victorian in preparation. Our house was never without large tins of Andrews Liver Salts or Eno's Fruit Salts on the cupboard shelves. The bathroom cabinet had bottles of dark concoctions labelled Parrish's Food and Gentian Violet. Like every household in the 1960s, we stocked TCP, Germolene and Anadin or Phensic tablets as standard. Away from over-the-counter remedies, Spud boiled up bottles of Hooper Struve Lemonade and would drink them while scalding hot in the belief it would settle a sore throat. Incredibly, it always seemed to work. Both he and Bet would talk wistfully about a particular cure-all that had vanished from the market and they made it sound like the key to eternal life. This potion was called, as near as I can spell it, Hepikepper Tonic Wine. The reason I resort to phonetics is because no Internet search has ever confirmed its existence.

Spud's right leg was prone to ulceration following a badly treated injury at the docks. When this painful affliction flared he would treat it with a bread poultice, made in the kitchen washing-up bowl, and applied amid a fusillade of swearing that I leave you to imagine. Indeed, whenever any of us kids gashed a knee, grew a boil on the back of our neck or even had a splinter in our thumb he would always offer to make us a bread poultice for it, though we never took him up on the offer.

'That's why you should always have plenty of bread in,' he would declare, as though an extra bag of Wonderloaf was right up there with the polio vaccine.

The most vivid memory I retain of Spud self-medicating is of him hunched over the kitchen table, attired in trousers and a vest, a towel covering his head, taking deep draughts of steam from a bowl of boiling water. Epsom salts, Radox crystals or Izal disinfectant were sometimes added to the formidable vapours. I never learned the lesson about not talking to him while he was 'clearing the passages' and would bother him with questions like where had Mum put my football boots. From beneath the cover, he'd bawl:

'Don't fucking ask me questions now! You can see I'm under here. What are you, batchy? Fuck it, I've lost count now.'

Oh yes, there was counting involved.

However, outside of witnessing these treatments and the products on show, there was never any display of what had caused him to resort to them. Admitting to my mum that he was 'feeling a bit rough' was the only concession to illness he made.

Another peculiarity – and bear in mind you didn't have to register with a GP in those days – was that while the rest of the family would be treated locally by either Dr Nath (three minutes away) or Dr Lauderdale (five minutes away), Fred would only ever use Dr Barry's surgery, which was a good few bus stops distant. This was because Dad visited Dr Barry for purposes ancillary to the state of his health.

The long and the short of it is, Dr Barry was a gambler and a piss artist my old man knew from the various pubs around New Cross. They were good friends and 'Old Barry', as Dad always called him, could be relied upon to sign sick-notes during Cheltenham week, or satisfactorily validate any injury claims Spud might have on the go. You didn't need appointments to see your doctor back then, you simply showed up in their waiting room and waited your turn. A buzzer would sound and everyone knew who was up next. Spud would always try to be the last person in before the end of the day's surgery, thus ensuring that, as soon as whatever bit of business he had come to see Dr Barry about was concluded, the pair of them could shut up shop and shoot across to the Marquis of Granby for a good session.

'He's as good as gold, Old Barry,' Dad would glow. 'Nine out of ten times he's writing me out the prescription before I've even sat down.'

In return, as soon as one of Dad's claims paid out, Dr Barry would always be his first port of call in the rounds to 'give a drink' to all who had assisted in the windfall.

*

Luck doesn't last forever and even Spud was no exception to that rule. In the mid nineties, he woke one day and found a trail of four or five little blisters behind his ear. The next day there were a few more and he showed them to me – in itself an indication that these were not the only symptom that something was amiss.

'What do you reckon they are?' he asked me, delicately fingering the tiny raw eruptions.

They looked suspicious, but I knew he didn't want to hear that so I concocted an answer that would make us both feel comfortable.

'Do you reckon that's where your glasses have been rubbing?' I said like the true research chemist that I am. 'Or an infection from them?'

Spud weighed this before accepting that this was the most likely diagnosis. However, he was concerned enough to want a second opinion. 'Old Barry' having long since retired, he conceded: 'I might ask Barry Albyn to have a look when I get down there.' This Barry Albyn was, by the way, a) another of Dad's friends and b) the local undertaker.

'Barry Albyn?' I couldn't help but respond. 'What's he gonna tell you? He's not a doctor, Dad.'

'No,' said Spud, gingerly putting his cap back on. 'But he's in that line . . . .'

The following morning my mum called me and said Dad needed to go to the doctor's so would I tell him that because he was taking no notice of her.

'Them blisters are stretching right out across his nut now,' she snapped in a no-nonsense way, 'and he's been feeling rough all this week, having bad headaches and everything.' In the background I could hear Spud shouting, 'Don't tell him that! I'm all right. I've just been overdoing it. I need a kip, that's all.'

It must have been pretty worrying because, without telling anyone, later that day he crept over to Lewisham Hospital A&E, where they quickly confirmed that he was suffering from a full-blown attack of shingles. The blisters, which more commonly appear on the lumbar regions, are the last stage of this infection of the nerve ends and would have been preceded by several weeks of great discomfort, low energy and sickness. I felt a little angry that once again he had masked an illness so defiantly, and yet what could I say? I was the one who thought a change of spectacles would be the solution.

Happily, shingles is very treatable, although the patient is required to take tombstone-sized tablets for three weeks and NO ALCOHOL. When I saw him forty-eight hours later with a small balloon of brandy at his elbow, I reminded him of this instruction.

'It's brandy,' he answered contemptuously. 'It's what they give you when you ain't well.'

Naturally, he recovered within that three-week window. In the last few years of his life, apart from acute periods of pain in his hip and knee that would be flagged by the wincing declaration that 'I might have to sit here for a bit', Spud's health and physical appearance defied his seventy-six years. Then one morning, after he'd missed out a few days walking the dogs because of 'a heavy cold', he came round looking distinctly unwell and, more alarmingly, distinctly yellow. We greeted each other and said nothing about it.

Spud sat in the big brown leather chair that looked out into our garden and I could see that even the whites of his eyes had an eerie tinge.

'Blimey, Dad,' I said, with as little concern as I could muster, 'you don't look right. You ain't half yella.'

He looked at me and swallowed deeply. 'Am I? That's what George just told me.' George had the butcher's shop nearby.

'I went in to see him 'cos he was rough a few months back. Thought it might be the same thing. He reckons I've got jaundice – you know anything about jaundice? Didn't one of your mates have that?'

I told him that he was thinking of Mancie when she was a baby.

'What did they give her?' he asked hopefully.

I explained that she had to lie in an incubator for two days.

'Fuck that,' he said. In the carrier bag he had with him I could see he had bought a bottle of Lucozade.

It was cancer. In his lungs, in his spleen, in his stomach, in his

Mum and Dad with my sister at the Festival of Britain, 1951.

Love this photo of Spud (centre & insert) pointedly ignoring pleas for dockers not to strike.

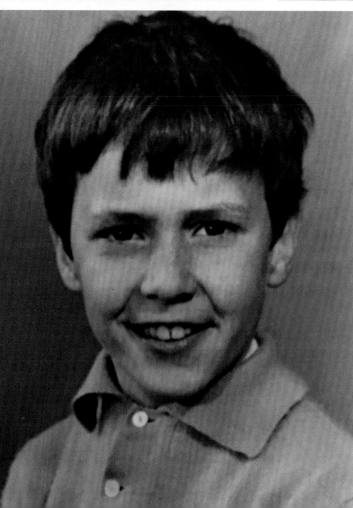

(*above left*) With Mum, 1960.

(*above right*) With Dad in our back garden.

(*left*) 1965.

(*above left*) 1974. Chugging a beer while ignoring the ectoplasm.

(*above right*) 1976. Oxford Street. Punk figurehead Mark Perry and I photo-bombed by old girl looking for her bus.

(*left*) 1979. At the NME.

(left) Bored of rock stars I began interviewing comics. Starting at the top with Bob Monkhouse.

(below) 1982. Spud overlooking the Thames from landing of a council block. The Mayor of London's office stands there today.

(*top*) Holding Bonnie and Sonny on our wedding day.

(*above*) I have no idea where this photo was taken. It looks like Holland.

(*right*) With Wendy in the 1980s. Note the tremendous product placement.

With Chris Evans and Billie Piper, Palm Springs 2001.

(*above*) Chris Evans and I late for a *TFI* script meeting. By which I mean they'd already been open twenty minutes.

(*inset*) Chris and I leaving the studio after the last ever *TFI Friday*.

(*above*) An extraordinarily amusing mask of a horse's upper jaw. You're welcome.

(*left*) I can't cook. But I enjoy butchery. Apparently.

(top) With Chas & Dave. Possibly the most cockney photo ever taken.

(right) Correction: THIS is the most cockney photo ever taken. With Tommy Steele in a pie-and-mash shop.

(above) Danny Kelly and I feeling absolutely no pain in the 1990s.

oesophagus. God knows how long he'd been putting up with it, but an earlier diagnosis would have made little difference anyway. The agonies and indignities were only beginning now.

The doctor at Lewisham Hospital, when delivering the terminal prognosis, asked me if Spud had ever worked with asbestos. I turned to him and said, 'You worked with asbestos a lot in the docks, Dad, didn't you? Bloke wants to know how much.'

Typically he squirmed a bit in his seat and looked at his hands.

'Oh, don't go on about all that, boy,' he said, irked as ever that someone wanted to know our business. 'It was fucking years ago. It's not that, anyway. I'm all right, it's the fucking flu, that's all.'

Five months later I was on the radio in the afternoon when someone came into the control room beyond the soundproof glass and began talking to my producer. Then they both looked grimly towards me. As soon as I put the next giddily upbeat song on air, she came in and said St Thomas' Hospital had called and said my dad's condition had worsened sharply and I needed to go straight there. The rest of my family had been informed.

I had spent the last few months since Spud's admittance visiting his bedside before and after my radio show. Even though his decline had been visible on an almost daily basis, I hadn't anticipated this news just yet. On arrival at the ward I found that my mum, my sister and her husband, plus a few other immediate family members, were already there. Spud lay unconscious, breathing strangely into a clear oxygen mask. I spoke to a doctor who told me that, in fact, the old man had rallied in the last hour and though 'it' could happen at any time, 'it' wasn't now expected to be imminent.

An hour later we were all still gathered around the bed and, in the way we are and the way he had raised us, we were making endless jokes about the awkwardness of the situation and whether Dad would want us to shoot over the road for a quick one. During one of the less suppressed group-giggles, the most incredible thing happened. Spud opened his eyes. Looking around, his brow furrowed and a quizzical expression developed. We stopped laughing.

'Dad!' I said, in the sort of everyday tone I know he would have wanted. 'How you doing, mate?'

He raised his arm, dragging the various drips he was wired up to with it. His reduced hand weakly grasped the oxygen mask and pulled it to his chin. In a voice that belied the shrunken state of his frame, he said, 'There's a lot of you here . . . '

He seemed frankly suspicious.

'Well, we thought we'd all come to see you,' replied my sister brightly, she being probably closest to Spud's temperament out of all his children.

What he said next were to be his last words.

'I dunno what for. There's fuck-all wrong with me.'

Then he put the mask back over his mouth and lapsed into unconsciousness. The breathing became shallow again and after another few hours we were all asked to step outside while he was moved to a side room. A different doctor then told us that, on most recent intelligence, it looked like he would now last another day at least, maybe two or three. We had a family meeting and it was decided I would stay there overnight, my poor bewildered mum would go home with Sharon, and I would call first thing in the morning to arrange the day's movements.

The side room in which Spud lay was on the eleventh floor of the hospital with a large window looking across into Waterloo Station about half a mile away. There was only his bed and a chair in there, and I sat in the dark switching my gaze between his face, the cheekbones – now very prominent on what had always been a healthy ruddy old dial – and the little red lights on the last trains making their way in and out of the terminus for the night. His breathing was wheezy but regular. At about 2 a.m. a nurse who had been popping in and out, mainly I feel to check on me, came by again with another offer of some tea. I said I was fine and she told me once more that I could go home for a few hours because there was little chance anything was going to happen tonight, and probably not tomorrow either. Thinking it over, I didn't need to try too hard to figure out what Fred would have said to me at that point.

What's the matter with ya? Go home! Fucking morbid, keeping watch. Stop being so dramatic. Fucking daft, staying up all night. I'm not going anywhere . . .

So I eventually got in the lift, aimed my Land Rover out of the car park and half an hour later climbed heavily into my own bed.

I must have lain there for all of five minutes before I got up again and started getting dressed. Wendy, who had only just finished listening to me explaining the current state of play, knew immediately why.

'You're going back, aren't ya?' she said.

Of course I was. The alarm on our front door barely had time to set itself before I punched in the code to let myself out again. Getting into the still-warm driver's seat, I started up the engine and headed for the hospital on Westminster Bridge. The same nurse was on the ward reception as I came back in; she must have thought I'd popped out for some fresh air. 'I'm back, Dad,' I chirped, taking up my seat once more. It was just after 3 a.m. and the black night outside was pierced sharply by the moon shining on the railway lines.

His breathing seemed to have a pronounced rattle on the intake now. I put my hand on his and told him I was there, even though I know he would have hated my repeated assurances.

Fuck's sake, boy, why d'you keep saying the same thing? I was in a lovely kip there – you do know it's gone three a-fucking clock?

I put on the sidelight but angled it away from his face because, out of habit, I didn't want the light to shine on his eyelids and disturb his sleep. I'd brought a book back with me, a biography of Al Jolson, and for the next hour I read it, reminding him every so often that I was still there. The rasp in his breath became noticeably more shrill at around four fifteen and the breaths themselves shallower yet, until the process sounded like a repeated gasp of surprise. There was a small toilet cubicle in the room and I walked over to use it, closing the door behind me as we always, quite properly, did in our house even when home alone. I flushed, slid open the lock and emerged from the cubicle.

And he wasn't breathing any more.

I could sense it immediately. I knew this was no laboured pause between gasps or a breathing so faint that my ears couldn't detect it. I knew it. He'd gone. In the thirty seconds or so that I'd literally turned my back, he'd slipped away. For a while I did nothing but stand on the spot, looking over at him, feeling a terrific sense of calm. *So that's that. There it is.* Then I spoke.

'I'm still here.'

I walked across to him and kissed him on the forehead.

'Thanks, Dad,' I said.

I sat down in the chair next to him and looked out at two lights that were all that were currently on in a tall building across the way. Probably office cleaners, I reasoned. Spud had been part of an office cleaning gang for a few years in the eighties. I immediately gave amused, silent thanks that, being his son, I could so easily nip that sort of maudlin observation in the bud. I then noticed the white tissue that had been clutched in his hand since I'd arrived at the hospital the previous afternoon. For some reason I thought I should now remove it, but as I tried to do so, it tore in half. The rest of it remained lodged in what I now saw was his still-clenched fist. This was a piece of symbolism I did allow myself to indulge.

Frederick Joseph 'Spud' Baker: 26 May 1928 – 17 January 2008.

He Who Would Valiant Be

At the service for my dad a few weeks later in St James's Church, Bermondsey, I gave a very lively address to a completely packed house. Indeed, I delivered it with such vim and peppered it with so many outrageous stories that afterwards the startled vicar said, in all sweet seriousness, that he'd never heard such laughter in the church and that I really should've been in show business. I told him that if I could work with raw material like my dad's life story every day then I would have considered that. I hadn't been morose or sentimental in the slightest and nobody who had ever known Spud could have felt otherwise. Besides, there was something about solemnity, even in death, that tickled him. I remember as a kid watching him fold back the *South London Press* at the obituaries column and read aloud, in a pious sing-song voice, the cloyingly worded tributes placed there by the relatives of the locally departed.

'"Your healing smile is with us yet,"' he would begin in a tone reminiscent of Derek Nimmo at his most unctuous, '"your blessed ways we can't forget. An empty chair, an unworn coat, not gone from us, nor love remote. RIP Auntie Fran from Kath, George, Terry and baby Rose." What a load of balls that is – why'd they do it?'

My mum would always rise to the bait on these readings. 'You're wicked, you are, Fred. They're being respectful, that's all.' Truth be told she could barely conceal her smile at his weekly performance.

'Respectful?' he'd come back. 'A shilling a word, that's all that is, Bet. This paper's robbing them blind! You've got to be a bit simple to go in for all this. Who wants to be remembered underneath an advert for a fucking garage?'

I must say, even at the tender age of nine, I thought he had a point there. Then he was on to the next one.

'"The rain it falls just like our tears / And in the sky your face appears . . . " Fucking hell, I hope not! That'd frighten the life out of ya, wouldn't it, boy?'

I'd laugh at this, as Mum would swiftly admonish, 'Don't encourage him, you. A bleedin' lightning bolt's gonna come crashing through that window one of these days while he's doing this . . .'

He'd plough on through the whole lot, relishing every last cliché and clunky rhyme. Sometimes he'd recognize the deceased being eulogized and offer, 'Fucking hell, that must be old Soapy Davis, that one! Unless they rhyme "missed" with "pissed" in the next line, they can't have met him!'

It was both extremely unkind and convulsively funny. In fact, during another of Dad's sacrilegious sprees, this time at the funeral of one of his own family members, I had to contain my hysteria so painfully that I thought my passing might be the next service at the crematorium.

Dad was born somewhere around the middle of a family of twelve children, most of whom survived into adulthood. There may have been more than twelve, but nobody talked about or even kept record of cot deaths in those days, but given that the fantastic matriarch of the Baker family, Alice, had her brood roughly from the First World War to the mid thirties, and that she seemed to have babies like shelling peas, I think there were probably one or two. I do know that my Uncle Teddy was killed aged thirteen as he ran across the road to the local picture palace and fell under a tram.

The first of my surviving uncles that I was aware of dying was Godfrey, who was, in fact, the youngest of all the brothers. To be honest, Spud was never that keen on his junior sibling, mainly because he chose a career in an office over the traditional Baker job of dockworker. He was a much slighter and marginally better-spoken man than his burly brethren and this, coupled with the fact that he dared call his first born Timothy, saw Fred reflecting, 'I just can't see it with our Godfrey, y'know. I'm sure old Alice played away there.'

Nobody expected Godfrey to 'go' first, but in the spring of 1993, 'go' he very suddenly did. On the day the substantial Baker clans were gathering for his funeral, Spud stood outside the church with his two closest brothers, Arthur and Alfie. Along with the three of them, I was to be one of the designated pall-bearers.

Now here's something. Have you ever been a pall-bearer? Well, up to that point I hadn't and yet, like most men, I had seen funerals on the news and in films and thought it looked rather a handsome thing to do. There's a status bordering on the glamorous in carrying a coffin, though at the few funerals I had attended up until that point it seemed that the modern way was to let the professionals take care of that end of business, and so I believed I would never get a crack at it. Now that day had arrived and as the hearse slid up to the portal we were briefed on how to shoulder the imminent burden by an attendant undertaker. He told us how to crouch and await instruction as the casket was decanted on to us, how to then stand and walk along the aisle, culminating in how to bring the thing to a dignified rest upon the bier. Dad, who hated to receive orders about anything, allowed the man to finish before chiming in with, 'Got all that, Chas, but we are all ex-dockers – we know how to stow stuff.' The undertaker then gave a heads-up for those of us who hadn't been pall-bearers before that the coffin would probably be much heavier than we anticipated, so to watch out for that.

Once the man had left us, Alfie looked across at the hearse and, with what he then said, proved to me that he had no need to take a blood test to show he was my dad's brother.

'You ever wondered, Spud, what they do with all the brass on the coffins once we've all gone out the church?' he asked in all seriousness.

Dad raised his eyebrows as he mulled this over for about two seconds. 'Well, it's fucking obvious. There must be a sack or something round the back that it all goes in. End of the week, you'd share it all out. Be a fair old whack, that.'

I laughed but nobody else did. I asked who might be doing this stockpiling.

'Oh, there'll be a little firm round the back, don't you worry about that. They're not gonna let a nice few quid go up in flames in front of 'em, are they?'

I never loved my family more than when I saw them regard propositions like this utterly seriously – enviously, even. Goading them on, I argued that there'd be no time to remove handles and unscrew plaques once the casket had gone through the curtains.

Spud was unimpressed at my lack of vision. 'That's why they have curtains!' he explained. 'So you don't see it being unloaded off the belt. You never see it going on the fire, do ya? That's all done downstairs, I expect.'

Arthur noted my incredulous face. 'Look at him. It's right though, boy. You listen up after Godfrey's gone through. See if you can hear an electric screwdriver going ten to the dozen.'

Now they all laughed, but there was no doubt they believed the grim racket was a going concern.

Shortly after, some of my aunts walked by to take their seats. From a young age I could detect that the greeting for my dad from the older of my aunts was always a degree or two colder than the one they extended to his brothers. Arthur had once told me, 'Bit of a black sheep, your dad, boy.' This possibly had to do with him once going to prison, or the fact when the Baker boys did get involved in punch-ups on the Isle of Dogs – often with each other – Fred was usually involved. Correction: make that 'consistently involved'. Unsurprisingly, as the women passed we could see that they had reacted to the hearse's arrival by shedding a few tears.

'I see Grace has gone early,' Dad said again, to some chuckles at the blackness of the observation.

'Well, it is her brother,' I floated, in an attempt to once again right the conversational ship.

'She loves a funeral, Grace,' he went on. 'Loves it. Her hanky's out as soon as she gets the invite. You watch when we go by with the coffin. She'll get an eight point five from the judges.'

The laugh at this set a new level of poor taste, judging by the looks from all around us. Fortunately, we were at that point called over to perform our pall-bearing duties. Spud and I were asked to stand on either side at the front; assuming the advised position, we crouched, awaiting the casket to descend. When it did I thought somebody must have put the hearse on top of it too. The weight was unbelievably punishing, shatteringly so, like shouldering one of the cross blocks from Stonehenge. When I'd seen this in films, the bearers seemed to glide along with no sign of the uneven struggle. Here in real life, far from being ready to stand I felt the thing was pushing me into the ground, planting me like a dahlia. How was I possibly going to unbend myself and manage to stand when my knees were already feeling like two grapefruits beneath a steamroller? While I internalized all this agony, Spud, to my right, was taking the opposite tack.

'Faaaaakkkkkkkin' hell! What they put in here, rocks? Fuck me, it can't be Godfrey, there was nothing of him!'

Suddenly all six of us in the team dissolved in a fit of complete irreligious giggles.

Dad continued to stoke this boiler: 'Alfie? Go and have a word with them, will ya? They must be trying to get rid of a job lot on us here.'

Somehow straightening to the upright, all of us began displaying tremors as though something about a seven on the Richter scale was going off under our feet.

'Easy, lads, easy . . . ' came an official-sounding voice from behind. This made the giggling even worse. I remember thinking that if I couldn't get this hysteria under control as we marched into church, I would have to pass off my wobbling mouth and my weeping eyes as uncontrollable grief. Everyone would be so touched by how close I must have been to my uncle (who I hadn't seen in over a decade). In this unfit state, off we went towards the transept.

We had barely passed the collection box on the way in before we heard, above the organ's drone, a short wail of grief. It was Aunt Grace. Dad turned to me in triumph and, in what just about qualified as a whisper, trumpeted, 'What did I tell ya? Eight point five!'

I thought I was now choking to death. Worse was to come. As we passed the row of pews that contained his sister, Grace gave forth an even louder sob. I shut my eyes tight and waited for his reaction.

'Nine!' I heard him hiss. 'That's a nine! A new record!'

All you can hope is that Godfrey, looking down or across from wherever his spirit may have been at that day, would have smiled a little too. 'Yep,' he might have reflected, 'that's my big brother, everybody.'

So on Spud's own funeral day the mood was suitably raucous, defiant and celebratory. Afterwards, there was, as he always liked to say, 'plenty of everything'. He would have loved it.

I know he would have summed up his own passing with the words he met all crises and calamities with – indeed, the very words I used to open his funeral eulogy: 'Well, there it is. Can't do nothing about it, can ya?'

About a week after his cremation, on a cold and rainy February morning, I drove a few of us down to the banks of the Thames. The tide was in, or 'making' as Spud always put it, and the water was deep. Removing the lid from the urn of my old man's ashes, I dropped the whole thing in and gave him to the river next to which he'd lived and on which he had worked for most of his life. Now he was part of it. Today, every time I cross the river or walk its banks, I'll always offer up a quiet, 'Aye, aye, Spud, how's it going?'

I'm pretty sure there are thousands of by-laws and environmental papers that prohibit life-long Londoners becoming part of the Thames after death, but to those strictures and the people who draw them up I offer a hearty 'Go fuck yourself'. It's only right and proper, and actually quite beautiful. And I give you fair warning: when I go, that's exactly where I'm going to wind up too.

That said, I couldn't have possibly imagined that barely eighteen months after my dad became part of his city's fabric, I would find myself so nearly reunited with him in the river's ebbing and flowing under Waterloo Bridge.

Somebody Said Your Name

I have very few regrets. In fact, as I sit here I can only conjure up two and I feel unless you carry these things around with you like Jacob Marley's cash-boxes and they are instantly memorable then they can't really be regrets at all.

The first that comes to mind features Vivian Stanshall, former lead singer with the Bonzo Dog Band, cultural conundrum, first-class British maverick and a screamingly funny writer. I had wanted to meet Viv all my life and yet, bafflingly for me, I cannot recall how we did finally connect. As described in *Going to Sea in a Sieve*, he had been a frequent and startling visitor to One Stop Records when I worked there in the early seventies, but I can't say we became friends then or that he would have even recalled me from, what were for him, those brandy-soaked occasions. It is most odd. Chief among the reactions to the two previous instalments of these memoirs has been people asking how on earth I could recall events and conversations from sometimes five decades ago. Well, I just can.

I have, and always have had, a terrific memory. I think I unconsciously began the brain-training from about the age of five when, typically, following a particularly well-plotted episode of something like *The Flower Pot Men*, I would repeatedly correct my infant school classmates as they attempted to relay the programme's action to another of our peers who had missed it, possibly because of a nap. It bothered me that they would casually say that the man who worked in the garden where Bill and Ben lived had 'gone somewhere', when the voice-over had specifically said he had 'gone into the house to have his dinner'. I felt this was crucial. If he had 'gone somewhere' then he might be away for ages, days even, and therefore Ben's discovery of the big pot of glue he had left behind – and the subsequent mess the flower pot men made of everything – lacked the race-against-the-clock tension of knowing the chap had simply popped in for his dinner and might be back at any moment. Couldn't they see that? It was all there in the script, for God's sake; you're supposed to pick up on such things.

It similarly infuriated me when they got the lyrics to theme tunes all wrong. I'd hear them trill, 'Andy Pandy's gone out to play . . . ' when the actual words are 'Andy Pandy's *coming* to play . . . ' There's a world of difference. If Andy Pandy had *gone out* to play, then why the hell was all the unfolding action taking place in his house? What was wrong with these kids? I wasn't being pedantic, *they* were being sloppy and allowing events of great moment to slither away half-documented.

Fast-forward a few years and I can remember when my old man brought home a ten-inch disc called *Max at the Met*, a recording of comedian Max Miller live in concert. It was, and remains, breathlessly funny, and even before we'd gotten to the end of side one, I knew I would have to learn it all by heart in the forty-eight hours before Dad had to return it to the Spa Road Record Library. And this I did, every word, every song, every pause for breath and slip of the tongue. Put it on right now and I can still perfectly mime along to it while conjuring up the disc's plum-coloured Pye record label, catalogue number NPT 19026 containing the small print *Made in New Zealand*. I have no idea why Spa Road Record Library had a Kiwi pressing of *Max at the Met*, but that information went in during 1963 and will never go back out again, short of a bazooka strike straight to my head.

And yet what should have been one of the most memorable moments of my life, my introduction to fellow Max Miller fanatic Vivian Stanshall, a man who had done as much to fashion my humour as Spike Milligan or P. G. Wodehouse, simply turns up a blank. It must have been some time in the mid 1980s, because I remember Viv coming with me during that time while I filmed a live insert for the *Six O'Clock Show* at the Hippodrome in Leicester Square, formerly the Talk of the Town. I was judging a talent contest, of all things, and I tried to get Viv on-air as a fellow panellist. However the producers of the item didn't really know who he was and, to be fair, his appearance and demeanour were, as ever, not the sort of thing to lay on an unsuspecting teatime audience.

One of my favourite Stanshall stories concerns the period during which he lived on a houseboat near Chertsey. One of the many ways in which the Great Man ran contrary to the rest of the human race was in the matter of those piles of bumf that one finds loitering inside magazines, the sort of advertising leaflets that usually contain a detachable form requesting you sign up for a newsletter or catalogue. Naturally, only lunatics ever complete these hopeful perforated pages, much less bother to post them off. But, even more naturally, that is exactly what Vivian Stanshall used to do. He would delight in providing ludicrous names and outlandish addresses, while filling out any questionnaires with a pattern of answers designed to totally baffle the recipients. Occasionally, if a home visit from a salesman was part of the deal, he would provide his mooring address on the houseboat and await their arrival. Sometimes they would even find him. So it was when one afternoon, upon the window of the vessel, came a tapping.

Viv, whose usual style of dress was best described as outré, was this day decked out in black cardinal-style robes with his flaming red beard woven into a long plait. With delight he looked through a gap in the boat's curtains and saw he had a caller. Feeling his appearance wasn't remarkable enough, he reached for the cover of a nearby record album and popped it on to his head like the pope's mitre. To complete the look, he then removed from its tank the toad he was keeping as a pet and held it to his chest. Lastly, he slipped on a pair of prop spectacles whose lenses magnified his eyes grotesquely, and then began to slowly climb the few steps from the galley to greet his visitor. It is fair to say that once Vivian stood fully revealed, eyes at full stretch, humming a discordant note and stroking his toad, the salesman stepped back a pace or two. It seems, however, that a sale is still a sale and so the intrepid caller reverted to his training. Raising his trilby in greeting, he cleared his throat.

'Um . . . Mr King-Penguin, is it?' he asked cheerily.

Vivian allowed a moment's more toad-stroking as he weighed this. Then, closing his eyes as if to mask some secret sorrow, replied in the lush bass tones for which he was famous, 'I am the same. What can I do for you, mysterious stranger?'

The salesman, after swallowing hard to contain his shock, continued undaunted.

'Er, I'm from Hawley's Bathrooms? And I was hoping to . . . um . . . I believe you contacted us about a quote?'

Viv leaned toward the man and issued a low, agonized 'Aaaaah . . .'

For a while nobody added to this exchange until eventually the man from Hawley's Bathrooms saw the way forward.

'Look,' he said, rising above his instinct to flee, 'I don't suppose Mrs King-Penguin is in, is she?'

Viv would become breathless with laughter recalling this indomitable response, his accent regressing from the polished tones by which the young Stephen Fry had learned to fashion his own voice, back to his native Southend. 'Amazing bloke. I mean, talk about fucking sangfroid. Asked him aboard for a session but he was off back up the towpath when he knew there was no commission to be had there.'

My regret with Viv is not that I cannot recall our meeting but that some time after we'd fallen out of each other's orbit I received a postcard from him, instantly recognizable by his magnificent curlicue handwriting. 'Dan,' it said. 'Been a bit. So. *The Face* magazine has asked to do an interview with me and want to know who should be the other half of the sketch. Better the devil you know. Fancy it?'

I never replied to that request. God knows why; I cannot think what else I would rather have been doing, and I certainly kept the card. Somebody else must have completed the interview but I never saw it. A year later, Vivian Stanshall died in a fire at his home in North London. Today I cannot believe we were, for a few years, mates. And I shrivel to think of him checking for a response to his postcard but then giving up with a light, 'Oh well. Hey ho.' So, yes, that's a big fucking regret I have.

The other one is less rueful and can possibly be seen as the karmic cost due the universe in the wake of my returning record collection miracle. Hold on to your hats, wigs and teeth, because this one requires we go right into the belly of the biggest star circus on the planet.

Ladies and gentlemen, come with me to Chicago where, in town for two nights only, are the Rolling Stones.

A measure of just how powerful *TFI Friday* had become as what we now know as a brand – something we never thought of it as, nor exploited it for – was that when the Stones needed to publicize their UK stadium dates in 1999 they invited us to make a film with them on the US leg of the tour. We said we could do this. Once again, Chris and I found ourselves heading across the Atlantic, but this time it was arguably less of a lark than the John Cleese episode.

On the way to the airport I had found myself stuck in traffic while passing through the Notting Hill area of West London. I don't know this area that well and only ever visited it in order to either call on Chris or trawl the many second-hand record shops that pepper the streets around Portobello Road. It was as the taxi crawled past one of these that I had, what struck me at the time, a good idea. Well, a fair idea, anyway. One of the rarer LPs by the Rolling Stones is *Their Satanic Majesties Request*, released in 1967 with a wildly psychedelic cover typical of the period, here featuring the band looking glum and uncomfortable in some ill-advised wizard outfits. The sleeve literally stood out because the first print run featured this hangdog image as a large 3D photograph. These originals are highly collectable and I could see one in the window of the Record & Tape Exchange as my cab idled in the traffic. Asking the driver to pull over for a moment, I went into the shop and bought it for £90. My plan was to get the Stones to sign the record, thus increasing its desirability to vinyl junkies worldwide, and then get Chris to present it to a complete stranger on the streets of Chicago. Ideally, this stranger would not have a clue what it was and wouldn't even want it. Any watching Stones collectors would howl in frustration at this outrage, and that would be that. As I say, a small gag at best.

Another thing I was bringing to Mick and Keith was the local newspaper from Dartford, the area in which they'd grown up. I figured it was probably a few years since they'd seen a copy and the image of them being reunited with their Kentish roots in Chicago struck me as rather sweet – and so it would prove.

Something Chris and I hadn't anticipated was just how enormous the Rolling Stones are in America. I mean, obviously they are the Rolling Stones and still capable of selling a ticket or two, but the sheer power their name and presence brings to the cities they are appearing in has no equivalent here in Britain. On our way from the airport to our hotel the radio was playing Rolling Stones records. Lots of them. This we thought might just be a special programme we had chanced on by coincidence, but as we learned during one of the jingles between 'Street Fighting Man' and 'Tumbling Dice', there would in fact be no other music on that station because it had been officially designated as Rolling Stones Day all over Chicago. Banners hanging over the highway intersections confirmed this.

When we arrived at the Four Seasons there were crowds, including whole families, milling around outside hoping to catch a glimpse of their idols. At check-in, Chris and I were greeted by a Stones assistant each and handed various wristbands, laminates, passes and itineraries. Itineraries! These included literal minute-by-minute instructions for where we needed to be in order to gain access to the stadium and the Stones that night. We had instructions such as:

7.02: Please be ready to leave your hotel room with all passes and documents needed for access.

7.04: Please wait next to elevator C which has been specifically commandeered for your use at this time. Failure to meet it may cause you to miss your slot in the cavalcade.

7.07. Once in underground car park area 3, please enter the seventh SUV in the line. Further ID will be given to you at this time.

7.11: Your SUV will proceed to the event arena. Please have ready wristband A and laminate 6.

I mean, the term 'military precision' doesn't begin to cover this sort of drill. This one gig would make the Concert for Diana look like a car boot sale in Dymchurch. I have to say, it was all devilishly exciting as every single detail followed the plan to the letter, although the real rock'n'roll element of this trip to the Enormo-Dome did not appear on the official schedule.

As the long line of black-windowed limousines and SUVs made their way up from underneath the hotel, each vehicle suddenly found itself flanked by actual Hell's Angel outriders. Chris and I – the only occupants of our motor – were stunned into a state somewhere between hysteria and open-jawed awe. Against the roar of the Harley Davidsons on either side of us, we managed to ask our driver if this was in any way normal. 'Absolutely not,' he replied solemnly. 'This is a show of respect. Only the Stones receive this in Chicago – just the Stones.' And how about this for respect? The itinerary had allowed exactly sixteen minutes for us to make the stadium. How could they be so precise? Because, ladies and gentlemen, every single traffic light on the route had been set to green by the City of Chicago so there would be no hold-up. THAT, my friends, is how fucking huge the Rolling Stones are in America.

So there we sat, in the back of a blacked-out SUV, smiling and drinking the provided cold beer, sailing past cheering crowds on the sidewalk, two enormous Hell's Angels gunning their hogs alongside us, the Rolling Stones in the vehicles ahead, 'Honky Tonk Women' booming out of the radio. In my decades of being around the music industry, I have never known a more complete rock'n'roll moment. I started to wonder if my little local newspaper gag might be misjudged.

When we arrived at the United Center – home of, among others, the Chicago Bulls – it became clear that the Rolling Stones don't have a backstage area as such, more of a backstage world. In the labyrinthine rooms and corridors that riddle these gigantic structures, entire sections had been designated for the families, friends and tastes of the individual band members. Suites of furniture, personal chefs and their kitchens, games rooms, artwork, vast wardrobes of clothing and children's areas are installed and later broken down again as the show ploughs on across the continent. Keith Richards' inner sanctum, you won't be staggered to hear, has the swampy decadent feel of a New Orleans bordello. To successfully achieve this sleazy red-light look in the stark utility rooms of sports stadia must take an advance party many hours of fussing with shade and fabric, drapes and sofas suitably distressed, lamps set to glow low, every skull-shaped candle pre-burned so as to effect the right amount of melted wax. It struck me that no matter how good a show the band would put on that night, the real spectacle would remain hidden from public view.

The Stones themselves were professional and charming. Mick, or at least a version of him, making himself available for a whole fifteen minutes, Ronnie happy to gabble to anybody around, Charlie not much bothered one way or the other. However, when they were all gathered to do a few promotional links and pictures with Chris, I took that moment to hand over the Dartford newspaper.

'Bought this off a bloke outside,' I told them. 'He said it sells better than the *NME* these days . . . '

Jagger and Richards fell on it like it was their old school reports returned, so much so that it held up the promo shoot for some minutes while they relished the parochial headlines, looked for street names they might recognize and, most of all, waded through the small ads. It was quite nourishing to hear the pair of them cooing over where a certain seller's location was.

Mick: I can't place that, where is it?
Keith: Yes you can, it's near where Barry Peak used to live.
Mick: Down by the church on the High Street?
Keith: No. You know the Rising Sun?
Mick: Yeah . . .
Keith: Come out of there and go right, yeah . . .
Mick: Past the laundrette . . .

Keith: That's it. Now turn down – what's it called . . .

Mick: Nelson Road?

Keith: Nelson Road, yes. Go down there and he'll be on the left
as you get to where the fag shop was . . .

Mick: Oh right, yeah, got you now . . . What's he selling?

Keith: Various covers and bedding, pillows, etc. As new. Eight
quid.

It was a privilege to have instigated such glorious mundanity and
also to witness the looks of confusion on the faces of the, mainly
American, staff all around us. I managed to get the copy of *Satanic
Majesties* signed, even if when I handed it to Mick he thought he
was about to be sent up for the three-foot starry wizard's hat he is
struggling to maintain dignity under on the sleeve.

Later that night I ended up with Ronnie Wood and assorted
company in a bongo bar somewhere in the city, still clutching the
album. I explained to Ron that we were going to be giving it away
at some point, a wheeze that he enthusiastically endorsed, although
he wouldn't sign it himself because, not having been in the band at
the time of recording, he would feel 'a bit weird' inking over Brian
Jones's picture.

Now a bongo bar, if you've had the lifelong luck to avoid one, is
the sort of place forged in a nightmare and that, for some time after
I experienced one, caused me to fret that they might take hold in our
culture, resulting in a situation where I would never be able to go out
again. They are perfectly good little bars that play a wide selection of
solid pop hits all night long but then add one further dimension to
this tried-and-tested formula. All over the premises are left percussion instruments – mainly but not exclusively bongo drums – and
the clientele are encouraged to join in with these to whatever song is
currently chugging its way out of the speakers. That's everybody and
to every song. Seriously, can you think of anything worse? A more
perfect vision of pandemonium it's difficult to conceive. Here is the
one portrait of hell that eluded Hieronymus Bosch.

The worst part of it was, everyone else in our company that night seemed to think it was a brilliant concept, drowning out some of the greatest 45s ever minted in a thousand different thuds, bangs, konks and crashes. Don McLean's 'American Pie' does not require the accompaniment of dozens of sloppily handled tom-toms, tambourines and maracas. Maracas! Some people were even hitting tambourines *with* maracas! These people were no more percussionists than Sooty is a drummer. Call me a killjoy, but at its height it was like being trapped in a tumble dryer with a canteen of cutlery. This was, after all, Chicago. I thought we'd booze away the small hours in some funky historic blues shack that had a sign on the men's toilet wall saying *Muddy Waters Slashed Here 1955*. Instead, here we were in a modern *themed* bar – and the theme was 'Hats Off to Paracetamol!'

Well, I promise you I did try to join in, hitting a pretty half-hearted cow-bell throughout 'American Woman' by the Guess Who, but during the free-for-all that greeted Grand Funk Railroad's version of 'The Locomotion' I decided to slip away into that good Chicago night. I could still hear the racket from about nineteen blocks away.

When I got back to the hotel, I pushed the lift button and about thirty seconds later the door slid back and there was Rod Stewart. Now I know Rod a little bit, had even drunkenly sung some of his own hits with him in the dressing room at *TFI* (and, yes, Rod will perform his own hits at the drop of a Jack Daniel's bottle top), and being not a little bamboozled by his sudden appearance in front of me, found myself saying, 'Rod. You're not in the Rolling Stones.' To which he replied, 'Am I fuck, Danny Baker, am I fuck!' And without another word he strode straight past me and out into the lobby. I inject this otherwise pointless titbit just to show you what kind of night this was turning into.

Arriving at my room with a pounding jet lag, I eased off my shoes with an agonized groan and then looked at myself in the full mirror opposite. Returning to one of my oldest themes, I then spoke to the person in the mirror like he was another character in this play. Very calmly I said to him, 'You've left the fucking record in that bar.' I had, too. Sometimes you are just so weary and find the idiotic things you do so stereotypical of a self only you truly know that you cannot even raise the required energy for the required self-reproaching. Falling back on the bed, I did toy with the idea of going back to the bongo bar to retrieve it but decided that one possible hindrance to this line of action would be the fact that I had absolutely no idea where it was. We had been dropped at the place via a couple of official Rolling Stones SUVs and I had arrived back at the Four Seasons by simply yelling those two words at a cab driver. All I knew was that it was eighteen dollars and seventy-five cents away. I didn't even know the actual name of the place beyond the two words Bongo and Bar. This, of course, prevented me calling them up to get the album safely secured until morning. That and the fact I could imagine all too well what it would be like, trying to have any kind of conversation with a barman who was speaking with that unearthly row going on in the background. In fact, where did they find bar staff willing to sacrifice their hearing and sanity so hordes of amateur timpani-thrashers could ruin 'Heard It Through the Grapevine', night in, night out? In short, Bugger the Bongo Bar.

The next morning I made some enquiries at reception about where the cacophonous dive might be located. Nobody seemed to have a clue what I was talking about.

'A bar I was in last night,' I tried to explain to the apparently interested yet strangely frosty woman at the concierge desk. 'Where you play drums.'

'Where I play drums?' she interrupted. 'I don't play the drums, sir.' She knew I didn't mean it like that. So it was going to be one of those conversations, was it? Anyway, I persevered and the more I talked the more it did seem as though I was in town for the Village Idiots Convention. I also began to believe that there must be an American Union of Hotel Reception Staff whose members had all been alerted that I was back in the country, because I don't think I've ever stayed in the States without having at least one flaming row with those gatekeepers at the keyboard, who seem to add extra layers of superciliousness as soon as I appear through their establishment's revolving doors.

Over the years I have won many hard-fought victories over room allocations, thermostat problems, drills (both fire and electric), noise leakage from the disco, twenty-four-hour room service that apparently means you wait twenty-four hours for the grub to get there, stupid malfunctioning electronic keys, lost restaurant reservations, breakfast menus that finish at 9 a.m., refusals to extend the checkout time when you've just spent a month at the gaff, non-appearance of repeatedly promised extra towels, sudden appearance of rat in the wardrobe, people upstairs who seem to be staging the Horse of the Year show, and countless other niggles, including my all-time bête noire – *fucking leaf blowers.*

Disney hotels are the worst for these ear-splitting devices. Every morning, as soon as you get yourself settled around the pool surrounded by the character-themed topiary in the lush sculpted gardens, out come the blokes with the bastard leaf blowers, looking like Ghostbusters and shattering the calm with what must be without question the most useless machine in Christendom. Intentionally loitering behind the sun loungers with a simmering hatred for we soft, vacationing loafers, they then proceed to rent the air like a phalanx of Norton 650 motorbikes with whooping cough. Of course the blokes wielding them don't give two shits because they have all been issued with ear protectors! Fuck off, mate! I'm paying four hundred dollars a day for this! And what's it all for? To blow leaves from the path! Not even suck them up. *Just blow them about!* Seriously, you people must have heard of brooms by now. I have given this tirade several times in hotel receptions at a volume that never fails to require the initially patronizing manager to ask me to lower my voice. 'Oh! Is it too noisy for you?' I'll hammer home in triumph. 'Then imagine I was charging you four hundred dollars a day to listen to it?' Usually the blowers are then forced to retreat. On more than one occasion, I have received a grateful round of applause from the rest of the people down at the pool.

Only once was I ever given pause over this cathartic exorcising of the red mist. We were staying in Disney's Grand Floridian Hotel on Lake Buena Vista. Outside our room was a short lawn leading to the lake itself. On about the second morning of our stay we were awoken by what sounded like a drag-racing car being put through a waste-disposal unit with every decibel being relayed via The Who's PA system. This, I immediately grasped, was our old enemy the leaf blower announcing the sun was up. Leaping from the bed, I yanked on some shorts and a T-shirt, bunged on my baseball cap and began steaming across to the manager's office. This journey took me past the main pool area, and as I navigated its banks I saw that, most unusually for a Disney location, there was an empty can of Budweiser bobbing away in the turbulence by the pool's filter. I reached down and grabbed it, intending to present this as further proof that the whole place was going to the dogs. Moments later, I was in my annual spot at the welcome desk – we stayed at the Grand Floridian a lot when the kids were young – impatiently waiting for an audience with the manager. Well, I made my case with my usual force and, disappointingly early in my monologue, before I had got round to some of the more choice barbs about a hotelier's responsibilities, received an apology and assurance that the work would cease.

Satisfied, I made my way back towards our room, looking forward to informing my wife that her husband had once again Put Things Right. As I came to the pool, I realized for the first time that in my fit of righteousness I had forgotten to make any mention of the beer can in the shallow end and had instead just stood there waving it about while making my point about the leaf blower. It was barely nine o'clock in the morning. I must have given the unmistakable impression that I was the most incorrigible piss artist. No wonder the manager had wrapped proceedings up swiftly.

Much as I wanted to go back and say, 'And another thing. This can of beer. I haven't just downed it, you know. I'm not some wild rummy, so you can take that off of my notes on the computer for a start!' I kept my head down and let myself back in the room. Even before I could relay the news of my victory over Corporate America, Wendy said, 'Why have you got a can of beer open at nine o'clock in the morning?' I explained the circumstances and even went so far as to admit it had probably weakened any further negotiations I may have to have with the staff over the upcoming fortnight. 'And you went out in that hat as well, did you?' was her next observation.

Looking at my reflection I now saw that the Budweiser was only part of my new mad person ensemble. The T-shirt I had scooped off the floor still had last night's red ragu sauce peppering its front and, worst of all, in my rage and in the half-light of our shuttered room I had snatched up, not my hat, but Bonnie's. Plonking it on my head and then fastening the Velcro, I had apparently laid down the law to the startled executive wearing a vivid pink baseball cap on which the fairy Tinkerbell was surrounded by the words: *Warning: Diva! Mood Liable to Change Without Notice!* For the rest of our stay I gave the reception area a sensibly wide berth, taking the altogether more scenic route via the luggage trolleys when leaving the hotel.

Meantime, in Chicago, I managed to keep my ire in check despite three separate concierge desk attendants – natives of the Windy City, one must assume – having no knowledge of a 'bongo bar' gracing their town. I next started calling the various rooms the *TFI* team were staying in – a hideously uncharitable thing to do, given that they had probably crawled into bed about half an hour ago. The only information I garnered was that nobody had picked the record up and that I shouldn't have left early anyway because they went on to several other great places afterwards. But as to where the bar was or what it was called, they hadn't the foggiest. Unsurprisingly, the hotel wouldn't connect me with Mr Wood's suite.

I was about to start asking along the long line of cabs outside when into the foyer strode Steven Tyler of Aerosmith. He had been a guest on *TFI* about two months previously and although there wasn't the slightest chance he would remember me, I knew that would be a card to play should his security people start punching my lights out for daring to speak to him. As we passed each other, I simply said, 'You don't know where the bongo bar is, do you, Steven?' This startled him and the scrambled phrase, delivered in such a casual way, caused him to stop and ask me to repeat it. I told him we had briefly met in London recently, dropped the name of the show, and thankfully his face lit up in an obviously fond memory of the experience. I asked him again if he knew where the bongo bar was. 'No, no, I don't,' he said with some regret, but then turned to address an enormous fellow behind him who was probably at that moment sizing up which of the plate-glass windows he would hurl me through, should I now suddenly whip out a cap-gun.

'Mark, you ever heard of the bongo bar around here?' Tyler asked him.

Unbelievably, Mark started to nod. 'Yeah, yeah, where you shake the shakers and join in the records?' he mused.

'Yes, YES!' I started to shout, like a man who had finally had his alibi corroborated as the noose was being put round his neck.

'Yeah, that's uh . . . ' Mark began to think. It seemed to me that he went on thinking for hours. Steven Tyler looked from him to me then back again.

'Sorry if I'm holding you up,' I said, hoping to fill the vacuum. 'I was there with the Stones last night and left something valuable behind.' Hearing this, Steven Tyler made an 'Ooh get you!' face. (Of course it had been just Ronnie Wood, but 'I was there with a Stone' sounds ridiculous.)

Then Mark delivered in full. 'Yeah down on Hubbard. West Hubbard. The Stones played there last night, you say?'

'No, just partied there,' I clarified, thus using the word 'partied' for the one and only time in my entire life.

Steven Tyler, wearing a magnificent full-length green leather coat, seized the opportunity to adjourn the meeting: 'Anyway, hey, great to see you again. Say hi to the guys for me.' And he swept away.

Ten minutes later I was in a cab going along West Hubbard Street asking the driver to take it easy lest we skate straight past the joint. Then I saw it. Screaming, 'This will do!' I paid the man and was relieved to see that the door to the place was open, though as I made my way into its gloomy interior it did not appear to be open for business. There was nobody around. After calling out a few times, I made my way towards the spot where I last remembered sitting in the wild hope my copy of *Their Satanic Majesties Request* might still be lying there. No such luck.

At this point I ought to let you in on a decision I had arrived at shortly before falling asleep the previous evening. It struck me that our film of the trip did not require the aid of a thin joke that, at best, might enrage a handful of vinyl collectors. The concert at the United Center had much rekindled my love for the Rolling Stones and now I believed that a signed copy of their controversial swerve into sixties psychedelia would be more properly honoured if preserved for the nation in my own substantial record collection. After all, I had forked out nearly a hundred pounds for the unautographed disc from my own pocket. Not that any of this would matter if the hallowed item was, at that moment, in the back of a reeking garbage truck making its way to the landfill.

A bloke appeared from a back room. 'Hi,' he said, 'we're not open.' At the very second he said those words, I saw my record. It was propped up among the bottles of bourbon, rum and vodka behind the counter like . . . well, like a trophy of some sort.

'That album,' I said with as much authority as I could muster, 'that's mine, I left it here last night.'

'Uh-uh,' he said. 'No. You. Did. Not.' He really put some force behind each of those syllables and started tellingly to take up a position directly between me and Mick Jagger in the big wizard hat. I was at a loss to see how I could substantiate ownership. I started to say I had been in there with Ronnie Wood last night and he shot that one straight down. 'Yes, I know Ronnie Wood was in here last night because Ronnie Wood himself gave me that record and I don't remember seeing you at all, buddy, so nice try.' He then took the LP from its perch and turned it around. On the back in enormous letters was scribbled: *For Phil, BONGO, BONGO, BONGO! Ron Wood.* 'I'm Phil,' he added as an unnecessary coup de grâce. There was no way back from that.

I remember thinking the always clubbable Ron must have been well alight to have overturned his previous edict not to moniker an album he hadn't been part of. Then again, I had told him that we were planning on giving it away to a total stranger, hadn't I? I can also recall my rueful mathematics, figuring I had paid – if you threw cab fares on top of the initial investment – about $220 for the privilege of this humbling charade. Today I reckon 'my' record has got to be worth at least five times that on eBay. Enjoy, Phil, enjoy!

There had been another US trip sandwiched between the 'working' ones – Chris with his then-partner, Suzi, and me with Wendy and the kids – to see in the New Year in New York. This trip is notable for two things. 1) we went on Concorde; and 2) I made the most dreadful horse's arse of myself shortly after we got there, chiefly because we *had* arrived on Concorde. Here's what happened.

Checking in at our hotel in Manhattan and immediately feeling the benefits of a jet-lag-free transatlantic trip – we'd left Heathrow at 10 a.m., flown for almost three hours and arrived at JFK at 8 a.m. local time – out we went to walk the streets of the SoHo district. We hadn't gone very far when Chris, who you may know enjoys the study of motor cars as a pastime, saw champion Formula One driver Damon Hill coming in the opposite direction. They vaguely knew each other and, though I had never met him, we had mutual friends. So we all stood there chatting and laughing a good deal in the crisp New York morning air and it turned out Damon was in town because he was guesting on the David Letterman show that night. Fantastically impressed, I told him that *Letterman* was just about my favourite show in the world. He invited us to come and watch, but we had to decline because, having only a few nights in town, we had made plans. Besides, children under fifteen were not allowed in the theatre.

'You'll probably be jet-lagged out of your heads by tonight anyway,' he said.

At this we all fell over ourselves to enlighten him as to why, on this particular trip, that would not be happening. Now it was his turn to be impressed as Damon Hill, apparently, had never been on a Concorde flight.

'Oh, it's incredible!' I enthused. 'It's tiny inside, like sitting inside a little Smarties tube. At first it's like any flight, until you get out over the Atlantic, then the old afterburners kick in and whoosh! – away you go. You can actually feel it, it pushes you back into your seat. Your ears register the pressure and for a bit it's like your heart is rising up your throat and you think, fuck, this is brilliant!' I could feel Wendy nudging me in the back. 'There's an LCD screen in the cabin and you can see the miles per hour keep going up and up and up,' I hurtled on, 'it's just the most fantastic sensation, you'll have to do it and . . .'

Well, I suppose I went on for about another minute, until Wendy finally interrupted me and said, 'Dan, I think you're telling Damon Hill what it's like to accelerate!'

Never in my life, and in the face of a mountain of other contenders, have I felt closer to that moment in a Tom & Jerry cartoon when Tom, having been hopelessly out-thought by Jerry, looks into a mirror and sees his reflection transform into a braying, goofy jackass.

At a hastily arranged dinner, I partially redeemed myself thanks to Damon's interest in my experiences in punk rock, an era he loved but was too young to be fully involved in, although he was later in a band called, spectacularly, Sex Hitler & the Hormones.

Spirit In The Sky

In 1984 I found myself doing knockabout reporting spots for TV-AM, ITV's first-ever breakfast show and one that had been flopping disastrously until turned around by former *Six O'Clock Show* editor Greg Dyke. In fact, Greg had achieved his rapid success at the station mainly by jettisoning its previously dogged persistence on analysis of the news and replacing it with the kind of breezy trouser-dropping hoo-ha that had made the *SOCS* tear up the ratings ladder each Friday night.

It was to entirely replicate this that I now found myself hauled aboard and taking part in such dimly recalled items as 'Searching for the Tonbridge Sea Monster' (in reality a large carp), 'The Great Cabbage Patch Doll Shortage' (the filming of which provided a great glut of them in our baby Bonnie's bedroom), and 'Hooray, It's Robin Hood Day!' In this I remember offering the suggestion that in one of the show's live visits to me I should become confused about the subject and believe it to be 'Hooray! It's Robin Day – Good!' This gloomy wordplay allowed me to deliver the entire link in one of the few vocal impressions I do rather well and also while wearing a prop bow tie. Viewers who had not seen the other instalments must have wondered what on earth I was doing. It is likely that even those who had seen them were similarly confused, however the crew and I had a tremendous time and the chaotic spirit of the thing would have sat perfectly on *The Big Breakfast* a few years later.

On other days I would be asked into the studio to sit and join in or jolly along with whoever the guest stars were. So it came to be that I found myself early one morning competing on the verbal high wire with Spike Milligan. As described in the previous book, I had hit it off immediately with Spike by, rather than showing deference when we were introduced, asking him if he were still alive – a gag I had heard him do himself on a few shows. We got on tremendously, on and off the air, and it was during one of the ad breaks that he turned to me and said, with all kindness, 'Man, you know I thought I could talk, but I think there's something properly wrong with you. In the army you'd have been sent to the MO for a thyroid inspection. An overactive thyroid, that's what has people rabbiting at your speed, watch out for it!' Then with his face crumpling in a huge smile, he added, 'You can get a huge goitre with an overactive thyroid, like a cabbage. You have to put a hat on it so people think it's just another head.'

I recalled such people from my childhood, with these enormous shiny swellings beneath their chin – and quite a common site they were too. There were also people who wore one giant boot that told you they had a 'club foot', and others who had suffered rickets and walked with bow legs. An old man called Pat Trower who lived at the back end of our estate was bow-legged to a startling degree and was forced to affect a walk like Charlie Chaplin. Naturally enough, this is what he was universally known as. I can remember my dad saying, 'Never send old Charlie to catch a runaway pig – it'll run straight through him!' One of the most tragic local unfortunates – if we may call them such – was a young chap called Jimmy Henry. He was generally known as 'Fingers' because he didn't have that many. What had happened was that in the 1950s he and his mates had gotten hold of several boxes of fireworks and, as kids will do, they'd grown tired of letting them off in the usual way. While the other members of his gang found ever more extreme methods of getting entertainment from the whizz-bangs, Jimmy had what he thought was a total brainwave and asked that nobody leave the bomb site on which they were currently camped until he returned. Running to the nearby flats, he let himself into his home and retrieved his bike that was leaning against the wall in the passage. Taking it down in the lift he then found a quiet spot round by the rubbish chute, because his spectacular plan required preparation in utmost secrecy. Firstly he set about removing the rubberized grips from the ends of the bicycle's handlebars. In my experience nearly every kid will at some time attempt to remove these, sometimes simply out of boredom but usually because the hollow insides of a bike's handlebars make a great place to hide things like secret maps, liquorice pipes or scrolled-up nudie pictures. Wrapping your mouth around the exposed tubing and trying to play it like a trumpet is also an option, although I have found this doesn't work and you have to resort to making the noise yourself and be satisfied with the resultant distorted effect. (Note to younger readers: Strumming the spokes of your bicycle's wheels in the hope they will make a noise like a harp is also a waste of time.)

The thing about removing the handlebar grips from a twentieth-century kid's bike is that it was the devil's own job. It took a fantastic amount of effort and concentration to get even a centimetre of give that then allowed you to part rotate them. If you were lucky, you might be able to turn one fully round on its spigot after about an hour's struggle, but that was about all you could do. No matter how noisy and desperate the struggle, these things would not simply pop off. I have seen teams of up to four youths setting about a single handlebar – one boy yanking the grip this way, one boy pulling the bike frame that way, the other two grasping their friends' waists and heaving them away for extra purchase, before the entire quartet collapsed defeated, the grip having moved not a jot.

Jimmy Henry was in luck that day, though – or so he thought. This was not the first time he had had the notion to take these fixtures from his vehicle, given, as I understood it, his fondness for popping ants, woodlice and earwigs down the pipe in the hope they would set up a nest inside or, better yet, form insect armies and battle to the death while Jimmy wheeled along at a hundred miles an hour. So he quickly managed the first stage of his plan and moved swiftly on to the second. Taking the box of fireworks he had with him, he began to crack open the cardboard exteriors of the various Roman candles, jack-in-the-boxes, screeching owls and aerial bombshells the package held and then deftly poured the exposed gunpowder into the handlebars of the bike. Now these were not your piddling firework starter packs. These were the top-of-the-range deep boxes of seasonal explosives that only a few kids' dads could afford. (Incidentally, Spud would never allow me to go asking for a 'Penny for the Guy' locally, the traditional way kids raised money for Guy Fawkes Night. 'If you want money, I'll give it to you,' he would warn. 'Don't go asking people in the streets, making it look like we've all got the arse hanging out of our trousers, thanks.') How Jimmy and his mates had come by such bounty a week before firework night, nobody would quite agree upon.

Anyhow, after ten minutes or so of decanting the black incendiary soot into the tubing on both sides, the narrow passageways appeared to be full. Snapping the stick off a rocket, Jimmy now began ram-rodding the mixture in tighter before selecting two of the rocket bodies that looked most likely to slide whole into the packed apertures. With some effort, two were somehow jammed in place with only their bottom halves protruding, the blue paper fuses hanging invitingly in the wind. Riding the now fully loaded bike back the short distance to the bomb site, Jimmy could see it all so clearly. From behind the partly demolished wall around the rubble dump he would announce his impending arrival through cupped hands, then after applying a match to the fuses he would screech into view, his chariot seemingly jet-propelled with sheets of flames and multicoloured sparks issuing from either side of the front steering column. Who knows, he might even take to the skies, sailing high above his puny earth-bound cohorts whose feeble brains could never have hatched such an explosive idea.

And I believe in the penultimate word of that last sentence we can at last recognize the one fatal flaw in Jimmy's grand vision. Far from taking his 1955 Swift bicycle into the space age, he had perfectly constructed what the terrorist classes like to call 'a pipe bomb'. Witnesses confirm that at least he was granted a few seconds of glory as he pedalled like fury around the corner with lengthy bursts of radiant fire trailing forcefully out from his flanks. However once the fuses hit the compacted gunpowder, the awful predictability of chemistry took over and poor deluded Jimmy awoke two days later never to properly be able to hold a fountain pen again. To boot, he had also gained a new and unwelcome nickname; one that would intrigue strangers whenever he later turned out on a Sunday to play up front for one of the local pub sides, always in gloves, and always for the opposition, ironically, a handful. A very good player was Jimmy 'Fingers'.

I thought little about Spike Milligan's thyroid warning until in the last year of the twentieth century, when I noticed that every time I shaved, the razor seemed to do a little shimmy at a certain spot as I ran it up my neck. After a few more months there was no disguising it; if I lifted my head up and stretched the skin taut, the bulge about halfway up on the starboard side was now quite visible. You'll note I said bulge and not lump. That is because the word 'lump' tends to panic people and I didn't want to panic people. Thinking the thing through one evening while in the bath, I diagnosed it to be a harmless cyst of some sort, possibly an enlarged gland. It was probably caused by stress, a condition that I genuinely never experience and so reasoned that it must be instead furiously channelling itself into this pressure point. Once the current intense round of work was over, the little hump would go down like a balloon after a birthday.

A few months further on and I started to notice that, while regaling guests with my latest good stories, they would greet my words with expressions on the sickly side of aghast while their eyes seemed to flick constantly from my face to my shirt collar. Retreating to the bathroom, I couldn't help but sympathize with their horrified conclusions that it did indeed appear as if a small bald-headed man was attempting to escape from my Ben Sherman. It was this social embarrassment rather than any dread of what the 'bulge' may be symptomatic of that eventually led me to Dr D'Souza's office for the first time.

After the usual happy formalities with a new doctor, a profession I have always found to be good company, I settled back and let him start pressing away on the swelling. I had already told him it was most likely a stress-related cyst that should respond to a well-placed lancing. Amazingly, he still seemed to want to have a guess himself. When he'd finished his Boston Strangler bit, he walked around to the other side of the desk and, without speaking, started to draw what looked like the first sketches for a daring new bow tie. At the point where I expected him to begin adding polka dots to the proto-type, he turned the drawing round to face me.

'This is your thyroid gland,' he said. 'One half of it has basically gone a little crazy and blown up.'

He explained that it was not an uncommon condition but it would require surgery to remove the lunatic half currently demand-ing *lebensraum*. So there it was. I hadn't worried about it being life-threatening because it wasn't life-threatening. All it was, was wages-threatening, seeing as how I'd have to take a few days off work – and in my game there's no pay if you don't play. The only other danger he was obligated to highlight was that, given the proximity to my vocal cords, the procedure might alter the timbre of my voice.

'Higher or lower?' I asked him.

His reply was that it might become a little more gruff. This was a shade disappointing, given that I'd always fancied one of those basso profundo deals that you often find given to bullfrogs and hippos in early Disney cartoons where they mournfully sing 'Asleep in the Deep' for the gathered species. Then he said something else.

'You will have no side effects from being left with half a thyroid, but do keep an eye on the remaining side. If that later goes rogue too then we have to take the whole thing away and you'll be put on tablets for the rest of your life.'

I promised I would watch it like a mother hen watches her brood. Having booked myself in two weeks hence to have the would-be goitre excised, out I went into the world whistling 'A Cockeyed Optimist' from *South Pacific*, a song that I believe holds Great Truth.

Now jump to several years later. I am shaving. Once again I note that the razor appears to encounter something alike a sleeping police-man halfway up the neck.

'Oh no,' I think. 'No, no, no. Not the other side too, now? Fuck it, when am I going to be able to take another three days off work at the moment? Well, sod it. Just leave it till it's getting remarked on.'

And that's what I did. Because it was my thyroid playing up again, wasn't it? Oh head and neck cancer, you sneaky false-flag-flying little bastard.

I left the lump to grow round and fat for almost another full year until even I had to concede I perpetually looked as if I'd eaten a whole gourd with one swallow. Booking another appointment with Dr D'Souza, I anticipated him being mildly cross with me for leaving it so long and hoped his removal rates wouldn't be governed by volume because this baby was twice the size of the last one. Entering his office at a crisp pace, I greeted him warmly and said, 'Look! It's back! I know what you're going to say – I promised to keep an eye on it and have broken that promise, but I swear this wasn't there yesterday.'

But I noticed he wasn't smiling. In fact he was furrowing his brow in concern.

'The old thyroid,' I said, settling into the chair. 'It wants to be reunited with its other half.'

Leaning towards me and cocking his head on one side, he stared at my neck. 'Mr Baker,' he said, 'that doesn't look like your thyroid.'

Like a buffoon, I continued with the larky act. 'Course it is,' I assured him. 'Don't you remember? You said the other side was likely to blow and ... you know ... tablets after that.'

Now he was feeling around the area but he didn't need long.

'Could you open your mouth for me, please,' he said. I quit the jabbering and felt the temperature in the room drop by about a hundred degrees. After pointing a torch beyond my teeth he swiftly withdrew it and, with an urgency that I should have read more into, he asked me to go down to see one of his colleagues in the basement and 'let her take some tests'.

'Now?' I asked.

'Yes, right away,' he replied, without looking up from whatever it was he was now speedily writing on a pad.

Well, I'll be honest with you, I still didn't twig that I was apparently showing all the signs of having a potentially terminal illness. I was leaning towards the cyst theory again; you read about them all the time. People let them get to the size of duffel bags, until they have to haul them about in wheelbarrows just to get to the corner shop.

Taking the stairs at my usual gallop, I loped up to a woman at a screen, gave my name, and within about ninety seconds I was having a hypodermic repeatedly sunk into the sac on my throat. It didn't hurt, though, as I put my T-shirt back on, the woman who had performed this revolting task did appear to regard my chatty demeanour as a little odd.

As I left, she looked at me with something approaching pity and said kindly, 'Are you OK with all this? Do you want to ask me anything?'

I said I didn't, wished *her* good luck and bounded out again. On the way home I bought a Cornish pasty and a slice of vanilla cheesecake. I had just washed these down with a cup of coffee . . . when the phone rang.

Could you bring someone with you.

****

'Dan? What's the matter, who was it?'

****

Dance In The Smoke

A Short Diversion into the Nature of Fate, Luck and Bad Vibes

Before we become immersed in the relentlessly grim months that followed taking that call, it might be wise to examine the question that many who receive such news ask of the cosmos: Why Me? I have to confess I never did ponder whether my illness was pointedly personal, but now that it seems to have buggered off again perhaps I can look at the whole picture with a more open eye. So. Did I do anything in the run-up to my contracting cancer that might have caused it? For example, was I a smoker?

Well, the answer to that is yes – I was a smoker from 11.20 to 11.22 a.m. one morning in July 1972. I was on my very first holiday abroad with my friends – if you don't count a school trip two years previously when twenty-five boys in our year went to visit, I promise you, a cuckoo-clock factory in Switzerland. (Later we went to a knife-maker's, where we all bought blades with the Swiss flag on their handles to take home as souvenirs. They used to wave you through customs in those days.) The '72 trip was a basic package tour to Arenal, Majorca, at the time the world's biggest roughhouse outside of the little fracas then being staged in Vietnam. I went with two pals of mine, Lenny Byart and Stephen Walford, who, to put it in the argot of the day, didn't mind a row. By this I mean that when the atmosphere in a bar or club would turn nasty and a violent mass brawl was clearly imminent, rather than take a walk around a nearby park until it all blew over as I would, Lenny and Steve were the type who would give the rebel yell, spit on their hands, run up the black flag and enthusiastically reach for their billy clubs. To them, a night without a punch-up was a night wasted. I, on the other hand, just wanted to rub up against as many teenage girls as possible. Of course these days if you say, 'Why, back in the seventies I just wanted to rub up against as many teenage girls as possible', the next thing you know you're being bundled in the back door of a police station with a blanket over your head as the national media jostle to get a clear shot of your pop-eyed expression. So I should point out that I, too, was a teenager when this was my one and only aim in life.

So, one morning by the pool, as Lenny and Steve were dangling their torn and bruised knuckles into a soothing ice bucket, I saw arriving on the far side an absolute vision. She was with two other girls and, because I was pretty quick off the mark, I lost no time in waving over at her. As so often happens when one forgets that dark glasses are concealing one's dotted eyeline, the entirely wrong girl waved back. She then called out something to us that sounded to me like a record playing backwards, but which Steve, who went to a grammar school, assured me was, in fact, French. Why on earth would she do that, I wondered. Did she think it was sexier? Was she showing off? Steve then furnished me with a third possibility. As it turned out, he was wrong. They were Belgian.

For a while, we three lads and two of the female trio on the distant shore called out incomprehensible messages to each other across the murky waters of the Arenal deep end. Our pointless questions soon became a little risqué, but judging by the uproarious squeals that followed whatever slogans the girls were coming up with, their replies must have been a bit ripe too. You'll note I said only two thirds of the opposing party were joining in the fun. Guess which one sat sullenly reading a paperback? Miss Dish Delish. The only movement she made was to occasionally lift her cigarette up to her wonderfully pale mouth, form her lips tightly around the filter tip, remove it, then exhale the smoke through a formed O so sensual the lenses of my Ray-Bans steamed up like a chip-shop window.

Clearly, some positive action was required. Waiting until she extinguished that lucky old fag in the plastic cup her friend had recently drained, I decided that it would be I who would offer her the next one. 'Be right back,' I said, rising from the lounger and making my way toward the kiosk on the hotel's patio.

Though never a smoker, this would not be the first pack of cigarettes I had ever bought, because since the age of about ten my mum had been sending me, often twice a day, round to Bill Hodges' shop to get her ten Rothmans tipped, so I knew all the lingo. Arriving at the stand, I searched for a brand that I recognized, but there seemed to be only two available. What could be the difference? Fortunately, the man at the kiosk was smoking at the time and the two inches of drooping stem that hung from his lips was giving off such a black noxious pong that I asked him to tell me what the brand was. When he pointed to the blue packet, I immediately asked him for the green ones. These were called St Moritz, which I thought suitably suave. Forking over the required pesetas, I strolled like Simon Templar back towards the loungers. On the way I attempted to open the packet but couldn't locate the thin strip that would circumcise the cellophane and so resorted to biting it repeatedly with my teeth – an image that must have added much to my cosmopolitan façade.

Settling down with Lenny and Stephen again, my image received further tarnish when, in the unfortunate manner of the times, they informed me that mentholated St Moritz was an appalling choice of cigarette with which to impress girls because it was well known to be smoked exclusively by homosexuals. Borrowing a lighter from a family a few beds away, I lit up the one and only cigarette of my life, blowing the smoke out before it had even passed beyond my teeth – though this wasn't swift enough to prevent one wisp making its way up under my sunglasses and into my right eye, which started off something of a flood. Taking another shallow puff, I grimaced at the taste. I had expected menthol cigarettes to be fresh and minty; after all, I had seen adverts at the cinema for Consulate Menthol and their slogan was 'Cool as a mountain stream . . . ' The only stream currently evident was the one making its way from my eye to the corner of my mouth. Two drags in and already it was like my head was made out of rancid back bacon, my tongue a strip of flypaper, the back of my throat a wall of flame. Yet somehow I found myself trudging around the poolside toward my intended *amour*.

Like all amateur smokers, I hadn't a clue how you got the toke-tempo right and so drew quickly again on the ghastly stick. All three girls were now looking straight at me as I approached, pale and sickly, tears cascading from beneath my shades and, in trying to suppress the inevitable coughing, making a noise like a workman's kettle coming up to the boil. Arriving at the girls' camp, the more welcoming of the triumvirate babbled at me in French, punctuating some of the more high-pitched statements with the sort of laughter that can't possibly have been complimentary. I remind you I was quite a good-looking kid and not used to young women handing me the lemon like this. Ignoring her light-headed companions, I focused on the bikini-clad object of my affection who by now was looking right at me as I loomed over her. Bringing forward the pack of St Moritz, I overcame my wheezing lungs and addressed her directly.

'Hello,' I said, with what I took to be devastating sangfroid. 'Cigarette?'

Unfortunately, I proffered the packet a little too energetically, with a heavy emphasis on the flick of the wrist. As a consequence about fifteen St Moritz mentholated fags shot out of the carton right at her. They bounced off her head or flew by to float bloating in the pool. Two settled absolutely upright in her cleavage. Now even as I look back on it today, forty-five years later, I still believe the three of them overreacted. Yes, it must have been a shock, but they were only thin cylinders of tobacco, not jets of liquid manure. Not that you'd ever know that from the way they all screamed. All three started to berate me in whatever Flemish variation of French it was as I fell into a sort of crouched scrambling, trying to pick up all the loose ones from the floor. I was repeatedly apologizing in the only French word I knew: *'Merci'* – something I now know isn't 'sorry' at all.

I leave you to imagine the howling coming from my friends, watching one pool's width away. Later on in the holiday Lenny did, if you'll again forgive the contemporary vernacular, 'grab hold' of one of the other girls in the party, which is how I know they were Belgian. Unfortunately, in the heat of their passion he gave her two love bites on the neck, something she was only confronted with when she saw herself in the bathroom mirror, and at the hotel breakfast the next day she walked in and hit him with her shoe.

Anyway, the point is that, yes, technically I had been a smoker, though I'll concede it's a slim chance that those three or four disgusting puffs in July '72 gave me cancer of the head.

Ruling this out, what else might have 'caused' it? Well, this one is less easy to dismiss because here we are entering the world of the occult and have to mull over the eternal question of whether inanimate objects can contain or transmit 'bad vibes'? And when I say 'inanimate objects', I'm not talking about a simple upside-down horseshoe or keeping peacock feathers in the house. No, the thing I brought into my home is pretty evil by anyone's reckoning. When I tell you this story takes place at the 2006 World Cup hosted that year by Germany, I think you'll get advance warning of where this might be going.

On 15 June, exactly one week before my forty-ninth birthday, England were due to play Trinidad & Tobago in Nuremberg. I had been covering the tournament for *The Times* newspaper, along with my great chum Danny Kelly, and we had arrived in Nuremberg the day before the match was to take place. Now Danny is exactly six months older than me, and even though there is this enormous age gap we find certain things can still unite us across this seemingly unbridgeable divide. One of them is the Second World War.

It seems incredible that Danny and I, having initially bonded over 1970s rock music, should have discovered this secondary shared interest, given that not many middle-aged men are that interested in Hitler and all that. I can recall the very first time I used words like 'Blitzkrieg', 'Anzio' and 'Operation Barbarossa' in his company. I had fully expected him to look bemused, but he said that he not only recognized the references but probably had some videos about the conflict somewhere. As it turned out he had 2,319 shelved and alphabetized videos on the subject – just four short of my own tally at the time. It is, as they say, a funny old world. And now, would you believe it, here we were in Nuremberg.

Checking in at the hotel, we immediately went online to find out whether this impressive old city had played any sort of significant role in those catastrophic events of the 1930s. Amazingly, after some thorough research, we found it had!

About twenty minutes later, the pair of us were climbing out of a taxi on the improbably named Zeppelin Strasse that runs alongside the old rally stadium. The city of Nuremberg, far from shrinking from its past and bulldozing this most Nazi of landmarks, leaves it standing stark and open to the public, who can walk among its vast and crumbling acreage, free, if they so wish, to mount the notorious podium where the blackest hearts of the twentieth century thundered and spilled their poison. It is a grim, sobering monument to the nation's atonement. When we entered the arena it was instantly recognizable as the monolithic setting of Riefenstahl's *Triumph of the Will* and it is almost impossible not to hear the murderous chorus of '*Sieg Heil*' echoing around the stones. You are inexorably drawn toward the focal point, the towering concrete podium, itself overshadowed by two gigantic doors through which the madmen strode to inflame the mob.

Mounting the steps leading up to this monstrous pulpit, Danny and I were unexpectedly tickled to find that upon these massive doors, once draped in slogans and swastikas, were now spray-painted the words 'Cypress Hill', a hip-hop band very popular at that time. There were about fifty or so other people there on this day, many of them German, and each of them apologetically took their turn to stand upon the very spot where Hitler stood, looking out across the entire stadium while friends captured the melancholy moment on their mobiles. When it came to our turn to feel the weight of history, Danny and I stood in silence for about twenty seconds before a group of England supporters down below recognized me.

'Dan!' one of them shouted. 'Put a comb under your nose . . .' As his pals all laughed, I tried not to react. His mate followed this up with, 'And then do what we all did, make out you're pointing at something in the distance.' It was, to be fair, a funny remark. Similar, I should imagine, to many made by the first British soldiers to walk around this infernal venue in 1945.

As we made our way back down the disintegrating concrete terracing I was nearly brought low when the edge of a step crumbled beneath my heel. I picked up the small chunk of masonry, tossed it in the air and caught it. 'Look at that,' I said to Danny, 'an actual part of the Nuremberg Stadium – I'm having that.' And I popped it into my carrier bag. In a movie, the camera would have slowly zoomed in on the space this purloined relic now occupied as it began to pulse a deep red, the soundtrack striking an ominous note on the synthesizer.

Back home, I took to keeping the stone on the mantelpiece in my office, where I would ask any visitors if they knew what it might be. Nobody did and when I told them, they would all pull the same face. 'How creepy. I wouldn't have that in the house . . . ' was a typical response.

When Spud became ill a year later, I can't say I immediately thought of the stadium fragment, but on coming back from the hospital one evening, feeling a touch low, it caught my eye and I figured that, though unlikely to be disseminating pure evil, the fucking thing couldn't exactly be helping either. The next day I chucked it over the wall of a building site in Lewisham. A new project now occupies that space, its occupants unaware that one tiny part of their foundations contains matter upon which Hitler himself walked. Then again, considering I sprang the rubble from a part of the stadium some distance from the VIP area, it's more likely to have been a pickle merchant from Mönchengladbach. No matter, may the record show that I too became seriously ill a few years down the line and so the Curse of the Nazi Stone may just have had the last laugh.

The final question we have to examine in the 'Why Me?' dossier, before we get on with the nuts and bolts of what it's like when you nearly drop dead, concerns my overall bodily condition at the time of the diagnosis. As far as I was concerned I had never felt better or lived higher on the Good Health Hog. Life was lush, sweet and delicious. Tellingly, though, when I now see photographs of myself from the first part of 2010 I am forced to accept that I had allowed myself to physically balloon to roughly the size of the Albert Hall. I don't remember swelling up to such dimensions and yet I plainly did because in photo after photo I resemble something on the scale of the beast that swallowed Pinocchio. As Wodehouse once wrote, 'These days tailors like to measure his waist simply for the exercise.' Why on earth didn't somebody tell me? When my underwear got hung on the washing line they must have lost an hour's daylight in South-East London. There's one picture of me and my mum where my head is a perfect circle. And not just a regular circle but one that could be filled with sawdust and used to stage circuses.

Quicksand

S tanding in front of the mirror, I looked at the person staring back and repeatedly told myself, 'I've got cancer.' Like a nervous best man rehearsing his wedding reception speech, I kept putting the emphasis on a different word. There was no dread, no anguish or panic, merely an unreal sense of having suddenly stepped outside reality with all its myriad useless concerns. A kind of conversation then developed in my head with the person I had been a few hours ago trying to get some sense from the person who had just got the news:

'So, what does this mean?'

You've got cancer.

'Hold on. Right. Hold on. What usually happens when you are in this spot?'

You've got cancer.

'No, there's a way around this. Think. There's a shortcut. A way of putting this off.'

You've got cancer.

'What's the story? What are you going to tell everyone? Where's the joke?'

You've got cancer.

'Dying. Is that it? No more. Gone. You're dropping dead. It's finished.'

You've got cancer.

'There's got to be something else. Something else happens now and this scare goes away. This is just an anecdote for later.'

You've got cancer.

'I can't have cancer.'

You've got cancer.

'Cancer. OK. Cancer. OK. Cancer.'

You've got cancer.

And then I looked out the window and for the first time saw that I didn't live in this world like the sky and those stones, I simply rented some time here. And now I was being evicted.

I swear to God, it was as if another part of my brain awoke from its stunned state and thought, 'This is all good stuff: Stones. Rent. Evicted. There's some good material there, so how does the complete joke work?'

But the complete joke for once didn't matter. Jokes didn't actually exist. Nor did thinking. Or feeling. Nothing did. And then I was putting on my jacket and placing my baseball cap back on my head so as to return to the hospital, and the ordinariness of these actions seemed utterly ridiculous.

Wendy drove and the silence hung over us as though we were bearing its weight like an ocean. Stopping at some traffic lights, she tried to lift the weight.

'Look. We're both presuming what they are going to say. We don't know. It could be anything. Maybe the tests didn't come out and they need to do it again. Let's not, you know . . . '

Neither of us had mentioned anything about cancer since I had said, with obvious implications, that they'd asked me to return to the hospital immediately.

And could you bring someone with you.

Other than my silent exchanges with myself in the mirror, we had gone into a sort of robotic efficiency, gathering our necessary bits and pieces, locking the back door, settling down the dogs, turning off the TV. All without a word, save Wendy asking, briskly and flatly, 'Do you think you might have to stay in? Will you need a bag?' I answered in the negative and the tone remained entirely without emotion because there were only two emotional choices currently available and the other option was simply unthinkable. Besides, nothing had been confirmed yet. Nobody had said anything about cancer yet.

Driving into the small car park at Blackheath Hospital, I saw Dr D'Souza, the throat specialist who had recommended the tests, getting out of his own vehicle. 'Oh, there he is,' I said, before adding with hopeless normality, 'Must have just come back from his lunch . . . '

Wendy pulled our car in close to his and he glanced up and saw me. He looked quickly away and marched smartly, but pointedly, towards the building. Whatever he had to tell me obviously was not to be shared in a pay-and-display. In that moment I felt the door of optimism close completely. I had cancer. Now I knew it. Had he asked me to return because, I don't know, because I had left my wallet on his desk, he would have stopped by the car, waved it at me and said, 'What are you like? Good job I'm an honest man!' No, mate. I had cancer. That big round lump in my neck? Cancer, all day long.

It was at that exact moment that I made the decision to suspend every intellectual and emotional inclination I might normally entertain in favour of complete subjugation to whatever process this diagnosis entailed. Walking towards Mr D'Souza's office, I began by asking myself if the strange numbness I now felt could be utilized as a sort of stoic calm. I found myself thinking of Robert De Niro's character in *The Deer Hunter*, holding a bullet in front of the face of one of his colleagues and saying, 'You see this? This is this. This ain't something else. This. Is this.' Because this indeed was. It's in you. You're in it. It's happening. Well, there it is.

I thought about the doctor's brisk departure when he saw me, and how he must be dreading breaking the news. Now I could relieve him of that burden, because I already knew. I felt Wendy's arm tight on mine as we went up the stairs and knew it must be worse for her, for the kids when they found out, so the last thing they wanted was me helpless and hopeless. This is this.

I'm sure this must all sound boastfully heroic, but this was the state that descended on me in the minutes before the result was confirmed. Mercifully, it remained in place for most of the upcoming awful year. In fact, I couldn't help but note a small moment of farce as we arrived on the required floor of the hospital and saw Dr D'Souza, now only a few paces ahead of us, going toward his surgery. I think he sensed it was us behind him, but nobody acknowledged this and he disappeared into his room at almost the same time as his receptionist said, 'You can go straight in . . . '

When we walked in on him, he couldn't have been seated for more than two seconds and yet none of us wanted to admit we had all arrived together. A normally welcoming man, he looked appropriately serious as he invited Wendy and me to sit down. In the seconds before he began what I imagine was to be a tactful and well-practised delivery of terrible information, I derailed the moment.

'So,' I said. 'Good news, I take it.'

I heard Wendy mouth a quiet, solemn 'Don't' and his mouth hung frozen upon whatever syllable he had planned to begin the dialogue.

All I can remember from the long explanation he eventually launched into is the phrase, 'It is, I'm afraid, a cancerous growth . . .' And how, though the lump was showing in my throat, the cancer was in my mouth. Or, to put it more accurately and bleakly, my head and neck.

As he continued talking, internally I found myself asking, 'Cancer of the head? Seriously? *Of the head*?' I had never heard of such a condition. Lung, bowel and stomach, yes, they got all the headlines, but cancer of the head? Oh well, goodbye cruel world. I knew you could get by on one lung, half a stomach and even a replacement bowel, but unless I'd missed that copy of *The Lancet*, I was pretty sure that even in the twenty-first century the old noggin was still all but irreplaceable.

Nobody was about to reassure me, 'Look I know it sounds bad but believe me we are making great advances in artificial heads these days. Take no notice of those old Frankenstein films – the bolts in the neck are barely half that size today and we've virtually eradicated the green tinge on the flesh!'

From the moment of that meeting I, like every person diagnosed with this most fearsome of illnesses, was suddenly entered upon a congested conveyor belt of appointments and treatments. At that stage, the treatments are little to do with combating the cancer directly but simply to get you into the best possible physical condition so as to help you withstand the terrible onslaught of science you are going to have to endure.

Dr D'Souza first handed me over to a specialist in the field of head and neck surgery, Mr Ricard Simo at Guy's Hospital. On meeting Ricard the following day, I instantly felt an unshakeable faith in his powers, chiefly because of his startling physical similarity to Donald Fagen of Steely Dan. This struck me as a fantastically important omen. After all, if one is entrusting one's life to an individual, one doesn't want them to pitch up looking like the late Pete Burns or the Crazy World's Arthur Brown, no matter how many letters they have after their name. Of all the rock stars Mr Simo might have resembled, had I been given free choice, I would have certainly gone for Donald Fagen or, if he was unavailable, something in the late period Joni Mitchell, when she stopped being poppy and approachable, and started withdrawing from the world. I am aware that both of these icons are heavy smokers, but one cannot have everything.

On that initial meeting with Wendy and me, Mr Simo outlined at length the type of cancer that I had and how it was manifesting itself around my head and neck. I barely heard a word of it. Not because I was in shock or denial but rather, in all honesty, because I had zero interest in the thing itself. Indeed, in all the time I was to be racked, tested and degraded by the illness over the coming months and years, I never once found it in any way fascinating or worthy of even a single Google search. My 'understanding' of it was of no more importance to me than understanding why the central heating in our house sometimes packs up. You ring a bloke, he comes and fixes it, but even they will make you stand in the hall while they explain about sumps, pumps and hosepipes. I owe my life to Mr Simo and another genius who we will meet shortly, but they soon understood that I saw the whole drama as something in which I had no real role. Science was fighting cancer. I was merely the battlefield.

If I may be presumptuous, I think they were quite relieved to find someone who had absolutely no questions for them or curiosity about the process. I never once enquired how I got it, what it was, who else had it, how the treatment worked or, the one everybody thinks they will ask immediately: is it worth me starting any long books or box sets? I think Ricard waited for me to 'go there', because after I had answered in the negative to his request for any questions he said, 'Well, I'm sure you want to know the overall prognosis, yes?'

'Go on then,' I said, in a tone bordering on the playfully indulgent. Quite why I felt so defiantly impish when, for all I knew, I was about to be told I'd better get my affairs in order, I simply cannot explain. But, as it transpired, the reaction wasn't entirely misplaced.

'Well, the good news is we have had some real success in recent years treating your particular type of cancer, Danny. It definitely can be overcome. However, the treatment itself, because of where the cancer is, is one of the most gruelling. It is going to get very tough for you. Very tough.'

'But that will be the treatment, not the cancer, right?' I said, seeking confirmation here rather than posing a direct question that would have broken my embargo.

'Yes, it's a very, um, *demanding* regime,' Ricard responded, quietly impressed, I fancied, at my resolution. 'You are going to need to be a very brave soldier at times,' he continued. Then to Wendy, 'He's going to need a lot of looking after.'

Then he smiled. And Wendy and I smiled. Then extraordinarily all three of us broke into a resigned but happy chuckling, as if to say, 'Oh boy. Cancer! What are you gonna do, eh?'

We shook hands, left his office and Wendy and I didn't say a word all the way down in the lift or even as we strode through reception and out of the building. I think we were both thinking the same thing. So. Not *necessarily* going to die then, eh? This was the option we had desperately hoped to hear but dared not entertain lest we jinxed its existence, and the next thing we knew we were hugging each other in euphoric relief on the streets of London Bridge.

Passers-by must have thought this entangled middle-aged couple were celebrating having become grandparents for the first time or maybe winning the lottery. How could they know it was even better than that?

And so it began.

Do You Believe In Magic?

The first appointment in my schedule was, rather surprisingly, with the dentist. I didn't actually have a regular dentist, though in imparting this information to those creating my schedule at Guy's I made it sound like I was merely between dentists rather than the shameful truth that I hadn't been to a surgery in seventeen years. And that visit was only because I'd developed a sharp edge on a back molar that was acting upon my tongue like a circular saw. Previous to that, I hadn't been in the demon chair for at least a couple of decades. Naturally, whenever I did choose to tell people this they'd make a face like I'd just revealed I keep the corpses of every dog I've ever owned under my marital bed. I would next see them trying to glimpse the interior of my mouth as I spoke in an attempt to confirm their worst imaginings – a festering black mire of tar and stumps or possibly a scene similar to the cover of Deep Purple's eponymous third album.

In fact, I have and have always had terrific teeth. Up until the age of about ten I did occasionally visit a local dentist whose brass plaque on the wall outside his office in St James Road SE16 proclaimed him as one Trevor T. Champtaloup – a name straight out of a W. C. Fields film but nonetheless quite a common handle in the antipodes, I am led to believe. It was the Champtaloup who extracted the only one of my teeth that ever had an eviction notice served on it for the entire first half of the century I walked this planet. Though only about eight years old – me that is, not Mr Champtaloup – I can clearly recall him asking my mother if I would prefer gas or cocaine as the anaesthetic. This was a standard enquiry at the time and I am not confusing the latter with the more likely-sounding Novocaine. They really did once ask eight-year-old children if they'd like to be dosed up on pharmaceutical cocaine in order to ease the agonies of tooth extraction.

Of course, the gas would put you to sleep, whereas I've found cocaine only puts the person you're talking to asleep. My preference was always to be wonderfully knocked out by the soothing gas. I can still clearly recall the small turtle-shell-shaped rubber appliance that would fit over a child's nose and mouth before they switched on the sleepy stuff. For a few seconds all you could smell was the frankly comforting odour of new wellington boots before a rising hissing sound sharply rendered you useless. There is no sleep like the one that followed, and even today I can't fathom why airlines don't offer this as an option to travellers on long-haul flights – they would only have to slightly modify the oxygen masks and, presto, demand for economy tickets to Brisbane would treble at the very least. I genuinely think it's a brilliant idea. Oh I know the authorities might highlight the dangers of allowing passengers to become totally overwhelmed by narcoleptic inertia for hours on end, but that's never stopped them from offering Swedish TV crime dramas as part of their in-flight entertainment, has it?

Anyway, off I went to the relevant department at Guy's and was quite surprised on arrival at the huge open-plan facility to be first asked about my general feelings toward dentistry. I said I was all for it. Of course what they were trying to ascertain was whether I was one of the three in five people who, upon being asked to 'open wide', burst into tears like a drunken debutante with a squashed cake in her handbag. I told them I was fine with it and was wildly impressed to then be informed that had I had a phobia I would have been funnelled off to a special section that came with counselling, soothing music and all manner of distractions including ceiling-mounted TV screens that would scroll through previously provided photographs of family and friends. I remember thinking that what would really help take sufferers' minds off events would be a troupe of magicians doing close-up tricks, roaming the booths, producing coins from cavities or pulling long strings of Flags of Many Nations from the yawning mouths of the patient opposite. Another option offered was hypnosis. Had I not already declared my psychological hand, I may have briefly toyed with the idea of giving that another bash. I say another bash because the only time anyone had ever attempted to 'put me under' previously was on live television and the whole thing had been an out-and-out farce.

This was during the days of the *Six O'Clock Show* when I must have volunteered for every aspect of light entertainment spectacle short of putting my head in a lion's mouth. These days, when I am often referred to as 'the veteran broadcaster' and even 'media legend', I can't help but feel such well-meant and respectful epithets slosh over great swathes of the broad baggy pants hokum that have comprised much of my career. Before we turn to the murky tale of my hollow hypnotism, how about this for a slice of bargain basement burlesque. One week on the *Six O'Clock Show* we had, for God knows what reason, a turn whose act was to hit stuff with a bullwhip. He'd snuff out distant candles and snatch cigarettes from proffered mouths, but the climax of his act was to incrementally reduce a page from a broadsheet newspaper down to a square the size of a postage stamp. For this he needed an assistant who would retrieve then hold out the ever-decreasing sheets until only one, minute fragment remained. Risky stuff, given the tip of the whip was travelling at the speed of sound when it split the print. In truth, I had not been keen to act as the stooge here until I was told that the pay-off on the act involved the assistant pretending to drop the last piece of paper. Then, upon bending to pick it up again, the star would perform one last whiplash that would tear asunder the rear end in a pair of specially prepared trousers, thus exposing the accomplice's oversized underpants emblazoned, quite correctly, with the Union Jack. Well, I ask you – what pro in their right mind isn't going to want to be part of the belly-laugh produced in response to that bit of business? 'Solid Gold' is the phrase I believe we're all looking for here.

On the night, everything was going as planned. I felt in no danger, though, as all the role required was putting on a convincing 'nervous

Nelly' routine. When we got down to the last small square of news-paper and the man with the whip said I should now hold that up for severing, to heighten the drama I protested, something along the lines of, 'Oh, now you're being ridiculous! You've proved your point – this is madness!' The audience guffawed and then held their breath as I eventually held at arms' length the last inch of *The Times* between my fingers. The drum rolled, the whip cracked and a pain quite as intense as any I have ever felt suddenly flew at warp speed from my middle finger to the very base of my skull. Yelping like a jabbed seal I thrust both my hands under my armpits and began running on the spot in sheer agony. This was live TV and, despite my brain urging me to do so – and as cathartic as that would have been – I simply could not scream, 'Christ Almighty, you silly old fucker! You missed!' However above the searing pain, another part of my brain was registering something else. I was getting tremen-dous laughs. The audience, believing it all to be part of the act, was howling.

As anyone in my game will tell you, when you hear that wonderful elusive noise cascading down it tends to override all emergencies. So rather than check to see how much of my finger he had amputated with his wayward bastard flick of the wrist, I milked the torture for all it was worth because – bonus! – I now remembered we still had the trouser-ripping pay-off to come! Despite my digit pulsating like the belly of a recently gaffed codfish, I submerged the suffering and dutifully doubled over to pick up the final sheet. Once more the whip cracked and this time, as instructed, I forcefully bowed my knees outwards, causing the Velcro on the trouser seat to split asunder, thus displaying our nation's standard in the wide-screen format. The resultant laugh, low and ancient though the source material may have been, brought the house down. As soon as it had subsided, however, and the show had moved on to the next item, the pain in my finger extended out into my whole hand. Without the adrenalin and, well, my *all-consuming ham* to mask its intensity, I literally felt like passing out.

The whip-master, an elderly chap who might well have learned his chops from Buffalo Bill himself, made his way over. 'Would I be right in thinking I caught you a bit at the end there?' he said in the casual manner of someone merely enquiring if we had ever met before. I attempted to reply but all that emerged was a long string of vowels passing across lips that, even if the errant consonants had been present, had lost the capacity to form the necessary shapes. In the end I held up my fingers so that he might see how ghastly and misshapen one of them was as compared to its brethren. Following a quick squint he said, 'Yes that happens sometimes. Bad luck. So crucial to hold that last one steady.' Bad luck? At no point previously had this indifferent old fossil ever hinted that the routine had an element of hit and miss about it. Also, was that last sentence designed to suggest that the entire fiasco was somehow my fault? Before sauntering away, leaving me to perform the rest of my duties on the show from behind a veil of torment, he chucked in, 'You'll lose that nail, by the look of it . . . ' And I did. About an hour later in the cab going home. The poor traumatized thing popped off in record time as I cradled my still burning paw in the ice pack the LWT nurse had provided. I was still wearing the Union Jack pants.

The hypnotism experience was a farrago of a different hue. In the first place, if hypnotism is a real thing – and I remain unconvinced – then my consciousness is about the least susceptible testing ground for such flim-flam. This doesn't spring from some bullish empiricism or the desperate desire to show that I am a no-nonsense sort of chap. Indeed, may the record show I am, if anything, an all-nonsense sort of chap. That this book begins with me behind locked toilet doors seeking to commune with other dimensions should indicate what a restless mind I have when dealing with the unknown. Consider also, that when I first arrived on television I was asked by a popular magazine to be the subject of one of those 'all about me' Q&A features, and under the enquiry 'What Is Your Preferred Choice of Hat?' I replied, 'A puffed-up turban with a large question mark on it.' There, if that doesn't identify me as an eternal seeker of truth then I don't know what does.

After seeing the film *Altered States*, in which William Hurt plays a man who gets into a flotation tank and turns into a monkey, I became extremely interested in the whole idea of sensory deprivation as a possible path to enlightenment. *Altered States* was not a comedy, I should add – it was a powerful psychological and philosophical drama based on a book by Paddy Chayefsky and directed by Ken Russell (though, to be fair, the overall plot did lean heavily on the 1933 Laurel and Hardy two-reeler *Dirty Work*).

Having spent a few months brooding upon and reading up about flotation tanks, I found myself in a hotel near Rye on the Sussex coast. Incredibly, one of the features of this hotel was such a tank. Housed in a refurbished basement, this immense coffin-like device called out to me like the door of perception it undoubtedly was. At the first opportunity I went to reception and with hesitant breath declared I wished to become as one with its mysteries. This, I learned, would have to be deferred until the following afternoon because the bloke who knew how to 'get it going' was off until then.

'Would two thirty be OK?' I was asked.

Two thirty, I declared, would be perfect.

Now for those of you who do not understand the general principle of a flotation tank, it is basically this. You climb into what is essentially a bath with a lid on it and lie flat out in waters specially infused with a secret blend of salts, herbs, nuts and spices that guarantee buoyancy for even the fattest old cove. Actually, I'm not sure why I added herbs, nuts and spices there, because I believe it is just salts. And far from being secret, I do recall seeing an enormous cement-bag-sized packet of these salts in the corridor outside.

Anyway, once you are settled in and gently bobbing like a piece of jetsam they bring down the lid and you are henceforth unable to see, hear, touch, taste or smell a thing. According to the books I had read, after a few minutes of this total sensory deprivation you start to wig out, or, to be more precise, *wig-in*. Your mind, suddenly freed from all its mundane responsibilities of keeping you from walking into traffic etc., turns inward and manifests itself in a dreamlike hyper state that ultimately reveals a deeper realization of ontological existence. Well at £12 for half an hour and £20 for the full sixty minutes (Monday to Thursday only), I was hardly going to turn that down, was I?

Needless to say, it didn't work for me. Like so many out-of-body experiences, I think you probably have to make a bit of an effort to at least meet the indefinable halfway. Suspension of the self is pretty paramount here and that is something I have never been much good at. During prayers in school assembly I could never manage to keep my eyes properly shut much beyond the line ' . . . and forgive us our trespasses . . . ' before opening them a fraction to surreptitiously peer around looking for whoever was truly lost in the moment. Once identified, I would then nudge a nearby chum and craftily indicate the zealot about whom we would both chuckle before resuming the blackout. So it proved in the flotation tank.

Moreover, the booking did not get off to the most tranquil of starts, given that I was forced to wait in the corridor for several minutes while the previous floater got dried and dressed. This corridor also abutted the ladies' hairdressers and you do feel a prize prune standing there in a dressing gown, holding a towel, big old hairy legs exposed to public gaze while a parade of well-dressed women flood by amid clouds of L'Oréal Elnett Satin.

Then when the extra-time-hogging guest finally emerged he was an enormous bearded bloke, plainly built by the same flesh-firm that delivered James Robertson Justice. Even though we exchanged a cheery greeting as he squeezed past, my only thought was that they might not change the tub water between shifts and I was about to surf into transcendence via a soup rich with his effluent.

Then, upon entering the magical chamber, I found a woman in attendance. Now this sort of thing I am no good at. One of the main reasons I am glad that I never pursued a life in the theatre* is because I could never be comfortable with the way actors are somehow entirely OK with being naked backstage. I have completed several stints as the narrator in *The Rocky Horror Show* and my

---

* *Going to Sea in a Sieve; Wonderland, Alice in*

pleasure in recalling this is always sharply tempered by memories of having to conduct conversations with men in the company who were seemingly unaware that their cods were on display. With the women it is a different kind of awkwardness and I cannot pretend for a second that it strikes me as in any way normal. There I'd be in full dress suit, trying to have a light conversation about post-show restaurant choices with an actress who was blithely climbing into fishnet stockings and very little else. I found it mortifying and yet they unfailingly found it amusing. It's not normal, as my mum would say whenever there was a sex scene on a TV play, usually followed by, 'I mean, sodding hell, where's the decorum?'

There was certainly little decorum in me being decanted naked into a recently vacated flotation tank by a woman to whom I previously hadn't so much as tipped my hat. She asked me if it was my first time in a flotation tank. I told her it was. She then asked if I had a fear of enclosed spaces. I told her that if I had it was unlikely that I would have signed up to be sealed inside a pitch-black torpedo for sixty minutes. Smiling at this, she then enquired if I had brought any music that I'd like played while channelling inner space. I must say this hadn't occurred to me and it struck me as cheating somewhat. I mean, when it comes to a thing like sensory deprivation, surely, in for a penny and all that. One can hardly become detached from one's physical self if one is simultaneously trying to think of the bass player's name on a track from *Now That's What I Call Music 28*.

Then she asked if I had any questions. Well I had two: 1) Will you be staying in here as I disrobe? And, 2) Have you hosed this thing out since old man-mountain took his trip? In the event, I posed only the first one, which, tellingly, I felt the most urgent. To my great relief, I was informed she would not be sticking around to assist my haggard old arse into the drink. She would, however, be coming back to check on me 'every fifteen minutes or so'. As it transpired, by the time she must have come back for the initial visit I was long gone. Having got naked in a strange room and then climbed the three steps that led up to the tank I could just feel that this longed-for event was not for me. Lying down in the tepid water I was at first all in turbulent motion, indeed all at sea, as I tried to achieve total buoyancy while endeavouring to stop my body from touching the sides of the tank and thus breaking the spell of being 'out of the everywhere'. This was almost impossible to achieve and my carcass repeatedly drifted over to bob up against the tank like a rudderless submarine. Eventually, I achieved the task of becoming an offshore island, but as soon as this delicate manoeuvre was accomplished I remembered the next instruction I'd been given: 'Once you're comfortable, close the lid on yourself.' This I had not done and so I now had to reach up, seal the deal, following which I was once again thrashing about like a buoy in a hurricane. A minute later I was once more becalmed, although the anticipation at knowing my foot might touch the tank at any moment was harshening whatever vibe I was trying to achieve. I even said out loud at one stage, 'Now come on, Dan. Let it go. Do it. Come on . . .' and may have even tried the mantra from the *Tibetan Book of the Dead* (via Lennon) 'Relax, turn off your mind and float downstream . . .'

Well no, I just couldn't do it. Far from 'floating downstream', it became obvious my brain has no such neutral gear. As I lay there, prone and preposterous, trying to achieve total consciousness but a few feet from the Do Or Dye Ladies Hair Salon, into my head popped the chorus from 'The Tiger Rag', that raucous trombone-led trad-jazz rip from which there is no karmic return. Why it came to me there and then, when an Indian raga would have fitted the bill so much better, I could not fathom. 'Tiger Rag' it was and I was stuck with it. I first smiled then began to uncontrollably giggle. What the fuck was I doing? I had made a monkey out of myself all right. Pushing open the lid again I dried myself, put the dressing gown back on and promptly left the dubious mental redoubt. Only later did I think that the woman in charge of the place must have 'checked on me' – found nothing – and thought I'd disappeared down the Matrix's plughole.

This private failure to launch stands in contrast to the very public mind game I was asked to play on the *Six O'Clock Show*. We had filmed a typically light and facetious report on the boom in 'alter-native' sciences then taking hold in the capital. Eschewing the fair and even-handed, we quite properly milked the subject for every last drop of quackery it traditionally held. One spectacularly batty old girl – who I now recall was about ninety-fifth in line to the throne – explained to us how she never made a move or decision without dowsing for guidance. Dowsing, of course, is usually associated with the search for water and requires one to ramble over the country-side holding a Y-shaped stick that will plummet like a nuclear bomb should so much as a dribble of moisture be detected underground. However, our titled host in this section of the investigation literally dowsed for everything, *everything*, using a crystal on a chain. She dowsed her shoe collection each day to locate the correct pair, she dowsed the meat in her fridge to determine if it was 'orf', she dowsed her cat every hour to understand its current mood. She even dowsed her phone before answering it in case the caller was someone she didn't wish to talk to. If the crystal spun clockwise it was a friend but if it rotated the other way it would most likely be the Gas Board or some other nuisance and so she would just let it ring. Remember – if a garden party at Buck House were hit by a meteorite and took out the top ninety-four members of the royal family, this woman would be on all our stamps.

It was during my interview with this grand dame that our cam-eraman – a wonderfully cynical Steely Dan fan called Trevor Salmon who had seen it all and worked with some of the greatest comedians of the age – had to call a halt to the shoot so he could leave the house and roll about in the street outside helpless with mirth. Our host was explaining that she was doing a bit of baking while we were there and, naturally, she did not trust modern timers, preferring the dowsing crystal, which knew when her fare was cooked exactly as she liked it. Every now and then she would break off from our chat and hold the bejewelled chain above her oven. I noticed it was slowly circling and asked her what that meant. 'Ah well, you see that motion tells me all is well, but it's nowhere near done yet. What we're looking for is for the crystal to really go whizzing around, so much so that I can hardly hold it – it's like having a puppy on a leash! And then I have to hang on to it like that for about ten minutes until it starts to weaken and as soon as it has come to a complete stop, I'll know my cake is cooked perfectly to my taste, moist inside with a slightly burnt crust. The crystal knows! The crystal knows everything!'

I asked what sort of cake she was baking.

'It's a fruitcake!' she beamed.

It was at this point that our cameraman had to leave.

At some point in the studio discussion after this item – the piece had also included fortune tellers, astrologers and the whole gamut of New Age fancies – I must have said that I couldn't even entertain hypnotism as a viable science. After the show we received a slew of calls from people affronted by this, with several offering to come and demonstrate the bona fides of the Great Science. Sniffing some show-filling hoopla, the producers booked a working theatre hypnotist to come on to the very next programme and give it to me live and undiluted.

I met him during rehearsals and he seemed an agreeable old pro, a little nervous and not dissimilar in appearance to the great Harry Worth. I didn't want to embarrass the man by tearing up his act live on air but I also knew there was no way I would actually succumb to the old 'your eyes are getting heavy' guff and this would undoubtedly result in professional loss of face for him. Still, the last thing I was going to do was play along like all those desperate volunteers you see on hypnotism stage shows who pretend to helplessly disco dance at the mention of certain words or imagine they get electric shocks from ordinary ballpoint pens. Frankly, I've always thought such hopeless end-of-the-pier showboating to be the physical representation of those signs in insurance offices that say 'You don't have to be mad to work here . . . BUT IT HELPS!' No, once we got on air it was either him or me that had to be put to the sword, and I set about trying to think of the kindest way to undermine his efforts while getting a good few laughs into the bargain.

Sadly, that evening as our spot in the show approached I could feel the ham in me start to sizzle and I suddenly realized that I had little choice but to make as big a splash as I could. I became resigned to total resistance and if that meant chucking the old pro overboard live on air, then so be it. However, never, ever underestimate those who have been in the game longer than you have. This sweet, avuncular, anxious bumbler had an ace up his sleeve that perfectly sucker-punched a cocky young pretender like me. Heavily trailed throughout the show, our moment arrived and in all honesty I was licking my lips at the laughs I was about to get at this old waxwork's expense. Following an introduction by Michael Aspel, the cameras zoomed in on the far side of the studio where I sat in the sucker's chair waiting to be transported into the fourth dimension. Behind me, and now in full dress suit, was my guide. Before I could say a word, before I could deliver my very first, finely honed, undercutting comic whizz-bang, he grabbed the high ground and picked me off like the sap I was. During the huge applause that greeted Aspel's intro, that old rogue leant forward and said, very softly, in my ear:

'Hope this goes well. That's my grandson in the front row. He's not seen me work before.'

What a bastard! What a brilliant, conniving, magnificent, blackmailing old bastard! And yes, sure enough, as I looked ahead, there smiling and fresh-faced was a kid of about seven that I hadn't noticed before. His eyes were wide, his hair neat and brushed, his face full of hope and he was applauding wildly because his granddad was about to be the star of the show. I repeat – what a sly old bastard! Now what could I do?

Well, I'll tell you what I did. I 'went under' meekly, compliantly, like the impotent stooge I was. Oh God. I clucked like a chicken and I ran around the chair like a rabbit. I sang like Frank Sinatra and I sat up and begged for a biscuit like a dog. Or rather, like the beaten mutt I'd become. All the while trying to catch my jailer's eye so I might indicate, 'Bravo, you slippery old genius.' When he eventually snapped his fingers in order to 'bring me back', I even did a bit of head-shaking accompanied by a little, 'What are you all laughing at?' Meanwhile, as the wild applause filled the studio, that little boy in the front row looked so proud of his ol' grandpop that he was fit to burst. I looked at his beaming grin and wondered if he would ever know what a humiliating sacrifice I'd just made for him. And then, as junior's eyes met mine, it hit me. Of course he would know. He wasn't there by chance. That kid was no more the hypnotist's grandson than I was. He probably wasn't even a kid. He was most likely some hard-bitten midget with a rap sheet as long as your arm that had been travelling with the act for about forty years. He was the guarantee. And I was the mark. What a heel. What a sap. What a sucker.

So, that first day in Guy's Hospital dental department, upon learning that one of my options was hypnotism, I soon dismissed any idea of giving it another crack as that whole painful episode came flooding back. Man, I suddenly believed I probably wouldn't need anaesthetic of any sort. Just tell the dentist to bung one of their junior relatives within my eyeline then drill, saw and yank away as much as you want. You won't get a peep out of me.

Solid Air

My teeth, as it transpired, were disappointingly sound. Disappointing that is for the wonderful operative who tapped and peered at them and who, as she openly admitted, would have loved to have given me a stern salutary lecture on so neglecting one's choppers. Even so, two were to come out. Not because they resembled moss-covered slivers of Stonehenge but because, even though they were healthy, in her opinion, they were the most at risk to go bad in the next few years. My mouth, indeed my entire head, was going to be in no state to put up any resistance to even the mildest infections for some time and so all suspect fixtures and fittings would be cleared out. This was to be the same precautionary conveyor belt virtually every part of my body was to be placed on in those initial few weeks. During this time I began to have the sort of dreams I was going to have to get used to.

Before cancer, I often had the kind of anxiety dream I know is common to many. In it, you have either murdered someone or done something so awful that the consequences can barely be processed and now it is all catching up with you. These dreams then reach some sort of ghastly crescendo before you wake up suddenly, heart pounding, slowly reassuring yourself of the glorious reality that none of it was real and you're lying at home having a kip in bed. When you have been told you have cancer, the opposite happens. You have dreams of fantastic everyday normalcy that roll along until you awake in the darkness without panic and feeling cosily sanguine. Then slowly you remember there is nothing blissful or even mercifully mundane about your circumstances. You have cancer.

That really happened. You've got it right now. It takes a while to drift back off after that.

Following a round of seemingly routine inspections – the teeth, the ears, the eyesight, etc. – things started to get a little more industrial. The most unexpected of these was an appointment to get fitted for a mask. Sticking with my 'no questions' policy, I merely nodded when I was told of this, although I sensed this approach was starting to drive the medical team a little nuts.

'Have you any idea why you are going to need a mask?' I was asked tersely. I said no, to which, in a tone that suggested I shouldn't make them drag this stuff out of me, they replied, 'It's because of where your cancer cells are. When the radiotherapy lasers begin their work, your head mustn't move so much as a thousandth of an inch. Therefore patients have to have a mask created for them that fits exactly so that we can bolt their heads down on to the theatre table and prevent any movement.'

Intimidating stuff, for sure, but also extraordinarily interesting and, I swear, just the faintest bit exciting. I have to say that I could not envisage what sort of mask it might be. My best guess was that it might resemble the kind of death masks you see of notable sixteenth-century archbishops and the occasional king. Blank, plaster of Paris affairs that make everybody look like Alec Guinness at various stages of his career. On the day of its creation I sat in the waiting room outside the 'workshop' looking for clues. The only information I could discern was the vigorous rubbing of a reddened face being performed by the man who exited prior to my appointment. He accompanied this with repeated, exaggerated gyrations of his jaw. A nurse called my name.

On entering the room I saw shelves of what looked like outsize versions of the facial protection Olympic fencers adopt. The mesh was a dull mustard colour with an off-white trim. Invited to lie on a medical bed, I was told that my mask would be created to the exact contours of my face and that though this process was routine, there was a small amount of discomfort involved. This was a description I would hear a lot over the coming weeks. What actually happens is you lie there while something like a tennis racket is heated to a very specific temperature and then placed across your face, lying initially against the tip of your nose. Then very slowly it is pushed down so that the fabric of it moulds into every bit of your dial. I was warned it might be a bit hot at first. This was not quite the truth. It was hot at first, in the middle and at the end. Though I bore it stoically – to wriggle or even wince would bugger up the fit – I began to have great sympathy with every bit of cod I'd ever seen fished out of a chip-shop fryer. You have to wear the thing until it's become cool and therefore set – a process the materials involved seemed hell-bent on resisting. The poor old tip of my hooter, which bore the brunt of the assault for the longest time, began to feel like a dead ringer for the last hot chestnut at Christmas.

Then there's the question of dignity. This would become a terrible recurring theme of my treatment. You might think worrying about how you looked would be absolutely secondary under such circumstances, but I have to say overall, on the few occasions I have ruminated upon this entire terrible period, it is the times when I felt utterly prone, exposed or otherwise bereft of majesty that have caused me to shudder the hardest.

So it was as I waited for my amazing mesh mask to pipe down and 'go off'. Initially, as I say, the thing seemed to be of a temperature similar to that of the space shuttle upon re-entry, but as soon as the heat started to ease off somewhat, say to that of a pound coin after a minute in the microwave, the staff felt safe to ignore me and go about their other duties. And there you lie while they gossip about workmates, fill out time sheets, trim other masks, choose what they want from Pret's, hum to the radio, every now and then saying, 'You OK in there?' and, because you can't speak, you gamely hoist a thumb, feeling not unlike Frankenstein's creation still waiting for his brain. I tried to picture what I must look like there, flat out, naked to the waist and wearing this ginormous mesh head with my exaggerated features bulging out of it, the top of my nose shining through the rigging like Rudolph setting out from the North Pole.

When it's finally done and passed as sufficient by the team, they tag it with your name and tell you you'll be seeing a lot of this thing later. They are right. Though, with reason, they don't add that when the radiotherapy is over and you are broken and reduced beyond imagination, you will never ever want to look upon it again.

I had an operation next to remove the cancerous parts of my throat and tonsils. This was routine enough and apart from being vaguely aware that I came around from the knife too quickly and was for a good ten minutes babbling the most toe-curling nonsense at the surgical team, nothing remarkable happened. I had been warned about the slight chance that my vocal cords would be irreparably damaged and my radio career would thus be over, but chose not to entertain this – with good reason, as it turns out. However, the next couple of 'pre-treatment' treatments were slightly more grisly. I wouldn't normally burden you with such butcher-shop details, but the fact is neither of them are without dramatic impact and a fair dollop of gallows humour, so here goes . . .

I was handed over from Ricard Simo to the consultant in clinical oncology at Guy's, Teresa Guerrero Urbano, a woman who was to save my life as surely as if she'd hauled me off a railway track moments before the Trans-Europe Express thundered through. In our initial interview she interpreted my lack of inquisitiveness as an attempt to avoid reality that, while not entirely true, certainly may have been part of it. In turn she proceeded to catalogue every revolting thing that was going to happen to me over the coming months in her care in an unvarnished monologue that thoroughly rattled me, and Wendy, with its brutal candour.

Chemotherapy could be tolerable but once radiotherapy began, because it would be centred on my head, I was going to become extremely ill, growing ever more ill as the weeks passed, until I would feel everything was hopeless. The inside of my mouth would become one enormous painful blister. A severe sore throat would have to be endured throughout. The skin on my neck would turn red and raw before becoming jelly-like and eventually sloughing off altogether. For many months it would be impossible for me to eat anything, drink anything or even talk. My saliva glands would be destroyed, so would my taste buds, never to fully recover. There would be a period of almost constant vomiting. I would have a hole punched into the top of my stomach, through which I could feed myself via a tube. This could also be used for administering morphine at times when the pain might become too great. The final few weeks of radiotherapy would be by far the worst. Though there was great faith in the treatments, there was no guarantee . . .

I could go on, but I think you are getting the gist. At the time, I thought Teresa might simply be laying it on a bit thick in an attempt to break through what she believed to be a denial of my situation. She later came to know that I really am as shallow as I appear. Equally, I came to realize that this cavalcade of horrors she had outlined were absolutely necessary so that when each disgusting symptom did eventually manifest itself, rather than think you were spiralling toward death, you knew you were reacting correctly and on track, just as she had predicted. This wouldn't help with the agony but, again, you could gratefully hold on to the idea that this torture was not being caused by the cancer; it was science carpet-bombing the cancer out of you. There were to be many times when I would cling to those awful, fearsome words of hers, literally for dear life.

The first thing I had to toddle along for was the stomach perforation. Far from being a big deal this didn't even qualify as an operation but came under the heading of a simple 'procedure', i.e. something that wouldn't require you to be previously knocked out with a cartoon mallet. This makes a huge difference, because immediately before your belly is gifted this new, dolphin-like blow-hole, you get to sit in a large waiting room with about ten others who have also been added to the same race card that morning. You chat and find yourself saying arcane phrases to each other like, 'Well, this is a fine kettle of fish!' One by one you go into the lab and, after only about fifteen minutes, out you come, newly drilled and reassuringly chipper for anyone in the waiting pack who still has the collywobbles about it. You don't actually see the carpenter's bradawl, or whatever it is they use to create this ventilation-shaft, doing its work because after a local anaesthetic they erect a screen across your chest, similar to ones you see when the council are digging the road up. Which, in a way, they are. There's a slight sensation of pressure being applied here and there before you are told to put your gown back on and send in the next chump. Of course, all you're dying to do is have a look at this radical new body piercing, but the relevant site has already been covered by a large square of gauze so you have to pretend you're not that bothered.

Naturally, as soon as I had waved a cheery 'keep in touch' to my new friends, I hastened to the nearest public toilet to examine the excavation. Disappointingly, you can't really see it, covered as it is by a sort of clear rubberized disc, not unlike the suction pad atop an arrow in a 1950s Red Indian dressing-up kit. Out of this extends a foot or so of clear tubing, coiled up and taped to your chest. This all remains in situ throughout the entire process. In the following days, dozen of boxes of large purple plastic syringes would be delivered to my home, specially designed to fit the end of this tube. Once loaded with the high-vitamin goop that would help keep my battered old bod ticking over, these purple syringes would pump the stuff straight into my then ample gut, thereby bypassing the top third of my frame altogether. Ditto water. Ditto morphine. A new syringe was required for every use. For the first few months I did this, our dustmen must have thought Keith Richards had moved in with us.

And the hits just kept on coming. Next up was to have what is known as a PICC line fitted. This is a thin pipeline that goes in at the wrist and plugs straight into one of the major blood vessels around the heart. By attaching a bottle of chemo to the end that hangs out of you, in theory, you should be able to administer the drug yourself and at home. I never got as far as that because on returning home from having this latest modification I began to feel pains right across my chest. I rang them up. 'Probably just a reaction, it should settle down,' I was told. That night I found it difficult to breathe, so I went back the next day. This turned out to be one of my better decisions because what was happening was that my blood had started to clot around the intrusive cable. Had one of those clots put on its hat for a holiday in my heart, I would have dropped stone dead.

The PICC was whipped out in an instant and I was given the dire news that my chemotherapy would now require me to travel each week to St Thomas' Hospital, with a few overnights likely. On top of this the clotting was something that needed careful watching from now on, so I was taken to a room where eventually a young woman arrived carrying a box of syringes quite different from the big cartoonish ones that I would soon use for numbing and nourishment. These looked exactly like real syringes – what would be called in schoolyard parlance 'needles'. Now needles have never bothered me too much, which was just as well, because over the next year I would have about five thousand of the things slid into me at various points. Thrice-daily blood tests took up the bulk of that number, with at one point even the doctors in charge noting that the backs of my hands looked like the camping site at Glastonbury after the last band had been on. These latest hypodermics being shown to me now contained Clexane, a blood thinner that I was informed I must administer myself, daily, and for the foreseeable future. The woman asked me to have a go at it there and then so she could see if I had the hang of it. 'Where's best to jab?' I asked, and was quite surprised by the answer. 'Most find the stomach is the easiest,' she said. Now I don't know about you, but I have only ever considered two bodily areas to be recognized targets for the pinprick: 1. The top of the arm. 2. The arse.

To be honest, I feared that second option would be her recommendation, because then I might have had to drop the trousers and expose the rear in a hangdog scenario familiar to low comedians since sketch comedy began.

'What you do,' she continued cheerily, 'is gather about an inch of your stomach between your fingers and inject directly and swiftly into that.' I saw her quickly look at the expanse of my girth and inwardly figure that when it came to 'gathering about an inch of stomach' I was spoiled for choice. Indeed, so large was my old gut in those days, I could have had the stuff punched home via one of those pile drivers that bridge builders secure pylons with and still comfortably absorbed the trauma. Taking one of the needles from the box, she handed it to me; though, as I say, I have no phobia of the things, there is something in the build-up to the actual jab that makes your backbone go a bit marshmallow. The tearing off of the paper around the swab. The noise the syringe makes as they fetch it in a steel kidney dish. The soft pop as they remove the protective cap from the needle tip. The studied way you look anywhere but at your arm as it is wiped with antiseptic. The endless silent moments before the thing eventually becomes embedded. These are the reasons people wig out at inoculations, because the slender invasion itself is not that painful at all and should you inflict exactly that degree of discomfort on yourself in any other circumstance you'd hardly register it, let alone bother telling anyone how awful it all was.

However, you can add to that suspenseful list a further level of exquisite ritual and that is: having to do the deed yourself. I rather shocked myself by becoming mentally all over the place at the prospect of this minor act of self-harm. Having taken my 'inch' between thumb and forefinger, I poised the syringe above the fleshy hillock and prepared to pop it in. But from somewhere deep in my brain I could hear a voice saying, 'No, don't! Don't do that! Why would you do that?' I suppose this is the same voice that stops us eating handfuls of drawing pins or putting Tabasco sauce in our eyes every five minutes. Through evolution, any override switch it may have been fitted with must have long since grown out because I found I couldn't argue with its reasoning and consequently still held the needle in mid-air like a darts player with the yips. The nurse to my side eventually said, 'Shall I do this first one for you?' This rather stung my pride and had the effect of temporarily turning me into Errol Flynn in *Captain Blood*. With a devil-may-care laugh I plunged the needle home triumphantly and withdrew it just as quickly. 'There you go!' I said.

Patiently, she explained that, though I had taken a big step, you do have to leave it in there while you push down the plunger part to get the contents into your system. All I'd done was unnecessarily stab myself.

I think, on the whole, my pain threshold is quite high, although like anyone else I can curse up an unholy storm when stubbing a toe or shutting a finger in a door. Actually, I think I can do that *better* than anyone else. Those requiring proof of this should be present when Wendy and I regularly perform a piece of traditional kitchen slapstick wherein I will squat down to get a plate from a low drawer, she will then open a cupboard above me and neglect to close it again, so that as I rise up it fetches my nut such a sharp wallop that even disinterested observers can hear the tweety-birds circling my throbbing bald head. This infuriating dance is somehow always my fault. In previous volumes of these books I have outlined both the Incident with the Caravan Tow-Bar and the Incident with the Balloons in the Cellar as evidence of my agony-tolerance, but as we are currently dealing with matters that the squeamish might skip let me complete my domestic accident trilogy with the Incident with the Hi-Fi.

One evening when the kids were small, we were all getting ready to leave our house in Deptford to go and have a magnificent slap-up dinner in one of the better restaurants down at London Bridge. I wasn't driving, for I intended to pretty much jump into a succession of wine bottles and sort of paddle about all night. A cab duly arrived and just as we were getting in it, Wend said, 'Make sure you turned off the plugs by your record player.' These outlets were specified because there were two sockets both crammed with three-way appliances and, as such, in Wendy's mind anyway, always on the verge of overheating and blowing up. I needed these extra juice boxes to power the amp, CD player, tape deck, turntable, radio, graphic equalizer and mini-disc that sat on the shelves at the rear of our front room – the bare minimum of kit in my eyes, but an arrangement that she felt turned her beautifully furnished home into a garish low-end disco-pub. Hence, even though her beloved Al Green would issue from it as much as my more difficult prog choices, it was always 'your' record player. A particular bone of contention was the mass of wires that hung from the back of each separate component like fat matted horse tails. Wendy claimed to have a memory of a 1970 edition of *Tomorrow's World* where they said you didn't need such appendages any more and my insistence that you did was merely an unnecessary holding with tradition. These copious industrial leads, coupled with the bulky plugs which meant an antique pine chest she had bought in Appledore would never stand flush against the wall, was a not uncommon source of marital friction in the Baker house. So, as we made our way out that night I knew I must go back and double-check everything was safe because, should I happen to hear the sound of a fire engine's siren hurtling down Tooley Street an hour hence, it would put me right off my starters. With a short huff of frustration I turned from the taxi, fished out my keys and began to unlock the front door again.

The sockets themselves were situated low down and about a foot to the left of one of the two grey marble fireplaces that sat either end of the parlour. Checking the plugs were neutralized was a function I had performed countless times without bloodshed, but on this occasion, possibly fuelled by a rising resentment of having to delay my appointment with the vino by all of forty-five seconds, I got my sums all wrong. Having dipped down to see that the pin-holes were vacant, I came back to the vertical at great velocity and entirely the wrong angle, thus sending my forehead crashing into the marble mantelpiece. The force of impact spun me round and brought me to my knees on the polished wooden flooring. Utterly dazed and on all fours, I watched in confusion as an altogether different type of claret than that I had been anticipating started to pool beneath me.

Now I don't want you to think that this blow, powerful though it was, is the focus of this story. As most people who have coshed, skewered or sliced themselves know, the actual severity of a wound may come as quite a shock, but rather than howl at what it feels like, your mind starts to compute what will be the tedious social consequences of this irreversible inconvenience. I remember once, in order to prove to an insistent cockeyed woman at a party that I really could not dance, I attempted to demonstrate the point by performing a single exaggerated dance step. Lifting my leg in a wildly over-the-top buck-and-wing motion, I brought it down heavily at the exact moment an empty rogue beer bottle rolled across the floor and into my orbit. Treading on the thing, I went flying, much to the delight of the drunk woman who thought I must have learned the move from Buster Keaton himself. As I hit the deck, the awful numbness at my ankle combined with that ominous fizzing sensation I had first experienced hunting for John Cleese on Broadway, clued me in that this was an injury that was not going to be made good with some vigorous rubbing. This was an injury that would now require the most soul-destroying, life-draining thing on earth: an immediate visit to a late-night A&E department. This bastard contusion was going to be moving in with me for a few months like some dull freeloading relative who insists on stealing one of my shoes every day. And so it proved.

The point is that, though the pain be acute, you can comfortably bury it under the teeming mass of details about what this stupid trauma is going to do to your diary. That night in Deptford, as the blood splashed steadily on to the parquet, I winced it is true, but not as much as I internally grieved that my rendezvous with a huge plate of seafood would now have to be scratched. On the upside, the row of stitches I had placed in my head temporarily gave me a dashing, piratical look that frankly made the whole episode worth it. So much so that I took a relaxed attitude to ever having them taken out. I even convinced myself that modern stitches could sense when healing was complete and then melt away of their own accord (a shaky theory I believe I originated and gave to the world), and so used to my little lace-ups did I become that, about six weeks after their insertion, I ignored their presence entirely while getting ready for another prospective night at the groaning table and flowing bowl. Laugh as much as you want, but I can assure you that in those days I had so much hair it would hang in my eyes and it was while trying to remove this lush pelmet from my forehead that I experienced the single most painful trauma of my entire life. With a grand arcing sweep of my stainless-steel comb I raked up not only my tumbling fringe but also the seven little stitches gathered underneath. Following the motion through, I yanked the recently restored fissure wide open again. Even worse, the teeth of the comb became lodged in the remains of the fibres and it dangled there crazily as I threw myself around the bathroom like a Native American appealing to the rain gods. Unsurprisingly, I have since measured all pain against that exact moment and, thus far, my Agony-O-Meter has never needed to mark a new threshold.

It was with regular reminders of the above that I soon learned how to deliver my daily syringe of Clexane straight to the gut with something close to cocky aplomb. A few days after starting the course I learned my chemotherapy was to begin. On the night before the first infusion Wendy, Bonnie, Sonny, Mancie and I went to an Argentine restaurant close to our home where I had a thick toothsome steak and a bottle of red wine. It would be four years before I could physically deal with such a simple meal again.

Remake/Remodel

When I pitched up for my first chemotherapy session I had no idea what it might entail. All I knew was that it was going to make me as bald as a balloon and I hoped this new appearance wasn't going to alarm Mancie, my youngest, too much. We hadn't told her how ill I was, and we weren't going to either. Another time, remind me to tell you how I think all this anything-goes openness between parents and children is a load of balls. Some things are none of their fucking business and vice versa. You are not a bunch of students who suddenly find yourself sharing a house. Frankly, when I hear that a parent and their child are 'best friends', I think it's peculiar. You are their parent – they should have a best friend as well and if those positions really are one and the same you should let the kid get out more.

Nobody could be closer than we are with our children but if I found out we were all each other's 'best friends' I'd figure Wend and I had created one of those cults that one day all take poison and flake out in the compound. On the occasion of my cancer it was obvious that our bright and bouncy Mancie, at twelve, was far too young to be burdened with the idea that the old man was on his way out. No, if I suddenly lost the little hair I had, I was going to tell her it was for a film I was going to be making in three years' time, but I wanted to bed the style in. Of course I had told her that I was going to get a bit mouldy for a bit, but there comes a point in even that conversation where an unspoken line is reached in both parties' minds that says, 'That's plenty of information, there. Anything else is hurtling toward the prurient and morbid, so let's move on, eh?' This strikes me as the healthy option. Parents can lack many facets, they can be uncaring or absent or even simply dull, but not talking constantly with flat-out emotional frankness, sharing every worry, fault and appetite with their own children, seems to be the flimsiest reason to blame them for life's later shortcomings.

I made my way to the relevant department at St Thomas' and was shown to a bright if cluttered room where about fifteen people, all hooked up to drips, sat around the walls in a selection of mismatched armchairs. I gave the nurse my forms and she showed me to a well-cushioned but frowsy old perch, saying she'd be right back. I got settled and unpacked the copious amount of magazines, books and iPod paraphernalia I believed would see me through what I'd been warned would be a long day. My plan was to treat it like a transatlantic flight, but rather than disembarking in Los Angeles I would instead be allowed to live another day. This seemed fair.

A bloke sitting across from me saw the mountain of distraction I had piled on to the small table to my right and chuckled. 'None of it helps,' he said. My face must have signalled bemusement because he went on, 'Clock goes backwards in here. Ain't enough books in the world!' This would prove to be one of the sagest statements I was to hear during the entire regime. The nurse returned and handed me a coarse grey cardboard bowl shaped exactly like one of the hats that Bill and Ben used to wear. 'Right. Could you pop off to the gents and pee into that,' she said breezily, 'making a note of how much you manage.' Wow. Here we were, not sixty seconds into my treatment, and already I wanted the ground to swallow me up. Attempting to bring even an iota of stateliness to the instruction, I asked hoarsely, 'And whom do I tell about it?'

'Just jot it down on the chart I'll give you and make a note every time you go after this,' she said, busily unpacking a series of valves and hypodermics from their sterile seals. 'We need to keep an eye on your kidneys and fluids. Have you moved your bowels today?' I reacted to this last question with an imperceptibly small nod of my head, as though it might minimize the appalling affirmative. Again, I know you will think it ridiculous that I might blanch and clutch my pearls under such circumstances, but that's just how I am. I was doubly glad that, because we had been a little late, Wendy had gone off to Boots to get me a few things. To clear the air, so to speak, I suddenly found myself making an enquiry that was only half in jest.

'Do I lose my hair during this first dose?' I asked.

'Oh no,' she smiled. 'In fact, I don't think you are having the kind of chemo that has hair loss at all. Let me double-check . . . '

As she walked away, it hit me that the only thing I thought I knew for sure about the process was now being shown to be false. Sure enough, when she returned she confirmed that 'my sort' of chemo did not entail parting with so much as an eyelash. In fact, and maybe you already know this, there is no such thing as 'chemotherapy'. Certainly not as a fixed brand of medicine anyway; as a term, it is as vague as 'surgery'. Everyone's chemo is particular to them and their cancer. Prior to that morning, I had genuinely thought chemotherapy was a 'thing' like penicillin or electric shock treatment. I had absolutely no clue that every single bag of the stuff that is dripped into your body is as bespoke as the Queen's gloves. It is specifically designed to attack what you've got, how much you've got, and where you've got it. Give the bloke in the next bed your bag of chemo and, in terms of curing his cancer, he might as well rub Worcester sauce into his right foot.

In fact, and I'll be completely honest with you here, until that morning I didn't even know how chemotherapy was administered. If they had stuck me under a heat lamp or asked me to drink from a glowing flask, I would have gone along with it. I knew there was an element of intravenous business but was this merely preparation or one of the stages? What nobody had forewarned me about was that chemotherapy is without question the most boring of all the treatments available to modern medicine. And when I say boring, I don't mean to be flip about either its study, field or superhuman results. It is merely a balls-achingly dull experience.

Here's how it went for me. A needle is slipped into a vein at the back of your hand, and – following dozens of checks that you are the intended recipient – this is then connected to a bulging bag of chemicals *that really does have skull and crossbones on it.* This slowly, extremely slowly, empties its contents one minuscule drop at a time into your system. You can neither feel any apparent benefit nor discomfort. You just sit there. A digital display counts down the hours you have till the bag is 100 per cent empty, which is a decision that gainsays all visual evidence. The chemo bag may shrivel so it looks like an old bit of bacon packaging that has been left for decades in the Gobi Desert, but that clock will tell you there is in fact more than another hour to go before the shrill pips of its alarm signal that not a drop of chemo remains. As a kid, I used to go to the ABC Cinema at the Elephant & Castle with my best friend Tommy Hodges, and as the main feature got underway Tom would sit in the dark sucking on a carton of Kia-Ora orange until his straw had hoovered up every last infinitesimal smidgen of moisture. The slurping noises as his final extended searches of the plastic container continued not only annoyed the people in the rows immediately around us but could apparently be heard in the Odeon across the road. Well, let me tell you, the chemotherapy machine makes Tom's efforts seem like he regularly left behind an entire reservoir of reachable squash.

Then, guess what? The hospital staff take the desiccated bag from its metal pole and replace it with one full of clear saline to wash both the system and your body through. This bag takes just as long to filter down. *Then*, guess what? The whole tortuous tedious imprisoning process has to start all over again. Don't let anyone tell you that there are only twenty-four hours in a day. A day on the chemo drip is as long as any on that notoriously dawdling planet Mercury – and a wet Mercury bank holiday one at that. No composer, no author, no director has yet created a work that can distract from the interminable hours spent being made well by this sluggardly miracle cure. How I cursed that snivelling blood clot whose attention-seeking actions had stopped me from having the on-the-go chemo that, as far as I could gather, allowed its beneficiaries to go water skiing while they got drip-fed the goodness. All I and my fellow detainees in that wearisome chamber could do was periodically rise and, still

Ah, that'll be Peter O'Toole and Ronnie Fraser with me, then.

Two old vaudevillians reminisce. My sunglasses and the trees make it appear I am wearing a wig.

(above) Knocking about with the Stones in Chicago.

(left) To be clear: this is me wearing a wig.

(top right) Emerson Lake and Palmer. Tailors would measure Greg and I, just for the exercise.

(*above*) On air and on form.

(*right*) And still I grow. Elton holding a picture of me from when we first met in the early 70s.

(*above*) This is David Kuo. You see, he is real.

(*right*) The Treehouse on air at BBC London with Baylen Leonard.

Producer Julia McKenzie would dress up the studio every single day. It changed with the seasons.

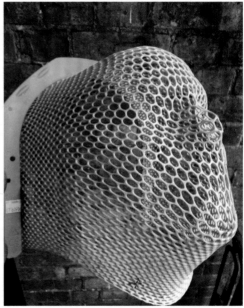

Peter Kay – probably the show's biggest fan. Note boxes of mini-discs in foreground.

The radiation mask into which I was bolted daily.

At the Sony Awards and telling Roger Daltrey he should have turned it in after 'Substitute'.

(top) Sony Awards, post-treatment, with Rhod
Gilbert. Dear Lord, I should not have been out.

(above) Ah, life seems to be returning once more.
A flagrantly hedonistic shot.

(right) Recovering in Portugal. The biscuit is a
prop. I could no more have eaten it than flown
home by flapping my arms.

(top) Sonny and I moments before I explained what hereditary baldness was.

(left) Back in the world. The whole family enjoying my bandana/wig combo over Mancie's halo.

(above) My gals: Mancie & Bonnie.

(*above*) Unaware of the camera, this reflective study
is among my favourites.

(*right*) The Bakers. Islamorada, Florida 2014.

And that's that.

harnessed to our clanking, cumbersome equipment, shuffle to the bog to once more fill our Bill and Ben hats to the measured brim. Through one window I could see people on the top decks of buses temporarily stranded in the dense traffic on Westminster Bridge and their studied boredom struck me as little short of rank impudence. Of course at this early stage the true physical side effects of chemo had not become apparent and I could not imagine that within days this debilitating ennui would be partnered by a woozy, gnawing sense of displacement, a feeling that combined fierce hangover and chronic jet lag while all the time managing to convince you that your feet weren't quite connecting with the ground.

During that first week I decided to make public why I had suddenly disappeared from the radio schedules. I was at the time broadcasting six days a week, but I had not been near a studio from the very moment of diagnosis. I typed up as cheery a missive as I could and placed it on the BBC London website.

Dear All

Apologies for the cloak and dagger over recent weeks. However as it appears this is going to continue for the foreseeable I really ought to offer up some sort of breadcrumbs trail as to what's going on. (As you know I am queasy about introducing vulgar real life on to the vaudeville stage so let's keep this crisp.) After a pretty mouldy cancer diagnosis about a month back I finally began chemotherapy on Monday with further radiotherapy from January. Yes, RADIO therapy; can you beat it? This being so, the old broadcasting baggy pants will be donned sparingly.

Once the quacks have soundly thrashed this thing I shall return like a rare gas and as if out of a trap.

In the meantime I am watching Tommy Steele box sets (and has there ever been a more lying title to a film than Tommy's It's All Happening?) and urge you all to keep yakking up a storm and laugh extra loud at the incumbents. Thank you for all the

*best wishes and concern from those who suspected as much
about my 'condition'.*
   DB

This, as they say, went over big. I began to receive bags of mail
that, while not comparable to those that the Beatles had dumped
at their door every half hour, were certainly on a par with a couple
of bundles that I once saw Billy J. Kramer posing beside. Listeners
to the show sent me cards, long letters, tapes, cuttings, books, even
their own artwork and tapestries, some of which still hang in our
home today. One morning the doorbell went and there on the step
was a fellow holding the type of outsize bouquet of white blooms
that mob bosses would send to Judy Garland when she opened at
Lake Tahoe. Manoeuvring the giant display into our hall, I fished
the card out from its clustered stems and read:

Dear Danny,
Wishing you a very, very speedy recovery. Get well soon, mate,
Emerson Lake & Palmer

I read this over and over about ten times. Wendy read it over
my shoulder. 'Oh, that's nice of them,' she said warmly, but with
what I thought was spectacular understatement. *Nice?* To me this
was colossal, stupendous, amazing. Emerson Lake & Palmer held a
place in my heart somewhere between my own mother and dear life
itself. Since seeing them at the London Pavilion, 15 December 1971, I
had been in a constant state of giddiness, shaking like a rattlesnake's
rear, the power and charge of that night remaining unmatched by
any other concert since. I have seen virtually every revered outfit
in my life as a music fan, from Bowie to The Clash, from Talking
Heads to The Wailers, from Steely Dan to the Sex Pistols, from Led
Zeppelin to The Ramones, from Springsteen to Sinatra, and in the
countless times over the decades when I've been asked, 'What is the
greatest gig you ever saw?' not for a second have I ever abandoned
the memory of that night with ELP in order that I might appear

more smart, niche or enviable. It was a fearsome thing, alarming and transforming, allied to more excitement and swing than was ever captured by them on record although it was, in fact, the beginning of their long journey into over-complication. If anyone had ever told the fourteen-year-old me that one day in the future Emerson Lake & Palmer would send a horseshoe of carnations to my home, along with a personal note that included the word 'mate', I would have floated over the moon on a wave of pure bliss. Had I then been told, 'Yeah but you will have to have cancer first,' I would honestly have had to sit in a chair for a good long time to weigh that offer. That's how much I adored ELP. And it says much about how my condition would swiftly deteriorate when I say now that, on balance, I would have forsworn their stunning floral gesture rather than have had to endure the next few months.

The descent was heralded by waking one morning to find the whole world had the tang of old pennies. While still able to physically eat the little my now waning appetite craved, I had been warned that shortly after care begins many patients find their mouths will only register a strong metallic taste, no matter what's on the menu. On rising that November day there was no escaping the fact that this sickly symptom had indeed kicked in. The only other possibility was that I had sleepwalked during the night and gone sucking on our Land Rover's exhaust pipe, though Wendy assured me that I hadn't moved. Shortly after this I was told that I could no longer have my chemo as an outpatient and that I would be spending every other week – you are given rest periods – on the wards. This was a blow. I loathe communal sleeping and can only achieve a dream state in conditions of total blackout and absolute silence. One cough, one sniffle or even the faint glimmer of a distant digital watch can send me into a spiral of inner brooding that will simmer for a period before erupting into a torrent of explosive swearing should my nocturnal torturer repeat the outrage.

I am also very picky about my pillows. As explained in a previous volume, I have learned to sleep with something over my face ever since the days when my brother and I shared a bedroom. This apparently suffocating affectation would serve to block out the harsh bedroom light and the sound of his loose change clattering on to the sideboard when he came home late after carousing with his friends. Later, when he got a job as a porter at the Borough Market, he would have his alarm clock set for 3 a.m., which became another riotous fanfare I would suffer each night in furious silence. Once Mike moved out, I swore I would never again tolerate my wee small hours being savaged in such a way and the pillow-on-the-face thing remains as both monument and bulwark to that testimony. Sometimes I feel all that has stopped me from entering a life of crime is the impending terror of a snoring cellmate. As a younger man, whenever talk about the return of conscription hit the headlines, I found I was less concerned about dying on the battlefield than how long it would be before I strangled the bloke in the next bunk.

The morning I was due to check in to my berth at Guy's for the first time, the omens weren't good. In a subconscious effort to disguise my fears under the cloak of efficiency, I had prepared my bag for the stay the previous evening. This is not like me. On mornings when we are heading to the airport for a family holiday I have been known to turn the taxi around up to three separate times because I have forgotten sunglasses, an essential book or even a battered and beloved old hat. Not only did I pack my bag the previous night on this occasion, I even went outside and put it in the boot of the car. Just as we were about to set off for the hospital I looked in it to make sure I had included spare batteries for the gadget on which I played Scrabble. What greeted me as I gazed inside was difficult to mentally process and I stared at it, prolonged and baffled, like somebody in a broad sitcom. Eventually I managed to say 'Oh' in a vaguely alarmed way. Wendy asked me what was wrong. I then produced a sentence that I knew would be unique in my time on this planet.

'My headphones have been eaten,' I said.

And they had. The ear cushions on my £280 Bose noise-reduction beauties were as perished as the pauper's pants. What were once two supple ovals of inviting black leather were now so thoroughly devastated that it appeared dynamite must have been used in their destruction. When I had placed them on top of my neatly folded pyjamas ten hours ago they had been pristine; what on earth could have happened?

At first nothing else in the car boot appeared to have been touched, but searching about I eventually found an empty packet of Jacob's Cheddars that I had noted had been stowed away there a week previously. Then it had contained crackers. *Now the crackers were gone.* What's more, the packaging, with its distinctive Jacob's branding, had been shredded like a deli cabbage. Weighing the mounting evidence, I deduced we had a serial product slasher on our hands. In truth we never have come up with a completely satisfactory answer to what went on overnight in the boot of my car. The best we could piece together was that a mouse, or possibly a small rat, had somehow scurried aboard after getting an intoxicating whiff of Jacob's flagship snack. After attacking the crackers, the beast found it was not yet satiated and his nose now twitched in the direction of what, in the half light, he believed to be the flesh of some prone and sleeping creature but was in fact the leathery cushioning on my high-end audio cups weighing in at close on a hundred and fifty quid an ear. Leaping on to the defenceless cans, the ravenous monster began tearing chunk after chunk from their circumference, his razor-like yellow teeth making small work of the pliant hide until, after one last mouthful of precious inner foam, he considered his work done and scuttled back into the night . . .

And now I didn't even have my headphones to blot out any thunderous rogue trumps the nights ahead held.

On arrival at the ward I was shown to my bed. Wouldn't you know it, it was smack in the middle of the row. Cannons to the left of me, cannons to the right. The curtains were up around the cot next door and within it a man was loudly hectoring some members of staff. From what I could gather, they wanted to discharge him but he was refusing to go until they had ordered him a taxi at their expense and provided him with temporary accommodation in a hotel and purchased him what sounded like 'a new tent'. Over the next few days this bilious character could be heard treating the various nurses and carers who came to him in the most brusque and appalling manner, demanding all sorts of things, most of which were wearily granted. They must have wanted him out of there pretty badly. It turned out he was the peace campaigner who lived in a tent opposite Parliament. I've since read that he was a selfless saint deserving of his own statue in Westminster, but, under the rules of speak-as-you-find, he behaved in Guy's like a grade A arrogant ponce.

He snored too. Everybody did. As soon as the sun went down, the barrage went up. During the day we all got on wonderfully – with the above exception – but man alive, I will never understand how the theory of evolution is supposed to hold water when humans still create such a prehistoric racket once their lids fall for the night. Maybe that's it. Maybe we still produce this frightening din in our kip to scare off any wild wolves that might happen by our cave. There certainly wouldn't have been a sabre tooth within a hundred miles of Blundell Ward while I was there. It didn't seem to bother anyone else. At one point on the second night the other nine occupants were all spark out, each making a different noise with varying parts of their anatomy until they fell into perfect syncopation like a rasping, gaseous symphony. After a minute or so I realized I could put the words to 'How Much Is That Doggy in the Window?' to it.

Dragging myself out of bed, I threw a blanket over my shoulder and went searching for sanctuary. As I shuffled into the nurse's station, the pair on duty asked if I was OK, so exploded did I appear. I told them I couldn't sleep with all the leaf blowers, tubas and power saws going full pelt. We chatted for a bit, then I asked if it would be possible to bring my own pillow from home in. Unsurprisingly, for reasons of hygiene, it wasn't allowed. They asked if I would like them to try and find a second pillow for me but I said it was OK. Truth was, it wouldn't have made much difference. The pillows as issued were so narrow and unbending I may as well have put a couple of Jacob's Cheddars under my nut. Then one of them said, 'No one's in the visitors' room . . .' and indicated with her head the small waiting room across the way.

'Can I sleep there?' I said, with a voice full of quivering hope.

'Well, you're not supposed to,' she said slyly, 'and if any visitors turn up you'll have to shift, but to be fair we don't get that many in at half two in the morning . . . '

I walked over and opened the door. It was dark in there. Pitch-dark. And cool. And so, so quiet. And so that's where I slept every night, along the bench seat by the TV, underneath a poster for a mobile breast-screening initiative. Once or twice an early bird would pop in and be startled by this old vagrant dossing down among the free magazines, but otherwise I would usually be woken by the night shift bringing me a cup of tea before they clocked off. I always accepted it gratefully and would sip it while we chatted, never having the heart to tell them that I had recently stopped drinking beverages because they all now tasted to me like the inside of my grandmother's coal scuttle. Then I'd waddle back to the boys on the ward.

'Where d'you bleedin go every night?' one of them eventually asked me.

'Home,' I said. And I wished it were true.

Strictly Confidential

As the chemotherapy sessions mounted up two things started to happen. One: the lump in my neck began to visibly reduce. I'd been told that, while this was good news, I mustn't conflate it with the actual cancer being beaten. That was still deep down in the cells and could not so easily be assessed. The second thing was that I began to feel properly ill for the first time. My energy was dropping, my appetite vanished, my concentration faltered. I found I could not form my hand into a tight fist and hold it like that. Permanent tubes ran into my veins to both put in the chemo and take out my blood. Boy, did they take out blood, like a pump on a Texas oil well, checking it every two hours while presenting an impressive array of tablets to be gobbled down en masse. The tube into my stomach remained still coiled and unused, a constant reminder that much darker days lay ahead.

My spirit remained buoyant though and I tried to greet every pill, prod and injection as though it were a surprise rather than a routine, and attempted to see the absurd in both the grim and mundane. I remember one wonderful conversation with the overnight staff when they asked what sort of thing I did on the radio. This is always a tricky one because the kind of scattershot and peculiar subjects I set before an audience can, to the uninitiated, just sound wilfully 'wacky' like the worst sort of gurning DJ cliché. I've found the only way to temper such enforced jollity is to treat even the most cross-eyed request – for example 'Has Anyone Ever Seen a Horse in a House?' – as though it were a discussion about terrorism. If you allow someone to simply outline why there was a horse in their house, while journalistically winkling as much information about the circumstances as possible, it becomes far funnier than pretending to be convulsed at how 'mad' your caller is. They are not mad. You have asked for stories about horses in houses and they have responded. You must treat the call as Great Truth. Ditto: What Have You Dried Yourself With? The Shortest Distance Anyone's Ever Gone on Holiday, Having to Hide as an Adult, Notable Places You've Had a Nap and Things You Only Usually See in Cartoons.

It was this last example that so lit up our late-night conversation. With all my other examples the two women appeared unresponsive to the point of disinterest, but after hearing the cartoon instance one of them, while still listlessly resting her chin in her hand, said matter-of-factly, 'I saw a kid come into casualty once with a saucepan stuck on his head. You see that in cartoons sometimes.' I immediately started laughing wildly, but her companion took the concerned, professional tack. 'How awful. Was it lodged over his nose?' Her friend, with but the faintest of smiles, explained that the child was quite calm about it but was reacting badly whenever anyone tried to remove the saucepan. She could add no more to the tale because it wasn't given to her to deal with, but she did add that, 'It must have been jammed right on, because he was in there quite a long time.'

'How about you?' she then drawled, eyes toward me. I thought she'd never ask and was ready with a real pip of a tale. The story takes us back to the 1970s when all of my friends had left school and were earning, in most cases, pretty good money. When I say 'left school', I do not mean college, or 'uni' as they say now, I mean secondary school. Until I joined the *NME* in 1978, I didn't know anybody who had been to university. Anyway, the point is that even though we were still teenagers we could all pay our way in the world, which made the concept of doing 'runners' from restaurants all the more baffling to me. I take it you know what 'runners' are? Running out without paying the bill. Certain among my friends enjoyed indulging in this risky divertissement as though it were a legitimate sport. I hated the gag, truly could not understand its appeal, and my stomach would flip as I saw the tell-tale signs that the game was afoot. No words were needed. As soon as the last drink had been drained, I would see the ringleaders' eyes flicker round the table and a Mephistophelian smile begin to form on their mouths. Heads would bob in the smallest of conspiratorial nods. I would always attempt to overturn the decision of the cabal.

'No, boys, not a runner. Not in here. This is a great place, come on, we've all got cash on us, what's the point in—'

I would get no further. Amid the sudden sounds of the table being shoved aside and loose cutlery tumbling, out everyone would dash like the rats of Hamelin. I was forced to go with them because otherwise you were left behind enemy lines to face a furious interrogation by aggrieved and out-of-pocket staff members who were never likely to buy the old 'But I was against it' line. To be fair, the moment you begin to run past shocked fellow diners helter-skelter for a restaurant door, you do find the most shocking fit of giggles consuming you. Even I, who could already hear a local magistrate sending me down for six months, would find myself overwhelmed by a riotous exhilaration that would find its climax in hysterical collapse only once we were several streets distant.

Given that our part of South London only had about five restaurants in it anyway, we soon ran out of venues to abuse and so the contests spread further afield. Before long the whole stupid lark started to fold in on itself and we would find ourselves standing outside various West End steak houses trying to decide if we could go in or whether we had 'played' there before. These unforgivable shenanigans were brought to a halt one night in a pizza place at the Elephant & Castle. This was one of the first such establishments to open outside central London, and even though it wasn't strictly on our doorstep we would hungrily make the journey by bus for slices of the delicious and then still strangely exotic pies. One night, having had to earlier wait about thirty minutes for a table, I noted the familiar impish glances being traded between the usual suspects. I could not believe it. Barely ten minutes beforehand they had all been saying that these succulent pizzas were so moreish they might one day stand alongside fish and chips and pie and mash as a local staple. (Of course nobody would ever do a runner from those traditional eateries because they were wise enough in the ways of the streets to make punters pay *before* they'd eaten their fill.) Yet here we were, about to cut off our culinary noses to spite our kamikaze faces.

Regardless of my usual spirited Perry Mason act, within seconds the flag had been dropped and the frenzied scramble was on. Now, had we been in a cartoon at that moment there would have been a few seconds of manic percussion noises before our legs began to turn like Catherine wheels and we exited to the noise of a speeded-up pistol shot. However we were not in a cartoon. Yet. We eventually entered one because, as opposed to all the other restaurants from which we had beaten hasty retreats, this one required you flee directly past the kitchen, an open-fronted workplace wherein laboured a couple of hard-nut pizza chefs.

When one of those guys saw a blur of snickering youths hurtling through the frame, he realized straight away what was going on and acted accordingly. Withdrawing his big, flat stainless-steel pizza shovel from the flames, he wielded it like a jackhammer and brought it crashing down full flush on Terry Windsor's head. The resultant noise from this formidable impact was a resounding Big Ben 'BONG!' straight out of an episode of *Scooby Doo*. Terry was brought to a sudden, shuddering halt by the blow and, in my memory of the moment, the outline of his body instantly became one big oscillating wavy line as the sound of that knell bounced around the establishment's walls. In other tellings of this story I have often added that the perfect shape of Terry's head remained sticking out of the pizza shovel, but I think I may have embroidered that detail over the years. Anyway, that brought an end to our years of being Butch Cassidy's Hole in the Wall Gang. No police were called, but amid an angry atmosphere we handed over much more money than our selected thin-crusts could ever have amounted to.

The tale got some minor chuckles from my medical company that night but their overall take was, 'Why would you want to stiff a hard-working restaurant like that?' Which is the correct attitude, but not necessarily one that goes down big in the music halls.

On a couple of my stays during chemo I was put in one of the small side rooms rather than on the ward. I know this seems terribly swanky, but these cubicles are subject to availability, not exclusive, and only suggested for me because of a reason I hadn't previously thought of. People can surreptitiously take pictures of you on the ward and some newspapers would pay handsomely for such a photograph. I'm not sure what the going rate was to get one of me, haggard, prone, unshaven, tubing at all points of the compass, the suggestion of balls lolling from baggy underpants but, as one of the nursing staff pointed out with refreshing directness, 'It's not so much yourself but you've had quite a few famous visitors, haven't you?'

This was true. Both Chris Evans and Jonathan Ross had made the trek in to see their ailing buddy, once both at the same time, which was an awkward coincidence given that they don't really get on and had recently had a big falling out in the press. I am a good friend to them both and so they sat either side of me like the heads of warring nations, politely observing the truce and even making each other laugh. I don't think they've spoken to each other since, but there you go.

Chris, knowing I couldn't work, had even popped a substantial cheque into my pyjama jacket pocket. Eighteen months later, as I walked on to the stage at the Sony Radio Awards where he was hosting, I put one for an identical amount into the breast pocket of his Armani suit as the audience applauded. Those who saw this action probably thought it was drugs.

While on the subject, because I had had to stop work the moment the diagnosis was made, there was something of a scramble to find people who could fill in for me on the radio. At BBC Five Live, Alan Davies initially filled the breach. He agreed to do it on one condition and that was that I, not he, would continue to receive the money for the job. Alan probably will hate the fact I've now made that public, but in all my years in show business I have never known a greater gesture.

It was while I was in one of the side rooms that my stock among the staff hit its high point. Lying in bed one evening, trying to figure out whether the tiny pay TV that hung over the bed on a massive metal-hinged arm would ever actually work, a nurse I knew well came rather breathlessly in the door, pushing a small trolley upon which was a telephone. Placing the trolley beside the bed she knelt down and plugged the phone's connection into the wall.

'Danny,' she said in a tone that suggested an urgent seriousness, 'there's a phone call for you. It's Elton John.'

As I whooped a chuckle at the preposterous circumstance, she seemed a tad disappointed. I think she expected me to react with a flushed panic, possibly even getting up to shave before lifting the receiver. In the event, I snatched it up from the cradle and entered into the sort of salty, forthright exchanges the great man has always revelled in, over the more than forty years I've known him. He told me he knew for a fact the whole thing was a cover for having a face-lift. Pretty soon we were on to the haemorrhoid references, but then the call settled down and he said some magnificent, warm things to me, assuring me if I needed anything at all, etc., etc.

On another occasion Paul Weller called, which again was utterly uplifting seeing as we hadn't spoken for about five years previously. Another evening I was watching *The Apprentice*, picture only, no sound (which was at least something), when the women on duty brought in an enormous hamper. Inside it was a five-course dinner for two, complete with the correct sauces, wine and champagne, direct and piping hot from The Wolseley restaurant in Mayfair. Alex Armitage, my agent, had organized the feast. Rather tragically, I had not twenty minutes before its arrival selected and eaten the World's Most Flaccid Lasagne from the hospital's dinner trolley and so the NHS stalwarts on parade in the corridor outside were forced to leave their sandwiches in the vending machine that night and selflessly make sure nothing was wasted.

Come December, however, and even listless lasagnes were proving beyond me. Though I could in this period still use my mouth, the depleting effect of the constant chemo was by now truly hollowing me out. Conversations required real mental effort, pins and needles wracked my hands and feet without respite and the once intermittent bouts of nausea now combined to form a day-long wave of sickness. All you do, hour after hour after hour, is watch the never-ending chemo globules as they dribble like raindrops from the swollen bag above with your name on it, along the clear cannula, and into the multi-headed catheter jammed into the back of your hand, its penetrating needles obscured by a thick criss-cross of medical tape.

Sometimes I would look over at the big pile of books on the window ledge. Beside them an equally impressive stack of magazines and behind those a portable DVD player. Peter Kay had sent me a laptop pre-loaded with all manner of great comedy shows and films and even the first episodes of *Sherlock* I had ever seen. None of this once-absorbing trove interested me in the slightest now. None of them seemed to hold even an iota of the old stimulation, temptation or flavour. I looked at the still-crisp dust jacket spines of biographies I'd been dying to read and morbidly reflected on the aptness, and the emptiness, of that sentence. It was not a feeling of hopelessness or depression but simply an absence of want. I could perfectly well remember where I was up to in the two books I was still reading, but I had lost the capacity to lose myself in their stories. I had forgotten how to be distracted. All I had was the drip, drip, drip. All that mattered between visits from the kids was whether I could make my way to and from the toilets, while still attached to the machinery, before the built-in alarm signalled it had been unplugged longer than the allowed four minutes and I might need assistance. Then you flop down on the bed again, useless and tired, listening to the shallow gasps of your own breath entering and exiting your poor pulverized body through your slack, open mouth. But here's the thing. You are still in there. By this I mean that even in the depths of my physical discomforts, my mind was not hobbled in the slightest and seemed to stand apart from my wracked old bones, observing and noting the grotesque theatre of it all, often robustly commenting on the scene in a voice not dissimilar to my father's.

'Fucking hell, this is ridiculous.'

'What must I look like?'

'Well, Baker, you're in schtuck here and no mistake.'

'I don't care how ill I am, at least I'm still better than this poxy show on TV.'

'Christ almighty, how hard did I just whack my leg!'

'Oh, this is bollocks. Bollocks!'

When I eventually lost the power of speech, I longed to let on that my mental pilot light was still burning strong but it was impossible. People see you shrunken, mute and wrecked and believe it must penetrate to your very core, but it doesn't. While any external stimulation remained of marginal interest, my own thoughts and reasoning stayed defiantly crisp. The genius Stephen Hawking lives his entire life this way, though possibly it might bring the humanity in his situation home with greater force if, instead of the famously computerized voice he uses to communicate, he instead tried the timbre of my old man.

Men Of Good Fortune

Towards Christmas my great friend Danny Kelly wrote a piece about me in the *Guardian* that even brought a blush to my grey and sunken cheeks. Once an editor always an editor; I'm sure Dan would have handed over the copy and told them that so fulsome was his encomium they might want to wait a few weeks before going to print because it would make a cracking obit. By way of thanks, and as men do, I sent a funny email to him full of swear words professing to be outraged at his earning a handsome fee on the back of my agonies. His reply simply said, 'Don't fret. I've booked the boat on the Broads with HF (handsome fee). You can provide the refreshments.' Now that *did* make me smile.

This mention of the Norfolk Broads alluded to a pledge Danny and I had once made that we would hire a cruiser with the specific aim of taking LSD amid the tranquil burble of the East Anglian river ways. We had been entirely serious about it and I'm not sure that the dream is even now 100 per cent dead. Why did two portly and contented old boys seek such reckless kicks? Well, having both spent a lifetime working in and thrilling to the machinery of rock, we both felt we had missed out on some of its required rites. Chief among these was that neither of us had ever smoked marijuana. Is it still even called marijuana? Anyway, despite being virtually surrounded by slow-talking, hazy, stoned goofballs for decades, Danny and I had never managed to take so much as a single draw on the omnipresent weed. Of all the remarkable feats and sights I have recounted in my career, it is this single fact that seems to most astound people. Then one morning in 1999, I received a call from DK and I could tell by the vim in his voice and the pace at which he spoke that he had something very hot to impart.

'Listen,' he began without even announcing who it was – the trademark of a Kelly call. 'In two weeks there is a record fair taking place in Utrecht and it says here in *Record Collector* magazine that the hall is going to be the size of THREE football pitches! If we don't go to this then we should hang our heads in shame.'

I agreed. Then said, 'Good morning, Dan.'

'And do you know what else I think?' he thundered. 'I think while we're there we should go into Amsterdam and finally get stoned. That's what I think.'

Wow. Again I concurred, but suggested we put off getting stoned until *after* we had been to the record fair lest we start buying up the complete back catalogues of Slayer, Player and Leo Sayer, just because it struck us as funny while off our bonces on weed.

Sure enough, a fortnight later Danny and I met up at Stansted Airport with but two aims: to hunt out and bring back only the rarest and lushest vinyl collectors' pieces, preferably from the 1970s, following which we would lose our hashish virginity in circumstances bordering on the sybaritic.

It was as we sat in the airport bar that Danny revealed this was but phase one of our New Awakening. 'After we've done this,' he said, looking over his spectacles, eyebrows raised, as is his wont when imparting important information, 'we are going to try LSD, yes?'

I must say this seemed to me to be a case of going flying before we had even learned to float but, in theory, I was all for it.

'Now where would be best for that, do you think?' he continued in complete seriousness. 'It should be a place full of happy memories. That helps, I've heard.'

It was here that I introduced the idea of a boat on the Broads, having spent so many wonderful childhood holidays there in the sixties. Danny liked the sound of it.

'Right, as soon as we've come back from this one, we should start looking into that,' he said determinedly, and we clinked together our first cold ones of the trip in anticipation of a weekend and a lifestyle that we felt even Hunter Thompson himself might approve.

Had we known what an utter fiasco the next forty-eight hours would be, that beer would have turned to antifreeze in our throats.

The record fair went well enough, though it was, at best, only about the size of two and a half football pitches. Danny, as usual, bought more than I did, because he has a mania for most every genre of music including hip hop and jazz, both of which are usually in abundance at such shindigs. We had some lunch and then made our way back to Amsterdam to first drop off our purchases and then drop out of our minds.

I met him in the lobby at seven and he walked toward me with a purposeful stride that said, 'Right, let's do this.' Then he actually said that.

The first problem was that we hadn't researched the area at all. When we had individually visited Amsterdam over the years in the company of various rock bands, the city seemed to be nothing but an endless parade of dope shops and whore houses – neither of which we required – and until we stepped out into the night air we both thought it would simply be a matter of selecting which puff parlour out of the millions available wanted to take us higher. Yet, looking about now, Brel's notorious Port of Amsterdam struck us as being not unlike Norwich during Holy Week.

And here's something else you should know about my best friend and me. We never ask anyone for help or directions. Ever. If we should one day build ourselves a grand stately home with a motto above the door, that motto would read: Numquam Dexter Numquam Sinister Semper Quaedam – Sometimes Right. Sometimes Wrong. Always Certain.

For about half an hour we charged up and down side streets, our eyes peeled for dreadlocks, our nostrils twitching like racehorses, hoping to pick up a whiff of the desired narcotic. At long last we saw a café that had a large red neon saying '*SMOKE*' next to a flashing cartoon joint. There was also a big handwritten board in the window declaring, 'Yes! We Have Cannabis!' Could this be the place we were looking for?

Well, as it turned out, yes and no. We had imagined our chosen opium den would be a tumbledown spot, full of pot plants – the legitimate sort, like your mum has – old sofas and warm lighting, where ancient hippies lay schlumpfed around to the throbbing beat of something produced by Lee 'Scratch' Perry. This gaff was harshly illuminated, full of stainless steel and glass, and was belting out insistent techno music that I still hold is no good to anyone. The clientele as we entered looked like they could all be our well-scrubbed young nephews. As Danny made for the counter, I told him the place felt all wrong and we should pretend we were looking for someone, then leave. Dan thought that would make us look like policemen 'casing' the joint before a bust. I reminded him that the café was selling perfectly legal hashish, not heroin.

In the event, we stood at the counter for about five minutes without looking like getting served and, with the pulsating soundtrack seemingly locked into a repeated sample sounding not dissimilar to a Zimmer frame falling down a lift shaft, we turned on our heels and left. Marching confidently around the corners of streets that all had names with four Os several As and a hat-trick of Gs in them, it took us certainly no longer than forty minutes to spot another tempting weed redoubt. On closer inspection, it turned out to be exactly the same one that we had flounced out of earlier that night, though since we were last there the flashing cartoon doobie had given up the ghost.

You may be wondering how two adult gentlemen, actual published writers no less, could be quite so hapless. Not to be able to locate grass in Amsterdam is, I agree, akin to not being able to find a beer in Berlin. Well, let us just park our Dutch Experiment there for a second – and there is far more fiasco left in that particular tank – and consider how, while working as football journalists covering an England international abroad, Danny Kelly and I also managed to wind up in entirely the wrong country, get mixed up in a riot, be hunted by police, become abandoned, then almost get killed by our own supporters.

The fixture was Germany v. England in the 2000 European

Championships and Danny and I were covering the tournament for *The Times*. The Euros that year were being co-hosted by Holland *and* Belgium so, despite what you are about to read, I believe it wasn't entirely our fault because such a crazed arrangement was plainly designed for maximum chaos. We were billeted in Brussels, though the match itself was in a place called Charleroi, which I had convinced Danny was a district within the city rather than the substantial urban sprawl forty miles away it actually is. When we found this out we had to leave a bucket of beer and two trawlers' worth of mussels behind on our lunchtime table as we scrambled for the train station.

We were in luck in that a train to Charleroi was due in about ten minutes, although out of luck in that once we got there we found the football ground, which we had been assured was within walking distance, could only be described as such if you had the stamina of Mahatma Gandhi marching to the sea for salt. We further delayed our arrival at the match by once again refusing to ask for directions, instead choosing to follow for twenty minutes a large group of German supporters who seemed to know where they were going. They did indeed. They were going to a bar to watch the match on TV with their friends. When we eventually made it to the game, footsore and angry, it had already started without us and turned out to be a bit of a damp squib even though England managed to win it 1-0.

The debacle started in earnest at the final whistle. Getting out of the ground was proving painfully slow because, rather than slog across Europe as Danny and I had, supporters were making the journey back to Charleroi-Sud via an enormous line of special coaches that seemed to be spectacularly inefficient at customer loading. I don't know which one of us it was who eventually came up with the idea of trying to find another, swifter exit, but we can trace all the appalling events of that night directly back to that one fateful utterance.

Leaving the herd, we began barrelling along a series of empty corridors and down any stairs that presented themselves. Eventually we arrived at some fire doors and opened them outward on to a darkened street that, while hardly deserted, did not appear to be a re-enactment of the Fall of Saigon like the previous area we'd been shuffling toward. Here were more coaches, though only a few, and people were boarding these intermittently. None of the vehicles were anything like full and yet rather than conclude these might be going somewhere less popular than the station, Danny and I congratulated ourselves on short-circuiting the crush, unlike those other idiots, and heaved ourselves aboard the nearest one. Like every other bus we had seen, this one simply had 'Transport' displayed as its destination. A driver sat leaning out of his cab window smoking a cigarette. 'Town Centre?' Danny asked him. Why he said that and not 'Gare' or even 'Station', we would have plenty of time later to reflect upon. However an even bigger conundrum is why this bored old nicotine hound at the wheel nodded his head at our enquiry. When, after about ten more minutes, he closed the coach doors and put the thing in gear, there were only we two Dannys and four other individuals in his care. True, DK and I did exchange a glance as if to say, 'Why are there not more England fans on this charabanc?' However we did not verbalize the thought because we both like to think things will always work out.

We began trying to spot places that we would have passed on our epic odyssey to the game and every now and then one of us would say, 'Yes I think I remember that little park,' or 'It's OK, there's that row of bins,' but none of it was delivered with too much conviction. Eventually, we started going along a motorway and the awful feeling of unavoidable catastrophe began to creep up on us. Yet even then we would not admit defeat. I insisted we needn't panic, because the driver was probably using a ring road rather than negotiate all the little alleys and backstreets we had criss-crossed. DK pursed his lips and said he hoped I was right. After going at around 70 mph for approximately half an hour, we both knew that, if this was a ring road, it must be a circle of tarmac encompassing the whole of the Benelux borders.

Danny staggered up the bus aisle in the dark and I saw him talking to our fag-dragging captain. After a short exchange, he came back and broke the good news to me. 'Well, we're not going to the station,' he said. 'His accent is impenetrable, so I'm not truly sure where we're going but it is a transport hub so maybe we'll be closer to Brussels or maybe we're going in the opposite direction. We'll just have to see when we get there. This might yet turn out to be the right move.'

It wasn't. We remained on that motorway for another forty-five minutes, every half mile punctuated by one of us saying, 'This can't be right.' When the driver finally put on his handbrake at our destination we were outside what appeared to be a small private airfield in the middle of nowhere. Well, not strictly nowhere. We were, it transpired, in France.

Our four fellow passengers made their way toward a small light aircraft, after which our driver, apparently uncaring whether we were still aboard or not, switched off the cabin lights and sat back for another smoke. There were absolutely no other vehicles around, no main building or even customs hut to report to for assistance. In fact, no outward sign of human life anywhere. What kind of 'special' was this? We both approached him and tried to get some information from behind the noxious fog wreathing his head. In response, he, quite naturally, was totally confused why these two tubby Englishmen had decided to go joy riding on the road to nowhere, and could not even make out what we were trying to say until after about the fiftieth time we had said 'Charleroi?' when some sort of penny dropped and he said, 'Oui, Charleroi, oui,' then, after pointing to his chest then out into the night, 'Er . . . Charleroi . . . one . . . er . . . heure.'

There was nothing else for it. Sapped, beat and sucker-punched, we returned to our seats in the dark and sat there for a whole crawling hour, during which time we saw not another living soul. Occasionally our chauffeur would rent the air with the most alarming guttural snorts, always bracketed by a series of barely suppressed burps. Otherwise, all was silence. Danny and I, utterly broken, had stopped talking. We were both still staring into the abyss when, at last and with a cheery Gallic 'OK!', old matey boy up front shut the chariot's doors and off we went again, back on the highway. Some time later he dropped us back at the exact same spot outside the stadium where we had so optimistically joined his company almost three hours previously. By now it was almost 1 a.m. and the streets were as deserted as the peculiar little airfield we had been ferried out to. In fact it was, as the cliché runs, almost too quiet. And to pile on the agony, we now had to endure the long walk back to the station. On the way we desperately tried once more to remember familiar landmarks that might reassure us we weren't steaming off to have a look at Luxembourg too. However something was not quite right. Things had taken an eerie turn.

There was hardly any traffic anywhere and every so often a police van or an armoured truck would draw alongside and kerb-crawl us for a hundred yards. The occupants of these vehicles would stare hard at us from their windows, as if daring us to start something. The first time it happened we waved cheerily at them but noticed they did not wave back. From within the vehicle's bulk came the sound of large dogs barking. Elsewhere we could hear distant sirens and once or twice a kind of massed caterwauling. As we passed the top of one long avenue the noise of plate glass shattering came echoing from the darkness, and yet we saw no one. To be honest, the atmosphere was so intimidating we didn't want to see anyone. We weren't even sure what speed to walk at, lest the next patrol that examined us thought we were trying to run away from or go to some trouble hotspot.

The sight of the station coming into view should have been a relief and yet all we could see were the blue and red lights of emergency vehicles bouncing off its windows and walls. On the concourse outside we could make out fifty or sixty silhouettes ambling about, some in couples but none in groups. Riot police were everywhere although there was no sign of any rioting going on. Danny and I took a deep breath and walked through the tense tableau as though it were invisible.

Once inside the station, we immediately noted a sort of pointlessness in the air. The few dozen people inside looked thoroughly dejected. We soon discovered why. The last train had left over an hour ago and there were to be no more until seven the next morning. Nobody was allowed to stay in the station itself, the city outside was in 'lockdown', and once you left the building you had to keep moving. There was to be no loitering and certainly no sitting on pavements. We were informed of this by a couple of exasperated England fans that had recognized me and seemed to think I might be able to do something about the situation. I once more took the increasingly ugly temperature of the evening and regretfully told them that, should the hooligan balloon go up in Wallonia this night, it was unlikely that being a British minor celebrity would cut much ice with the local constabulary. That said, DK and I wanted a proper confirmation of this unannounced curfew and so for a good few minutes we simply gawped like a pair of gaffed pike at the station information board in the vain hope that its complete blankness might be because it just couldn't cope with the amount of trains due to arrive at any moment.

Surly policemen were rousing people who had been lying on the station's benches and shoving them out into the square. Then they set about looking for other minor miscreants to bully. Danny raised an eyebrow at me. This, he seemed to imply, was what he had told me about when on his reggae albums they spoke about 'heavy manners in-a Babylon'. What were we doing here?

A wizened German gentleman of around seventy, wearing a rumpled suit, nervously came over to befriend us, probably because we were the only people around not wearing replica football shirts. In faltering English he said, 'Pliss. This is not good. May I schtand vit choo?' We replied in the affirmative, but even this turned out to be a bad move because the old coot had only one topic of conversation: the dreadfully narrow seam of Victory V Lozenges. Producing an enormous packet from a carrier bag, he began by asking us if they were popular in England. (Quite, yes.) How much were they? (No idea, old fruit.) And was the brand still in the hands of its originator, Ernest Jackson? (Probably just a front these days.) Meanwhile, as the hands of the big clock overhead shuddered on to quarter past one, a member of the Police Locale headed toward us with an Alsatian on a leash.

Once again turfed out into the night, we made a few weak enquiries about taxis, even though we knew it was the longest of shots. Trying to appear cheerful and civilized to the grim law enforcers the conversation got no further than:

Me: Hello we're journalists from the London *Times* – where
    would be the best place for getting a taxi back to Brussels?
Cop: No taxi. No taxi.
DK: What would you suggest?
Cop: Go. Move. Move now.

Which is what we were obviously condemned to do all night. All hotels had put shutters up, quite literally, and the one or two whose night managers did react to our knocking peered through their windows with amused contempt at the sight of our proffered credit cards. This had now gone beyond the kind of silly inconvenience where, though initially there is a degree of shock at finding oneself on the back foot, deep down you know sooner or later you'll come up with a Plan B. This was real, total and dangerous desolation.

Now far from the station, the sounds of chaos somewhere worryingly close by would continue to flare up as we trudged ever on through avenues and deserted market squares, destination absolutely nowhere. Shouts rang out. Bottles smashed. We passed a pair of café umbrellas that were completely on fire. Indecipherable orders were being barked through loud hailers. Were we walking towards them or away? Had there been some sort of coup? A helicopter continually hovered in the inky night sky, but we could never see it. Exhausted and frightened, neither of us felt we could take another step, but to sit even momentarily on a wall would bring a personnel carrier from out of the shadows and a barked cry of 'Move! Move!' I hesitate to reach for 'Kafkaesque', but I hope you will forgive me just this once. Walking now many yards in front of Danny I looked up at the moon and thought of Wendy and the kids at home and I welled up.

At around 2 a.m., Danny's mobile rang. It was the other journalists we were travelling with, now on the umpteenth boozy round back at the rollicking hotel bar in Brussels. Danny spoke to them with a tone in his voice I have never heard in all the years I've known him. Flat, hopeless, humourless, vacant. Getting nothing but screams of laughter upon relating each syllable of the nightmare we were undergoing, he smartly snapped the phone shut.

'Danny, will you promise me something,' he said to me with pale and quaking lips. 'Promise me that you will never tell this story in an amusing way. We must never forget exactly how we feel right now. And it is: Not. Fucking. Funny.'

I don't feel as though I have broken that promise. It is for the individual to decide whether these events are uproarious or worthy of sympathy. However, the finale to the night, I think we can all agree, is right out of Frank Capra.

We found ourselves limping once again back along the dreary parade of closed shops and bolted hotels that faced the wretched station. I say limped, because both Danny and I had now developed, and much built upon, the excruciating inner thigh 'rub' that men who weigh a few pounds more than they ought are particularly prone to. By 2.30 a.m. I felt as though the area below the crotch-seam in my jeans was giving off enough frictional heat to fire up every domestic boiler in Britain.

Our ghastly perambulation took us one more time past a line of badly parked vans with UK number plates, most of which I suspected housed hung-over supporters sleeping themselves sober before leaving town the next day. At that low moment in my life, their fetid interiors appeared to me every bit as lush as the Presidential Suite at the Ritz Hotel. Music was coming from one of them and at the very moment I eclipsed its rear, the side door whined open and a big chap of about forty with close-cropped hair and wearing a bulldog T-shirt dumped a mass of burger-shop detritus out on to the street.

I didn't notice him glance my way, but he must've done.

'Uppleize,' he purred almost softly.

'What?' I replied, swivelling round.

'Uppleize!' he said, this time brightly and with eye contact.

Now then, 'Uppleize', in case you don't know, is the correct local pronunciation of 'Up the Lions', the accepted way most Millwall supporters casually greet each other.

'Gernawall . . . ' I fired back, this standard slurring of 'Go on the (Mill)Wall' being the acknowledged response.

'What the fuck you doing here?' he beamed while washing something off his hands with a bottle of Evian.

Enjoying this sudden break in the monotony and, if I'm honest, eyeing what seemed to be a Baker-sized space invitingly vacant on the floor of his van, I provided a precis of the night's burlesque so far.

'Ha! So where you supposed to be?' he chuckled at the end of my sob story.

'Brussels.'

Without a moment's hesitation he said, 'Brussels? Get in, we'll take ya!'

I simply could not believe it. Here, beaten and numb, at twenty-five past two in the Belgian morning, there were suddenly angels singing and sunlight all around.

'You can't take us all the way to Brussels,' I dangerously offered by way of a get-out for him.

'Course we can. We only just got here, cos we thought it might be kicking off, but it's pretty quiet, innit? Might as well go back your way. Here, Des, look who it is!' At this, not one but two people emerged from the front seats. 'Danny fucking Baker! We can take him and his mate to Brussels, can't we?'

'Easy!' smiled the presumed Des, holding out his hand. 'Danny Baker! What you doing here? Uppleize!'

And but moments later DK and I were lying on sleeping bags and pillows, stretched out in the back of a darkened van turning on to the motorway, heading for our beautiful soft-lit hotel rooms where the buzz of the mini bar would bid us to harvest from within. In the meantime our hosts offered cold water and packets of powerfully flavoured crisps, together with some spectacularly profane non-stop conversation of the type middle-class film makers fantasize proles might naturally deliver.

Driving at speeds that made our earlier highway trip seem as though it had been conducted in a milk float, we went flying through the blackness, narrowly avoiding crashing into other cars and overpasses on no more than five occasions, each of which seemed highly hilarious to this strangely invigorated, footloose crew. Nevertheless, it had been an almost holy deliverance. The chances of passing that van at the precise moment our champion decided to gift his old chips and pizza crusts to the rodents of Charleroi were surely astronomical. That he recognized me in the darkness and had no plans for the rest of the night, I still find staggering.

Who were they? Suffice to say they had spent the day driving from Antwerp to Brussels, then to Charleroi, then back to Brussels then back to Charleroi and that their commuting wasn't done yet. I suppose it's possible they were touring notable church buildings in the region, but a more likely explanation was, as Robert Duvall's regiment are described in *Apocalypse Now*, 'they were tear-assing round 'Nam looking for the shit'. After they dropped us back at the hotel, we did both notice they urgently began driving toward the police sirens wailing a few blocks away rather than away from them.

The night porter let Danny and me in and, even at that hour, asked if we might like a late one. Why not? There is something deeply comforting about nursing a cold one in the wee small hours by the glow of the only light on in a hotel bar. Even better if one can also massage soothing ice cubes against the raw skin at the top of one's lacerated inner thighs. And of course, within minutes, the pact DK had insisted on about 'never ever finding anything remotely funny about this night' had been discarded like a Belgian railway timetable.

Meanwhile, back in Amsterdam on the Trail of the Elusive High, Kelly and I hit on an acceptable compromise to our 'never ask directions' policy. We hopped in a cab and asked him to take us where 'all the cannabis coffee shops are'. This didn't admit we didn't actually know where they were, it just meant we wanted him to take us there.

At first he didn't seem to want to take us, insisting, 'They are every-where!' So we modified our request to, 'Take us to the best one and we'll each tip you ten euros.' The wheels of the taxi only seemed to go around about six times before he announced that we had arrived. Twenty-one euros, that cost us. Entering the place, it immediately seemed more like what we had in mind. For a start, the place stank of the stuff, a smell I have never warmed to, that dank sickly fug like somebody's hair had caught light and then they'd extinguished it with some boiled sweets. The room was disappointingly modern in its décor but at least its customers looked well seasoned. We strode up to the counter and made no bones about why we'd come. 'We'd like some marijuana, please,' I said, half expecting the kid behind the counter to hiss at us to be more discreet while signalling with his head that the good stuff was kept in some secret back room. Instead he gave us a couple of menus.

Neither of us had been expecting this and neither of us could make head or tail of what we were looking at. 'Which one do you suggest?' said DK, as though addressing the head sommelier at the George V, Paris. The bloke shrugged his shoulders and left us to it. The jargon on the menu was utterly bereft of meaning to us and the last thing we wanted to do was order something so insanely powerful that they would be fishing us out of the canal in an hour's time.

'We've got to be careful,' Danny further ruminated, 'because it's not all like tobacco, is it? Sometimes it's solid, like an Oxo cube that you crumble with a lighter.' I added to the dilemma by introducing the word 'bong' to the conversation and the thought of us sucking on elaborate paraphernalia or tiny pipes started a fit of giggles that would soon become the hallmark of the evening.

A decisive man, Danny then called out a choice to our indifferent host. 'This one here,' he said, pointing to the second name on the list. 'Is it very strong?' We received the shrug again and, after a hap-less glance at each other, confirmed that this blind selection would indeed be our mood fuel for the evening. We asked for a small bag of it, which was duly tossed on to the bar in front of us, then paid and went and sat down in one of the booths. 'Right,' said Danny. 'How do we do this?'

'Well, you have to have cigarette papers,' I replied, thinking back to one of the scenes in *Withnail & I*. 'And you sort of build a big rectangle with them.'

Danny asked me – a little optimistically, I felt – whether I had any cigarette papers on me. I didn't, so we both went back up to the counter. There were quite a few people in that night and we had to wait some minutes to get the weed merchant's attention. When we did, it went like this.

DK: 'Papers?'
Weed Merchant: 'What papers?'
Me: 'To build our joint. Cigarette papers.'
WM: 'OK, but which ones?'
DK: 'Aren't they all the same?'

The fellow waved his arm at a cabinet with about two hundred different brands in. Suddenly I understood why the rain forests were losing areas the size of Switzerland every week.

'What would be the best ones to go with the stuff we just bought?' said Danny. Even I knew that was a hopeless question. Looking along the various people puffing away at the bar I asked for whatever ones the stoners nearest to us were using. The required packet was dispensed to us and back to our booth we went.

'Right,' said DK, putting the package before me, 'I'm fat-fingered at things like this – you'll have to make it.' In return I reminded him that I'm the bloke who once screwed his own sock to the bedroom floor while assembling some flat-pack furniture. There then followed the most pathetic sequence wherein the pair of us attacked the construction individually, placing out the thin little skins this way and that on the table top, trying to achieve some sort of acceptable square that might possibly then roll up into what I've heard described as a 'Victorian Vase'. Yet it eluded us. No matter what variable geometry we employed, there always seemed a bit to spare sticking out, or else we had over-licked an edge and made it soggy and useless, or just torn the stupid things. In the end we agreed that my latest effort, even though it looked like the ragged remains of an old treasure map, was, at a pinch, roadworthy. Then this:

DB: Right, how much do we fill it with?
DK: Not much, I think. You just add to the tobacco, don't you?
DB: What tobacco?
DK: From a normal cigarette.
DB: What normal cigarette? Do you have any normal cigarettes?

So back up to the counter we went again. Eventually we managed to get old matey boy's attention once more and he gave us an old-fashioned 'What now?' look.

'A packet of cigarettes, please,' said Kelly, brusquely heading off any sarcasm. 'Anything will be OK – you choose.'

Our man gave us some Marlboros and once more into the shadows we retreated. Breaking open the individual cigarettes we began piling up their contents into a mound until we seemed to have a pile like one of those coastal beacons they light to mark bicentennials. After adding four pinches of weed to this hillock it suddenly became very obvious that my tatty raft of Rizlas was not going to easily encompass this copious foliage. But we did try, and soon the stuff was all over the table with the papers rent asunder as completely as if a cat had been at them. It should be noted that every stage of this increasingly pointless exercise was accompanied by the pair of us shuddering with hopeless laughter. The other patrons must have thought we'd been on the bong all day. Starting from scratch again, it only took us about another twenty minutes until we finally hoisted aloft a limp blimp of narcotic promise.

DK: Right, who's going first?
DB: You.
DK: OK then. Light it for me and I'll 'toke', man.
DB: (Pause)

DK: What's wrong?
DB: Dan. We haven't got any matches.

And so, I promise you, back up to the counter we went where it took absolutely ages to get served. We had now been in the place approximately forty minutes without so much as a magic puff passing our lips. Getting back to our seats, surely there couldn't be yet another barrier to stave off this high so delayed that the gear was probably legal back in Britain by now. Well there was. As soon as I applied a match to the crude swollen stogie in Danny K's mouth, the twisted end of it went out almost immediately, while a kind of wildfire zipped along the underside like the fuse of a cartoon bomb. As it reached a few centimetres from his mouth, the whole thing went up, bringing to mind the cover of *Led Zeppelin*. Spitting the blazing torpedo clear before the conflagration had a chance to engulf his nose, it flew out on to the floor where the pair of us set about violently stamping the thing out.

My God, but I don't think I've ever laughed harder than in the few minutes after that. Everyone in the bar was looking in our direction and a smiling young woman, having witnessed the farce, asked if she could be of assistance. 'Yes,' I replied, 'I'll give you ten million euros if you roll us a fucking joint, would you?'

She sat down in our booth and completed the task in under thirty seconds, leaving us with the perfect specimen. I said I would try it this time. I lit it, tried to gulp down some smoke, retched, coughed and blew the disgusting effluvium out explosively before it had a chance to get anywhere near my lungs. I lay my head on the table, arms outstretched and declared this entire venture to be 'fucking ridiculous'. Danny took up the torch and had a go himself. This time, along with the inability to physically inhale, a wisp of smoke found its way under his glasses and directly into his eye, causing him to throw the spectacles off and jam the palm of his hand into the socket. As he did so, he echoed my review that this was 'absolutely fucking ridiculous'. Once more we found ourselves the cabaret for our fellow consumers, but this time we had no interest in being rescued. Standing up, we needed no further cue to exit the stage and with a cry of 'It's all yours!' motioned to the various piles of materials we had pointlessly purchased that in other hands probably would have helped the evening go with a swing. Leaving the café, our helpless giggles surely said only one thing to the people passing by and that was: here were two happy hoppy heads from the seventies who undoubtedly knew their stuff and were veterans of the underground art. Innkeeper – roll me up whatever it is they've been smoking.

I remind you. Our next venture was to have been with LSD. On a boat . . .

Not Dark Yet (But It's Getting There)

My chemotherapy was scheduled to end, with film script neatness, on Christmas Eve 2010. That final day seemed truly interminable and I didn't get signed off from the hospital's care until almost nine that evening. It had been snowing in the days previous and as I stood with Sonny outside Guy's waiting for Wendy and the girls to bring the car round, the cold penetrated my bones. I attempted cheery conversation but I could tell my reactions were slow, my gaiety sounded hollow. I knew that no matter how many times I said that I couldn't wait for Christmas Day, my eyes showed I was desperately weak and unwell.

Arriving home the house was, as it is each Christmas, like something out of a Norman Rockwell painting; candlelit, welcoming and dressed for the season better than any Hollywood film. Bonnie later told me that nurses had told Wendy that once home I would be very susceptible to infection and so in the seventy-two hours before I got back she had virtually bleached the house inch by inch with a toothbrush. Going room to room I marvelled at the exquisitely stylish touches she had decorated each surface with and yet I think she could see that I wasn't really there. My head seemed to be packed with cotton wool and my body strangely unoccupied. My lower neck and chest in particular were experiencing an anxious sensation like a perpetually collapsing void that delayed both speech and any natural reactions. I slumped down into a soft chair and hoped my satisfied sighs were conveying to my family that whatever discomforts I had been prone to in hospital were now all dispelled by simply being home – but that just wasn't so.

'There's plenty to eat if you're hungry,' Wendy said quietly and with not a great deal of hope. She could tell all right.

'No, I'm OK, mate,' I replied. 'I know it's a drag, but I might have to go to bed.'

Taking the stairs very slowly, I found our bedroom was a glittering, pristine seasonal centrepiece. I subsequently found out that all the sheets on the bed were brand new, but even so Wend had washed them all twice. Everyone came and sat with me while I tried not to worry them by being such a wash-out. I think my inertia was perceived as tiredness and yet, though I had not an ounce of energy, I didn't crave sleep at all. I did crave Christmas, my favourite time in life and one I was acting my socks off not to depress, but every sign of tranquillity I faked just seemed to further confirm my utter dislocation from it.

The next morning I joined in the ritual of the present opening wearing a frozen expression of elation like a man trying to follow a joke being told in a foreign language. I leafed with a perfunctory enthusiasm through books I had been bought, tried on slippers and designer pyjama bottoms that this Xmas held a deeper meaning, cheerfully measured up against shirts presented to me, most of which were already too big, and took thanks for gifts that Wendy had bought for others in my name but that, once unwrapped, were as much a surprise to me as they were the recipient. Christmas breakfast in our house is traditionally a huge affair, one of such largesse that local supermarkets demand forty-eight hours' notice from us each December before we swoop by and empty their shelves of eggs and bacon and all manner of friable delights. Simply buttering the bread necessary to accompany this meal can take up to an hour. Secretly I was dreading being asked what I could manage at this early feast because I knew my answer would have to be 'nothing' and this in itself would begin to cast a pall over the great day. Eventually, and tentatively, Wendy asked me.

'I fancy some egg and beans,' I found myself saying, although it was a lie, albeit brightly delivered.

'Not even a bit of bacon?' said Wend, trying to inject a rasher of normality into events.

'No, in fact I might give it a miss altogether. I don't want to take the edge off dinner,' came my desperate response, and I sensed behind my back the kids were exchanging glances.

'Don't worry, I'll have double next year,' I added swiftly, hoping to deflate the tension but too late realized the words 'next year' not only presumed my presence at the breakfast table but on the planet. As discreetly as I could, I touched some wood. Wham's 'Last Christmas' would have to be deleted from any playlists too, lest that get taken literally.

Reversing my decision, I eventually did sit down at the heaving kitchen table but the beans tasted like squidgy ball bearings in Vaseline and the sliver of egg I did manage may as well have been a parboiled half-inch of my granddad's watch strap. Placing my knife and fork down in a deliberate manner I decided to address the artificiality of my presence.

'Listen, everyone,' I said in something approaching my normal tone, 'I feel unusual.' I knew this particular choice of word, lifted again from a scene in *Withnail & I*, would be wryly understood. 'I'm going to go back to bed because otherwise I might keel over before the turkey comes up. Nobody make a big deal of it, I'll just be upstairs reading.'

There was a flurry of replies to this, all designed to make me feel that whatever I'd decided was fine by them.

'And another thing,' I declared, 'Merry Christmas.'

Everybody laughed. A lazy pairing of words in any other circumstance, but we really, really did laugh. Then they all raised their teacups and wished me Merry Christmas in return. And for a few moments around the piled-high breakfast plates, it actually did feel like a Merry Christmas.

Later that day we pretty much went through the same pantomime at dinner. I showed up, allowed my plate to be moderately filled, went through the motions of eating it, i.e. chewing two small mouthfuls, cunningly hoping that time spent would equal appetite restored, before announcing that I would be departing the festivities but on no account should anyone make a fuss. Then I rose, tottered upstairs, pushed a syringe full of blood thinner into my midriff and lay on my side in bed staring with unseeing eyes at the book cabinet opposite. This was how the whole of Christmas passed. I didn't feel ill; I didn't feel at all. My family has since assured me that, other than a certain slowness of wit, my demeanour over the period wasn't that peculiar or alarming. That, however, was about to change dramatically.

Going into 2011 I had a few further weeks of the zombie-in-the-house existence, punctuated by mounting ancillary hospital appointments, before radiotherapy, the apparent bad cop to chemo's good cop, beckoned. I was urged to begin feeding myself through the external tube anchored in my stomach to become familiar with the process. This was a straightforward piece of care that I would always retire alone to our bathroom to undergo because I was under no illusions about just how nauseating the spectacle was. A fresh pump/syringe was required for each 'meal' and Wendy allowing her bedroom drawers, usually so full of linen, to be commandeered for my mass of medical equipment I felt was sacrifice enough. Elsewhere we had to store pallet-loads of the 'food' that would be shooting through my gut lining three times a day. This was, in essence, super-infused milkshake that came in various flavours – not that this matters when it's getting introduced to your system some eight inches south of the mouth.

Every trip up to Guy's now required me to go to their pharmacy directly afterwards to pick up more bags full of soon-to-be-essential medicines and equipment. Wendy made careful note of what they all were, what they would do and how I should take them. A week before the first radiotherapy session, I was given a prescription for morphine, with careful instructions about its strict dosage limits even when suffering extreme pain. Neither of us said very much on the way home after that one.

Then, on 10 January 2011, I walked down into the basement of Guy's Hospital and presented myself to the receptionist in the radiotherapy unit. In many ways I still consider that moment to be the actual start of the fight, the hell and, eventually, the miracle. Having made myself known, I was guided to a waiting room no bigger than a normal GP's, wherein sat a small group of people, some noticeably more frail than the others. One man, about my age, was having frequent coughing bouts that verged on seizure. Between these attacks he would lean over exhausted towards a woman that I took to be his wife and desperately address her in short, agonized, barely audible sentences, most of which seemed to be requests for tissues. Every so often he'd emit an undulating tortured wail as he tried to control, without success, the endless waves of eruptions rising from his lungs, every fresh bout wracking his entire frame. This unnerving scene culminated in him gasping, with what remained of his hoarse and shredded voice, 'Oh God. Oh God. Oh my God.' His wife held his arm tightly as he repeated these pleas and Wendy held mine.

There were various sorts of cancers in the poor souls around this room but as this one distraught patient writhed, buckled and heaved we both silently recognized that he most likely had his cancer where I had mine: head and neck. I couldn't be sure how many weeks he had already been taking the radiation, but without doubt, sooner or later, his torment was coming my way. I pretended to read my magazine but, as any observer would have spotted, I wasn't actually turning the pages.

After twenty minutes, I heard my name called and a nurse with a clipboard and a resigned smile bade me follow her. Wendy was not allowed to come with us. I was led into one of the two radiotherapy chambers, a sparse yet scientific space with low lighting, dominated by a huge machine very similar to the body scanners I'd only previously encountered when watching Hugh Laurie in *House*. After confirming my name and a few other health details, the nurse turned and retrieved my mesh mask that I hadn't seen in three months. I had lost some weight and so she held it to my face to make sure it still fitted where it should. Satisfied it did, she asked me to change into a medical gown and then hop up on to the gurney that protruded from the imposing equipment. I sat cross-legged on it while she went through a speech I suppose they give everybody on their first visit. Claustrophobia seemed to figure predominantly and also how, once the work got underway, I could visually signal either distress or satisfaction. The machine being used on me was called Electra and none of the staff could remain in the room while my dose of radiation was in progress but would observe from a gallery above, rather like George Martin producing the Beatles.

The session would last twenty minutes each day, I would feel no real effects from it for the first week or so but it would become 'pretty uncomfortable' subsequently. I asked about the fellow I had seen struggling in the waiting room and she confirmed he had the same illness and, if it was the bloke she was thinking of, he was on week five of the six-week course. She then surprised the life out of me by saying she was an old school friend of my daughter Bonnie and that we had met, briefly, a couple of times before at parents' evenings. We started to chat informally now, though I must confess I suddenly felt a bit of a berk in my green surgical gown with my hairy old legs hanging out and everything. A second surprise came when she said, 'I'll put a Hawaiian beach video on for you to watch – is that OK?' and she pointed to a TV screen in the ceiling. 'There are other choices, or some people like to bring in their own ones. Whatever relaxes you, you know?' I said Hawaii would be just fine.

Next it was down to business. I lay flat on the gurney and the mask was placed over my face. I was told to say when I was completely comfortable because once the mask was secured I would not be able to move again until the treatment was over. Inside the mesh it was like looking at the world through a tennis racket and after a few seconds I signalled I was OK, whereupon my peculiar head façade was bolted down tightly on to the stretcher bed.

'Right I'm going outside now,' I heard the nurse say. 'Don't forget, if it gets too much wave your hand or give us a thumbs down. You won't be able to see us, but we'll be watching you the whole time.'

A few moments later I heard a heavy door thud closed and the lighting reduced still further. I lay there in silence, head totally encased inside the mask, my heart beating faster than it had for some time. Then her voice came through a speaker somewhere.

'OK, Danny, we're going to move you in now to the machine and then you'll hear it start – it's quite noisy. It'll seem longer than twenty minutes, but I promise you we aren't going anywhere.'

Again I lay in silence until the thin mattress on to which I was strapped and bolted began to move backwards into the cavern of Electra. There were some minor jolts of adjustment but soon all was dark and still again. Seconds later, a short shock, as through the lattice across my eyes, the TV screen above flashed into life and there was a palm-lined beach, the fronds waving gently with the sound of waves lapping against the sands. This continued to play for about a minute and I gulped, nervously awaiting the laser beams or whatever it was that I was to be bombarded with. There came one final message from the gallery.

'OK Danny, sorry for the delay, it's going to start now.'

What started was a noise almost identical to the squeaks, bleeps and electronic stuttering that used to occur on old Internet dial-up services or on being connected to a fax machine. It was slightly more shrill with a wider range at the lower end, but otherwise that was exactly what it was like. There would be ten seconds of this, then a three-second pause, then another burst. I awaited some sensation to accompany the work in progress but nothing came, not even a slight detection of heat, just the repetitive whine of the device's robotic rifle sniping away at the individual cells of cancer. Once underway, any nerves I did have vanished completely and back flooded my soothing sense of the absurd. Again I found terrific comfort in the simple thought, 'What must I look like?'

Contrary to finding the time drag it was all over in what seemed like barely five minutes. Hawaii faded from view, up went the lights, in came the nurses again, I was unbolted, asked how I felt and then told, 'That was it, see you tomorrow.' I must say I fairly skipped out and as I passed the sombre huddle still waiting their turn I felt the most dreadful showboater. Compared to the draining monotony of chemo, what I had just been through was a walk in the park and an extremely interesting one at that.

Wendy of course wanted to know all about it and as we exited Guy's I excitedly babbled like a kid who'd just gotten off Splash Mountain in Disney World. I think I may have even allowed myself to believe that the haggard fellow with the atrocious cough may have been just that – a bloke with an atrocious cough. By the time we had arrived home the adrenalin had levelled out again and I found myself swallowing repeatedly and slowly trying to detect even the faintest glimmer of a sore throat or even a numbness, but there simply wasn't. A week later there still wasn't and I started to believe that against all the odds I wasn't going to have the extreme reaction to radiotherapy that the team had warned me about. In my meetings with the nurses at the Electra machine each day I was positively chipper, not even heeding their caution as they tactfully said, 'Well, it's early days yet!'

Early days it may have been but I had now completed one and a half weeks of a six-week course – that left just over thirty days for any notable deterioration to get stuck in, and as far as I could see it hadn't yet even got its boots on.

Then, at the end of the second week, I woke one morning with saliva overflowing from my mouth. I ran my tongue around behind my teeth where they met my gums and the area felt tender, the tip of my tongue raw. 'It's started,' I thought. Then I made to swallow and in two discernible spots in my throat there came a sharp dragging pain like pulling on tight jeans over recently grazed knees.

Oh, it had started all right. I went downstairs and tried to tell Wendy as brightly as possible that I believed the treatment was 'kicking in', but became aware that my tongue wasn't as nimble in forming the words as it had been twenty-four hours previously. Was this involuntary or was I just taking extra care not to aggravate the parts of my mouth that were increasingly sore? With gentle fingers I felt around my throat. The lump had all but gone, but something else was now definitely going on and in a total reversal of my earlier optimism I started to think, 'If it hurts like this barely two weeks in – how bad will it be by week six?' I also remembered that Dr

Guerrero Urbano had said that it was once the course of radiation stopped that the worst weeks of suffering began.

Happy days.

I was by now taking the tube to the hospital – a bit of a risk, given the number of people who sneeze like howitzers in every carriage, but the journey took eight minutes from our local underground station, whereas driving could add anything up to another hour and a half. Exiting London Bridge station, I would observe the hordes of people charging for their trains, chatting wildly into mobile phones, queuing for juices or wolfing down thick Cornish pasties on the hoof. The sweet mundanities of their days looked positively exotic to me. Once somebody asked me the way to a church in the area and the pain in my mouth was so acute I just had to wave my hand at them and make an apologetic face. 'Oh for fuck's sake!' they snapped and dashed off to find a local less lunatic. Rather than feeling ostracized by this, I actually found it funny – not that I could physically conjure up anything as taxing as a laugh.

When I got home I would invariably go straight to bed where I would lapse into a pitch-black and dreamless sleep for a couple of hours. When I awoke from this I would lie for a few moments and discern how much the destruction of my oral tissue had progressed in the interim and every time the results confirmed that it was happening with alarming swiftness. By the end of week four, the roof of my mouth arcing down into the tonsils felt utterly excoriated, scorched like a severe sunburn – which, in effect, was not far from the truth. My tongue hurt with every movement and to try and swallow the diminishing amounts of saliva I produced took determined effort, always accompanied by a grotesque wince and dreadful agonized groan. I didn't talk unless I absolutely needed to. I didn't move unless it was to make minor shifts in my bedridden posture. I couldn't even hide the deterioration from the kids any more; the best I could manage was a barely audible 'All right, mate' whenever they asked me how I was.

Poor Wend felt helpless, regularly coming into our once beautiful bedroom, now a stuffy shuttered sickroom, to ask if I needed anything. I would reply with a shake of my head without even opening my eyes. And yet all the terrible daily regimens still had to be observed and endured: the shuffling up to Guy's, the bolting into the mask, the blood tests, the inspections, the injections, the questions, the weighing, the assessing, the invading – sometimes tubes through the nose to shine a light on the devastated soft palate, the ghastly feeding through the stomach, the constant trips to the toilet to blindly vomit until you reached the very limits of consciousness, followed by coughing fits that threatened to rob you of your reason.

By the fifth week I was in an identical condition to the man I had both feared and pitied in the radiotherapy waiting room. I never thought I was going to die but completely understood that this, for many, was how it happened. At the beginning of week six everything above my shoulders but below my eyes was completely broken, dry and useless. That awful prediction about 'one big blister' had come to pass and the impairment was now absolute. I could not move my jaw at all, oral muscles atrophied, taste and saliva glands gone, my tongue a useless static piece of wood. On the Monday of week six, I went into the bathroom to feed myself and then, having barely strength enough to put away the equipment again and make my way back to bed, I reached for the bottle of morphine for the first time.

In the years subsequent to my recovery I have been asked a few times to talk to people who have recently been diagnosed with neck and head cancer, but I've always hesitated. I hoped that my public return to annoying ebullience would speak for itself. Addressing any gathering of nervous newcomers to the dreaded sect, I knew that the only honest thing I could tell them would be, 'It is going to be so much worse than anything you could possibly imagine.' And nobody would want to hear that. At the start of that sixth week I could not conceive of how this appalling torture could become any more acute or distressing. And yet, they had warned me back in October that it was from now on that I was about to enter the truly gruelling period. Surely that couldn't be right? I was by anyone's standards at the very limit: stupefied, scourged, done with. This could NOT get any worse.

Which just goes to prove: I am no doctor.

I have few recollections of the final radiotherapy sessions. I do recall that by then I needed assistance to get on to the gurney and that the Hawaiian beach scenes were now deemed too absurd to require playing on the ceiling TV. The staff in the radiation room no longer attempted conversation but instead just made sympathetic faces as I shuffled in to theatre to be locked into my mask. Usually this would have to be delayed as another expelling of matter convulsed me for minutes on end. I use the word matter because I have no idea what it was or from where I could be producing it; it appeared to be simply water, but in such copious amounts that at times made it impossible to grab even a single breath. A nurse would stand beside me as I sat doubled over and retching, handing me wad after wad of paper towels. And yet, even in that degraded moment, I could hear me, the real me, saying from behind the barricades in some deep defiant mental redoubt,

'Fucking hell, Dan – this must look choice.'

On the last day, when the shrieking laser completed its ghastly song for the final time, I was helped from the machine, told to rest if I needed to, and then got dressed at the speed of a two-toed sloth after an absinthe binge. Exiting the theatre to the genuinely moving good wishes from the team, I stood at the entrance to the waiting room looking for Wendy. Hunched, grey and tight-mouthed, I couldn't even turn my head to scan the assembled faces, so my eyeballs made laboured progress from left to right then back again. I couldn't see her and my death's door demeanour must have truly spooked everybody present. A nurse came and took me by the elbow. With my other hand I motioned toward the small reception desk and though only about twelve feet away I think it took the best part of the day to get there. I reached for a pen and on a piece of tissue tried to write 'My wife?' but my hand wasn't quite up to it, moving like a Ouija board indicator being powered by a particularly clapped-out and illiterate wraith. I also left off the question mark and so the nurse looked at me as though there was more of this spidery message to come.

'You want me to tell your wife something?' she asked.

With great effort I managed a small shake of my head and then, in desperation, reduced the preposterous exchange to a game of charades, indicating that I was looking for Wendy by holding my hand above my eyes in the manner of somebody searching the far horizon. This failed to translate and as far as I could tell the nurse now thought, in my delirium, I had taken to saluting her.

'Come and have a sit down,' she said. The untouched inner observer in me was scribbling all this comic gold down for later, healthier recollection.

We hadn't yet made it to a vacant chair before in came Wendy, cursing herself for trying to save time by collecting my latest dispatches from the pharmacy while I was under the light beams. During the drive home she tried to lift my spirits, expressing joy and relief that we were now finally finished with chemo and radiotherapy. We arrived to find all the kids gathered at the front door and gently applauding as I was helped up the front steps.

'All done now, Dad.'

I couldn't respond much but began the slow ascent of the stairs to our bedroom thinking that even if I could talk I wouldn't have dampened their optimism by saying that, far from dispersing, the dark clouds of my sickness were in fact regrouping for the ultimate great storm.

Turning into our bathroom, I closed the door and placed both hands on to the sink top. Lifting my head I looked in the mirror at the sunken travesty of my face with its flat dull eyes, putty-coloured skin and deathly bone-dry lips. Stubble grew only in tiny isolated patches now, the majority of my beard follicles long since nuked into oblivion. I tried to open my mouth but could part my teeth no more than a matchstick's breadth. Reaching out, I turned on the cold tap. I stared at the powerful torrent until it filled me with an overwhelming desire to plunge my head downwards and let the stream flood directly into my mouth, restoring new life to my desiccated dead teeth, to somehow wash away both the cancer and the devastation of its cure. I now turned the tap on full blast and studied it as though it was some new force of nature. The urgency of the cascade sent occasional tiny droplets on to my arms and even up as far as my face and neck as I became mesmerized by its wild, liberated invitation. This one moment as the water flooded into the sink, peppering me with its exiled magnificence, explosively churning in violent orbit before rushing out of sight, remains for me the single most potent image of my entire illness. I stayed transfixed by the forbidden deluge for quite some time until Wendy knocked on the bathroom door in concern.

I took a syringe full of morphine and repaired to bed where, for the next six weeks, I would exist in a semi-conscious state today only recollected through the various pinnacles of suffering as the two armies, cancer and science, did battle inside my very atoms. There were two soundtracks to this blearily remembered period. The TV in the bedroom remained almost permanently on and tuned to a sports channel, not because I could have cared less about the games shown or indeed possessed the ability to even watch television, but the low burble of something seemingly urgent taking place somewhere gave the otherwise suffocating sick space a glimmer of vibrancy. It also marked time for me, though that had no real meaning. I might fall asleep during a Spanish domestic football fixture but wake to hear a re-run of an old Aston Villa game. If it were a live match I would drift away during the build-up and find myself coming to during the post-match analysis. I might hear a sentence about 'darts coming up at eleven' and then next find myself surfacing to the noise of arrows thudding into the board. Another hour gone. I rarely ever lay facing the screen, and even if you were to put a gun to my head to ask me to recall any of the hundreds of events I must have dipped in and out of during this time I would be at a total loss to respond. Tom Waits was once asked about his favourite kind of music and he said, 'The sound of a ball game on the radio.' I totally understand that. In my case it was also a whispered, welcome tone poem reminding my fractured spirit of a temporarily lost world.

The only other outside occurrence to find its way on to my radar during the early spring of 2011 was the catastrophic meltdown at the Fukushima nuclear plant in Japan. During the weeks of rolling news about the threat of radiation sickness I managed, while watching the scenes of a panicking population and clogged motorways, to form a pretty good joke about how I had spent the last few months walking towards what these people were now running away from. I heard more than one expert detailing the various signs of exposure to radiation and could confidently tick these symptoms off one by one like the veteran I now was. Had anyone run a Geiger counter over my battered old frame during March, it would have wailed like a Theremin.

My health now declined so dramatically that for the first time I wondered if something was not quite right. My breathing became so disrupted by bouts, sometimes a full hour in duration, of continual vomiting that I was provided with an oxygen tank and mask. Any respite granted by this would be cut short when my mouth began quickly filling up with water that seemed to be drawn from some inexhaustible well near my lungs. Unable to swallow, I just had to let the liquid pour into tissues and soon filled dozens of carrier bags of the disgusting things that Wendy would dutifully clear ten times a day. The constant agony of the blistered mouth and throat made true sleep impossible without my stumbling gratefully toward the morphine bottle. From the bridge of my nose to the edges of my shoulder blades a fire raged under my skin similar to those subterranean coal seams in Kentucky that have been burning since 1931. This resulted in a terrifying development one night when I woke to find I had apparently cut myself below the ear and was bleeding on to my pillow. Limping into the bathroom I turned on the light to see that I was not cut at all but rather one side of my neck was, to all intents and purposes, melting. The skin there, which had been growing increasingly sensitive to the touch, was now simply dissolving and the neck of my T-shirt looked like I'd had my throat cut. Over the next few days the liquefying spread until no part of my neck was unaffected. To make the revolting malady even more exquisite, a visiting nurse warned me I mustn't cover the area because any gauze or pads would become stuck to the surface and thus later be excruciating to remove. Now I couldn't even lie normally in bed and securing my oxygen mask in place was as delicate an operation as defusing a bomb. And yet still the sickness. Still the stomach injections. Still the feeding through the tube.

Reader, I think we've had enough of this don't you?

Resurrection Shuffle

There was no one moment when I detected a corner had been turned. The sheer amount of symptoms and areas of battle made it so that any scaling down of individual torments could go unnoticed. However I do recall one moment of revelation that happened deep in the night as I lay there, freshly awoken from the latest sliver of morphine-induced relief. I breathed out heavily, and as I did so I produced an involuntary sigh through my long-dormant vocal cords. This note, like a brief push upon the lowest key on a harmonium, startled me in that it sounded like me. Not the usual me, for sure, but at least the me of when I have a heavy cold and Wendy asks if I'd like some tea. A sort of affirmative 'Hmm'.

Now I know that a single basso profundo 'hmm' coming from a three-times winner of Broadcaster of the Year doesn't sound like much of a riff, but it encouraged me to try again. This time I extended the hmm and, with a racing heart, even stepped it up an octave at the end. It worked, and for the first time in many months I began to feel something approaching excitement. I decided to test myself. There in the dark, and while still feeling chronically unwell, I sent the noise up my throat and as it exited my barely open mouth I forced back the pain barrier to push my tongue upwards. The word that emerged sounded like 'Hell-a'.

I repeated that a few more times, even though each lift of my tongue rasped with a raw flash of pain. Next I tried to flex the edges of my lips inward. Again, the motion felt punishing but I kept at the exercise, still with unopened eyes, until I thought I might be ready. Then I said 'Hell-a' again but now brought my lips in.

This time I heard 'Hell-o'. The next time even a little clearer. On the third attempt there came a soft but discernible, proper, unbroken 'Hello'.

All I wanted to do was rush next door and wake Wendy up. In the event, I simply repeated the word to myself several times and salted the moment away as possibly significant.

About a week after that I decided I would surprise everyone by walking down to the kitchen. I had been attending to some vile routine or another in the bathroom and could hear everyone gathered below and, though doddery, was confident enough to attempt the journey under my own steam. This would be the first 'unnecessary' journey I had made in months and progress was slow. If I left the bedroom in March it must have been July by the time I got there. As I appeared at the top of the kitchen stairs everyone's immediate reaction was a kind of horrified shock, the assumption being that there must be something wrong, an emergency to which I was attempting to alert them. Noting their panic, I waved weakly and produced the thinnest of smiles. Then everybody burst into tears.

Recovery is a tricky process to quantify. If you find yourself coughing to the point of blackout only three times an hour instead of five, or using an oxygen mask in bursts of two minutes instead of three, are you entitled to consider yourself well? In everyday illnesses like flu there definitely comes a point when you can detect it departing, where you wake one morning and feel pretty normal. With head and neck cancer there are so many fires that need to be brought under control, so many physical areas that have been thoroughly gutted and now require building again from the ground up that no true moment of 'getting better' can be declared.

However I am extremely impatient by nature and as my mobility returned to that of, say, a 109-year-old man, and my rasping voice managed to overcome the, still, acute oral distress to put together sentences of sometimes three words, I began to, as my mum would say, 'overdo it'.

The first thing I wanted to achieve was to come off the incessant morphine injections. Ever since I had first pumped a few spoonfuls into my stomach tubing I had had a nagging worry that the legacy of my nightmare would be a drug habit like a beat poet. If Danny Kelly and I ever did make it to Norfolk to indulge our LSD fantasy I would by then be so chemically dependent that dealers would flock to our craft in a broads-blocking flotilla. So I went cold-turkey and stopped taking it. Enduring the raw resultant pain I would remain vigilant for any signs of parallel withdrawal pangs. None came, there were no side effects of my short junkie period, and I now realize I went through several unprotected, murderous weeks with my throat that I needn't have.

Then, in April, I received the news that, despite not broadcasting for over six months and currently being 98 per cent mute, I had been nominated for, get this, Speech Personality of the Year at the Sony Radio Academy Awards. The ceremony was scheduled to take place in May. For some reason, for some utterly fucking ridiculous reason, I decided I would attend. Actually, I think we know exactly why I made that idiotic choice – because how heroic a moment was it going to be when my name was read out and I made my way to the stage? Let me tell you, people, nothing temporarily overcomes a degrading, life-threatening malady like a sense of the cinematic. Of course everyone from the medical team to my family gently tried to make me see that it was at best an ill-advised option while at the same time trying not to deflate my newly resurrected gung-ho.

A few days before the excursion, following a subtle suggestion from Wendy, I gingerly tried on the suit I planned to wear on the night. I had suspected I may need a belt for it now and perhaps one of my double-breasted jackets might wrap around me better but was simply not prepared for the shock of what greeted me as I climbed inside the material. There had to have been a mistake. Whose suit was this? Staring into the mirror, appalled, I saw Stan Laurel wearing Oliver Hardy's costume. How could this expanse of blue serge have ever fitted me? I knew I'd lost some weight, but the suit made it seem that I'd shrunk in all directions. I looked like the child Tom Hanks returns to at the end of *Big*. At the collar, my head stuck from the gap as if it were a ventriloquist doll's head on a stick. Everywhere great swatches of material cascaded in billowing swathes whose sheer weight threatened to drag me to the floor, whereupon search parties would be sent in to find me. How could I possibly have ever been this fat? How could *anyone* have ever been this fat? When I released my grip on the waistband, my trousers promptly fell to the floor.

Wendy took some measurements and drove to a gentlemen's outfitters to purchase a new miniature outfit for me.

On the night of the awards I left the house for the first time for something other than a hospital appointment. Walking out into the waiting black cab I felt unusually capable, although this, as we shall see, was an illusion created by the unfamiliar sensation of having even a modicum of energy. By the time we had arrived in the West End I didn't feel right at all but did not share this with anyone. The cab dropped us at a bar a few hundred yards from the venue, which was the arranged rendezvous with my agent and workmates who'd be sharing the table with me that night. Now then. When you've been utterly bedridden and as ill as I was, a sensible first trip back into the world to acclimatize might be a park or perhaps the local library. Pitching up at a Mayfair hotspot full of media people out on an orgy of self-congratulation makes as much sense as a manned spacecraft planning re-entry over Mexico City. I literally took two steps into the place and felt a sort of plunger drop violently from my knees to the soles of my feet. In the wake of this detonation the fiercest pins and needles I had yet known occupied everything from thighs down. I came to a complete stop and wavered like a tightrope walker caught by a sudden zephyr.

Alex, my agent, saw this and said, 'Have you gone?'

'I've gone,' I croaked as the muscles behind my eyes started to slacken and sag.

Putting his arm around my waist, he marched me straight back out into the street where passers-by must have seen my buckling legs and assumed I had been on the Martinis since midday. Taking in breaths as big as my still-lacerated throat could bear, I announced I was now OK but would have to give the bar a miss. The truth was that I was far from OK and needed to abandon the whole farcical expedition. The pins and needles were now chronic, making it impossible for me to judge even whether my feet were in contact with the ground. According to Alex, shortly before I collapsed I was walking like a show pony with my knees coming up to pelvic height on every step.

Anyway, collapse I did – ace, jack, king, queen on the deck. I hadn't blacked out and can remember every moment of it, but I had come to the point where the single energy briquette in my boiler room could no longer power the hubristic *Titanic* of my ambition. So now here I was. Enjoying Piccadilly from a dachshund's point of view. People gathered around me and more than one was asking if they should phone an ambulance. This really cut through my woozy state of mind and I started insisting I was fine, only needing to 'recharge' my batteries. Still, the incessant firework display taking place in my lower half continued with all the force of water pouring over Niagara Falls, and yet I could harness none of its power to get me back on the vertical. I tried a couple of times but my legs crumpled like a pole-axed boxer hoping to beat the count. Finally, placing a hand squarely on the concrete, I attempted one last determined effort but my shoes could not gain the required purchase and I found myself just going round in a low half-circle like a Cossack dancer. As I slowly pivoted on the pavement to the horrified cries of the assembled crowd, I inwardly nominated this moment as probably the most ignoble of the entire period. Eventually I was helped into the Ritz Hotel who at first didn't know what to do with me, figuring like everyone else witnessing the spectacle that I was just another piss artist who had hit the wall. When it was explained that I was actually an invalid in denial, I was taken to a vacant conference room and laid out on a banquette. Here I remained until the neurological rapids in my legs retreated to merely ankle level and once more I was helped to the upright.

Everyone assumed I would now go straight home, but being so close to my accolades and hosannas, I insisted that the storm had passed and we try and retrieve something from the wreckage of the evening. The award I was up for was mercifully early in the programme, our table charitably close to the stage. When I was announced the winner an enormous cheer went up and I submerged the turmoil within to appear to, if not quite skip, then at least walk normally on stage. Some old friends in the room were giving me a standing ovation and when it had all died down I did what was expected of me and claimed I was only getting the award for still being alive. As soon as I was off again I made for the exit and a taxi home. Of the few photographs I have seen of myself on that night I look like an absolute ruin; gaunt, sweaty and crazed. It took me a full week to get my rickety health back to where it had been right before I'd pulled on my new size-zero suit, and when I told the doctors at Guy's of my jaunt they were indulgent but not impressed one iota. But do I regret doing it? Yes. Totally – 100 per cent. However, six weeks later I did something equally as impetuous and half-witted.

At the invite of Chris Evans, my family and I had gone to stay at an apartment he keeps in the Algarve. My cancer meant that there could be no suggestion of even limited exposure to the sun and so I knew that I would arrive resembling an exploded old waxwork and return home looking like a slightly more rested gargoyle. However the break for everyone away from the pallid palace of sickness that our house had come to represent was a blessed relief. I also knew I would not be able to join in any of the wonderful eating and drinking such a trip should revolve around. I was still feeding through the tube and even though the blistering of my mouth had receded somewhat, my throat remained raw and tender. That said, the act of swallowing was at last not an impossibility and I had been taking tiny infrequent sips of my nutrition drinks as well as the occasional hit of water. Though not technically swallowing, what I'd do was tip a little liquid into my mouth, wait for the stinging to stop, then tip my head backwards, forcing the liquid to tumble down the windpipe. Finally I would push the pulverized throat muscles at the very back to make the weakest of spasms – which never failed to give birth to a shriek from me – that hopefully would help the minute pool on its way. The first few times I did this, I'd next check the hole in my stomach to see if it was jetting back out again. It didn't, but in two out of five attempts the tortuous ritual would trigger a coughing fit that sent it all back through my nose. It was slow and painful progress but it *was* progress. The important thing, I feel, is not to rush these things.

So for the love of God will someone tell me why on the second night of our stay in Portugal I felt the moment had arrived for me to try drinking wine again? I know. Following such a lunatic stunt if Wendy had pushed me over a clifftop I think people would have agreed her only crime was not throwing a few rocks at me on the way down.

We were in one of those perfectly positioned restaurants that are accessed via a little stairway from the beach. Seated at a white linen-draped table with an uninterrupted view of the ocean, the warm evening breeze blew lightly over us, causing the three little candles at the centrepiece to flutter but never extinguish. The daylight was beginning to fade, leaving a pale blue sky generously streaked with pink. It was totally idyllic. Indeed it was one of those utterly serene instances of existence where, it soon became obvious, even the most expensive of table waters would be found wanting. The company, the setting, the occasion warranted only one thing and that was, to quote Withnail again, 'the finest wines known to humanity'.

The only stumbling block to achieving perfection was of course that, since the violent scourging of my upper inner linings, I had the oral tolerance of a newborn. Also, even the dribbles of water I had managed to tip down the gullet had carried the distinct tang of a pig iron and musket milkshake. And yet still I eyed my companions' half glasses of chilled white Rioja as though they contained the very elixir of life. Even the angle of the wine bottle, as it sat soaking in the silver bucket, cold rivulets of condensation beetling down its length, seemed to beckon me: 'Come, dive in.' Were I prone to fantasy sequences, this powerful tableau would have next had me frolicking about in there, gaily sliding down the green glass neck on to the giant ice cubes bobbing about in the clear lake below, before turning to camera and toasting my audience like Esther Williams in *Million Dollar Mermaid*.

Taking my wine glass, I tipped out the inch of still water on to the sands below me and, without saying a word, reached for the siren vino. My fingers had barely made contact with the bottle when I heard Wendy ask me what I was doing. Pulling the dripping vessel from its icy port, I croaked that I needed to try something. Now everyone around the table was begging me to abort the experiment and attempt something less impulsive – a half-teaspoon of natural yoghurt, perhaps? I once more assured them that I felt up to the task. Indeed, I fancied this was going to be the snifter of a lifetime. As I lifted the glass to my mouth, it is true that I hesitated, and all watched with bated breath.

'Dan . . . ' Wendy said in a tone that usually indicates the next words are going to be, 'Put. The gun. Down.'

Resigning myself that it was now or never, I placed the rim on my lower lip, tipped, and let a goodish glug of the straw-coloured ambrosia flow to the back of my mouth from where it tumbled across the uvula and into the dark valley below.

Now then. Being a voracious reader of Second World War biographies, I have always wondered how the cyanide pellets issued to Nazi leaders as a suicidal last resort could possibly have acted so quickly that as soon as, let's say, Hermann Goering bit down upon his he was the very next instant standing at the Gates of Hades being handed the keys to his room. Surely the human body needs at least a few seconds to process alien ingredients before deciding whether to shut up shop or request a refill? Yet from all reports, the exact moment when Himmler's teeth broke his smuggled capsule of poison, he was beyond the actions of even the swiftest of his guards. Instantaneous is the word usually applied and it was something I was always a little sceptical about.

At least, I always was right up until the second that single slug of Rioja entered my battered old kisser. How to best describe it? Well, next Guy Fawkes Night, if you are entertaining at home, instead of nailing a Catherine Wheel to the fence at the back of your garden, why not place it somewhere between your tonsils and then apply the match? This may give you but an echo of the sensation that I was engulfed by as I assaulted myself while overlooking the Atlantic.

I may not have had any saliva glands left but in those searing seconds after once more embracing Bacchus I knew there was nothing wrong with my tear ducts. I shook so violently I fell off my chair. Waiters came running over, believing I was choking. If the scene had been in a situation comedy, some of the same people who had seen me carried through Piccadilly a few weeks earlier would have now been at a nearby table regarding my latest 'drunken' collapse through disapproving lorgnettes.

Propping me back up on to my chair again, Wendy frantically tried to explain the problem, trying to make herself heard above the wordless fusillade emanating from all parts of my body. One of the quick-thinking staff dashed to the kitchens and brought back a long glass of cold milk and, momentarily overcoming the physical difficulty, I chugged at it gratefully. Though not providing total relief, it certainly brought the conflagration under control and more importantly seemed to contain no side effects of its own. Milk would from that moment become the universal panacea and magic lubrication that made mealtimes viable again – an arrangement that continues to this day. Though I can manage a lot better now, for years afterwards I never took even a single mouthful of food without it being accompanied by a swig of semi-skimmed, though it is surprising how many restaurant servers have been baffled by the request and have had to check the kitchens first before accepting the order.

Back in the Algarve, so rattled had I been by my spectacular act of self-harm that I sat the rest of the night out, smoke issuing from my clothing, a low generator-like hum detectable from my still vibrating teeth. I think it says something about my fighting spirit though that I didn't let this setback send me any sort of wider message and, unbelievably, quietly persevered until the very first taste that returned post-cancer was with wine. To be absolutely honest, if I had been given the choice between food or drink and could only welcome back one, I would always have taken the sweet sociable liquor. On subsequent nights out I found I could happily sit there while all around tucked into steak or pizzas, even bread, but I loathed the period when nursing a cavernous chalice of the deep red was denied to me. Today I can eat and taste most things again, although I'm never entirely sure if the intensity is at pre-2010 levels or merely a sense memory boosted by my gratification at being able to detect any flavours at all. Strangely, only chocolate, biscuits and ice cream remain completely neutral to me now and some people react with horror when I tell them this. I find I can absolutely live with such a privation – mainly because I am not eight fucking years old.

For the next five years I remained under the care of Mr Simo and Dr Guerrero Urbano as an outpatient. The way it works is that at first you have hospital appointments every six weeks, then every three months, then biannually and then, one day, they are sitting across the desk to you and, after a conversation that has been 20 per cent medical and 80 per cent catch-up chit-chat, they say, 'Well, that's it, we don't need to see you again. Take care. If you have any worries, come back, but you should be fine. Goodbye and good luck.' And it's over. The cutting, the coughing, the needles, the tubes, the pain, the sickness, the indignity, the separation, the worry, the dread, the loneliness; all ended. The most devastating period imaginable is finished. You are well. You are strong and fit and without symptom. You had cancer. Now you don't have it. You don't have cancer. You don't have to come back here any more. You didn't die. It didn't win.

And now the people who did that for you are holding out their hand to shake, smiling at the enormity of the moment reflected on your face. They will not be going anywhere, of course. They are the ones still looking fraught and frazzled as, mid-shift in one of the busiest hospitals in the world, they now want to wave you off and get back to dealing with the long line of poor wretches outside who are at all the varying stages of this disgusting, miraculous process they dispense. What on earth do you say to such extraordinary people at a time like that? Well, you try to come up with a speech but in the end just say thank you. Then you say thank you again until you realize you are saying it over and over and can't stop. Then you stand up dazed and walk the few paces to the door of that small familiar scruffy surgery and turning to them once again say it a few more times, quite unable to leave. Then they perform one final service for you. They hand you some tissues.

Roll Away The Stone

It is surprising how soon after a major illness that every bad habit that you swore would never plague you again returns, hangs its hat on a peg in your psyche, sits back on its perch and says, 'Now then, where were we?'

Within weeks of re-entering the world, there I was once more, screaming at the bloke in the car in front for not indicating when changing lanes, while takeaway deliveries of hot food failing to show up on time would be declared 'a nightmare'. I can also remember confidently stating that trying to get through to the same person at the bank was 'the worst thing in the world'. (This by the way is still under review and may not be simply hyperbole.) In short, while some sainted souls do indeed emerge from a crisis in their lives more rounded and reflective than they had been previously, I seem to have rejoined the zip wire every bit as bumptious and shallow as when I first ignored the lump in my neck.

At the time of writing there are several legacies from the dreadful blight that I have learned to live with, chief among these being the constant whine of tinnitus. Other than my spectacular teeth, in all those tests prior to the treatment starting, the examination for which I was most proud of getting 9.5 from the assembled judges was the hearing test. The chap in charge of me that day said because of my career in and around rock music I probably had no idea how blunted my hearing had become. Yet after fifteen minutes of asking me to stick a finger in the air whenever I detected a sonic blip from his tone box, he seemed dumbfounded at the results. It turned out that, despite a forty-year bombardment, my old lugholes were in superlative shape, correctly identifying several of the lower registers that normally only get a thumbs-up from elks in Yellowstone Park. I can't quite remember the exact day when this pristine reception was wiped out and replaced by a shrill pitch that neither rests nor wavers but, as I say, we're cellmates now. Day and night, my ears try to convince my brain that I have just walked out of a prolonged concert by The Who.

Another victim of the cure was my singing voice. Now I know the form is to pretend that one's singing voice is a hopeless howl that when in full flood sets chandeliers rattling three streets away, but I'm afraid mine wasn't. Both my mother and father could sing and would do so constantly. Their styles varied wildly, with Mum's being a sweet and gentle trill, something along the lines of a more delicate Deanna Durbin, while the old man had a powerful technique and would go at every tune like it was a contest that could only be decided by three falls or a submission. He was a popular singer too in local pubs, always in demand, though in truth he only liked three songs from the entire history of recorded music: '(Wrap Up Some) Red Roses for a Blue Lady', 'You're My Everything', and Max Bygraves' 'Back in My Childhood Days'.

This last one also incorporated 'Back in My Young Man's Days' which was the B-Side to the single that, as far as I know, was the only record Spud ever bought in his whole life. We played it at his funeral, but in providing the CD for the service I neglected to separate parts one and two, which meant it went on for over eight minutes. As Max launched into yet another verse I could sense a certain restlessness setting in among the congregation who, as Dad would have noted, were all gasping for a drink.

Strangely, Spud was otherwise no fan of Max Bygraves, genuinely believing that the much-loved working-class entertainer had stolen from him an alternative future. Watching the latest TV special featuring Bermondsey's own favoured son he would bristle with scorn. 'That's not singing! Hark at him – anyone could fucking do that! Tell you what, he wouldn't have lasted ten minutes in the old City Arms. He must have put a nice few quid about to get on like he has, I'm telling ya. Look at all the silliness with his hands, you don't need to do any of that . . . ' And so on.

Though the least frustrated man on earth, I did suspect that Dad felt had the right talent scout walked into any of the pubs on the Isle of Dogs in which he acted as weekend compère post-war, then Max Bygraves would never have happened. And if you had ever heard my dad singing at full-throttle, bottle of Guinness swinging wildly to emphasize the big notes, you would have given a good deal of credence to his theory. It was only his refusal to learn any lyrics to songs that might possibly have been a stumbling block. Other than the previously stated trio of exceptions, Freddie Baker reacted to all song words as one might the serving suggestion photograph on a microwave meal. There wasn't a single syllable from the pens of Cole Porter, Lorenz Hart, Irving Berlin or Sammy Cahn that Spud felt couldn't be better replaced by one of his own stock phrases. These would invariably be 'Oh baby mine', 'In the old-fashioned way', or perversely for someone of his generation, 'Rock and roll me all night long'. So, for example – and so you know these definitely were not the original lyrics – let us enter the realm of science fiction and imagine my dad standing on the stage of the Duke of Suffolk and singing Queen's 'Bohemian Rhapsody'. He might start by acknowledging the original but would soon veer into the Lexicon of Spud. Smiling broadly and with absolute confidence he would've then belted out the following:

> *Is this the real life?*
> *Oh rock and roll with me!*
> *I'll take you round, babe*
> *In the old-fashioned way, oh baby*
> *All night long!*

Now I know you might think this doesn't fit the melody, but that was another thing that didn't vex him in the slightest. I've seen seasoned pub piano players looking toward him in sheer terror as the agreed tune would suddenly turn a hairpin bend and go off in another direction entirely, often to a completely different song that was also a travesty of its popular rendition. Occasionally, he would notice that he'd left his associate behind and swiftly turn from the mic, snap his fingers and berate them with a terse, 'Come on, fucking keep up!' Another example:

> *Hello darkness my old friend,*
> *I've come to rock and roll with you again*
> *In the old-fashioned way, oh babe!*
> *All night long around again, oh babe!*

Now neither of these originals would be anywhere in Spud's repertoire but they are both perfect examples of his cavalier attitude to the songwriter's art. What stopped him from being simply a madman at the mic was his voice. People would forgive his wayward ways with tune and poetry for the handful of times in each song when he did remain on track and his pitch-perfect lungs would forcefully match his undoubted onstage charisma.

Mum, on the other hand, only ever sang indoors. Against this, and in absolute stark contrast to her husband, she could remember just about every popular song ever written and knew not only the complete lyrics but their long-lost opening verses too. (The opening verse would be a few stanzas at the start that would literally give the upcoming song context. Almost every hit from the thirties and forties had one of these. Think Ella Fitzgerald setting up the song 'Manhattan' before the melody proper blossoms.) Effortlessly tripping through these intensely crowded mini-librettos, she would ply her Hoover like Fred Astaire nimbly animating a studio prop or wiggle the iron along a shirtsleeve in time to whatever melody she was duetting with on the wireless. She seemed to only need to hear something once and every phrase would be committed to memory. It is a trait of hers that I have inherited and, when applied to anecdote and conversations, it has provided the essential core to my broadcasting career. Watching her dance through the chores, I would often remark on her total recall and in reply she would underline to me how important were the words to a tune.

'It's the main thing, boy – you don't learn the words and you might as well be humming any old thing. It's so important to know what a song means. Without the words, it's only half finished. Mind you, some of 'em ain't worth a light . . . '

Spud could not see this. 'If you spend all your time wondering what comes next you'd never sing a fucking note!' he once explained to me. 'Just get on with it. People don't give two fucks what you're saying, so long as they can join in at the title. That's all they want. Take no notice of y'mother – make the fucking words up.'

And that gunshot you just heard was Sir Tim Rice walking off into the woods. Anyway, the point is that between Mum's gift for melody and lyrics and Dad's unfettered gusto, I ended up having the best of both worlds and could actually perform pretty impressively. While not blessed with a complete six-octave range, I was surprisingly flexible and rejoiced in singing not only growlers like Lee Marvin's 'Wanderin' Star' but also 'A Cockeyed Optimist' from *South Pacific* in Mitzi Gaynor's stratospheric original key. Similarly, I could do a passable Barry White, as well as the falsetto parts from the Stylistics' hits without going overly cross-eyed. The only song in this higher pitch that ever defeated me was Kate Bush's 'Wuthering Heights', a setback that bothered me until I found there isn't a man – and very few women – on this planet who can successfully tackle that notoriously tricky timbre.

I came a terrible cropper on live TV once when I attempted to sing Bowie's 'Life on Mars' accompanied by none other than Rick Wakeman, the song's original pianist. Now I suppose I must have sung along to 'Life on Mars' a couple of hundred times in my life, so perhaps that was why I charged into it in front of a huge studio audience without even the most cursory of rehearsals. I mean, 'Life on Mars'? We can all do 'Life on Mars', can't we? Well, let me tell you we most certainly can not.

It came as a huge shock to me that I could not sing 'Life on Mars' and it was made all the worse by the watching crowd exploding into helpless laughter, like the entire performance was some kind of slapstick gag. It most certainly was not; in fact, up until the crash I had entertained visions of people nudging each other during the number and saying, 'Hey, this kid can really sing!' If it had been any other song – apart from 'Wuthering Heights' – they would have, too. However, the thing with 'Life on Mars' is that it contains a vocal leap that, in everyday renditions, most of us tend to craftily duck. It comes right after the phrase 'Take a look at the' and just before the word 'sailor'. As Rick and I unrolled the classic that night I began strong enough but could soon sense trouble ahead as, for the first time, I noticed how right from the off the tune ascends a sort of harmonic stairway. Normally, I suppose, I would have started this stairway at its base, which would have meant I could soar to 'sailor' about two thirds of the way up, though at the limit of my upper range. However, because he was there at its creation, Rick launched into 'Life on Mars' in its original key that even Bowie found a bit challenging after 1973.

Almost forty and as fat as a house, I stood no chance. By the time I got to the bit about spitting in the eyes of fools my face had already gone purple and my neck muscles strained so grotesquely I was waiting for my shirt collar to give way. I should have backed out then but, well, everyone was watching, cameras were turning and somewhere deep inside I still held hope that I might yet somehow successfully scale the north face of the sailor. Suddenly, there it was. Gamely I used every beat of 'take a look at the' as though it were a pole-vaulter's run-up and then flung myself across the chasm. To be fair, I think I made it about a third of the way over before I realized I hadn't a hope in hell of making the note. Instead I emitted a noise like a stricken narwhal as my throat first ruptured then appeared to implode in on itself. The audience fell about and Rick shot me a look as if to say, 'Oh, are we playing this for laughs? I wish you'd told me', his genius hands now hanging motionless above the keyboard.

There are various other examples of me singing on TV and radio where I manage to complete all sorts of songs, many extremely complicated in both tone and structure, without ever once panicking the paying punters. However, I know it will be this moment of me squawking, buckle-eyed, puce-faced and with the veins in my neck bulging like dockside ropes that will one day be the very last thing left on YouTube acting as permanent testimony to both my hubris and apparently tin ear. Sadly, today I can no longer muster a performance to counter this sole outrage in my once proud canon, for what was once a sweet nightingale's lilt is now a coarse raven's croak.

In terms of outward appearance I came away virtually unscathed. True, the skin of my neck, from certain angles, does concertina rather, but this is my own fault. So thorough is the care provided by the National Health Service that, when well enough, I was offered a course of one-on-one meetings with a masseuse who was going to guide me through a regime of exercises that would help prevent the ravaged areas from visually becoming like an Ordnance Survey map of the Lake District. Out of courtesy, I attended the first meeting but knew I wouldn't stick it out. She was a wonderful professional working in a small room in Guy's, but as soon as our pleasantries were over and she began to show me the peculiar jaw and head swivels I needed to perform three times a day so as not to go baggy in the throat area, I bailed on her request. In fact, the idea that I would even attempt a few of the movements that morning while she looked on brings a blush to my cheek even now. Imagine a sort of New Age gurning contest crossed with one of those acting classes where everyone pretends to be a Digestive biscuit and I think you'll see my problem.

Elsewhere, I still have a pronounced pea-sized dimple at the top of my stomach where the feeding tube had made its entrance, and, though not quite an outward sign, the pads of skin on the soles of my feet beneath my toes both still tingle away with pins and needles. The sensation is constant and is exactly like half a dozen electric toothbrushes are scouring away under the skin searching for the exit. And that's it really. Not a bad final bill for what I went through.

Perhaps the biggest blessing, though, was that my speaking voice returned without blemish and I returned to my regular radio shows undimmed and, as far as the audience reaction went, like Lazarus upon a solid gold chariot. The general goodwill extended as far as newspaper articles describing me as 'a national treasure' – a proud term I currently share with about 59,000 other old fossils still cluttering up show business – and being asked to appear on *Desert Island Discs.*

It says something about my insatiable cultural curiosity that up until I received the *Desert Island Discs* invite, though fully aware of the show's august reputation, I had never actually heard it. In fact I don't think I'd ever heard anything on Radio 4. Radio 3 either, come to that. Or, and I know you won't believe me here but it is absolutely true, Radio 2. (That Radio 1 and I parted company about the time Thunderclap Newman was in the charts is a given.) This of course is not to my credit, but the radio wasn't much of a feature in our house growing up and so I have never learned to romance the medium in the way so many broadcasters do. *Housewives' Choice, Family Favourites* and *Sing Something Simple* were the only wireless staples back in Debnams Road, with the 'gram otherwise only getting fired up for a midweek cup-tie or heavyweight boxing bout. Even the comedy greats that so nourished and nurtured me in my formative years were originally brought to my ears via vinyl records loaned from the Spa Road library and until I was about thirteen I thought Tony Hancock and The Goons had only made about twenty shows between them.

Of course I knew about the *Desert Island Discs* format – you give them some records and the host will, in turn, reveal your soul – but even though this seemed like a good enough gag, I'd never been curious enough to actually dial the show up. Similarly, I only recognize the theme from *The Archers* because of its use in sketches parodying Ambridge on TV. I retain the information that *The Archers* is set in Ambridge because that stops one looking like a total chump when the reference gets dropped into conversation, but that's as far as it goes. However, when it came to my song selection for *Desert Island Discs* I did feel a certain amount of pressure – as I'm sure all its contestants do. (Actually 'contestants' makes this revered programme sound a bit like *Supermarket Sweep*, doesn't it? 'Subjects' is a better fit possibly.)

Anyway, after a few days of trying to pare my life's obsession down to essentially twenty minutes of ragtime, I threw in the towel. There was no point in attempting to impress the assembled lorgnettes by taking a mallet to my musical tastes and hammering in both Emerson Lake & Palmer and Ella Fitzgerald, or welding Mountain to Mozart just to prove what a rounded repertoire I possess. So I decided to go with the first eight songs I remember liking before I reached the age of five. These magnificent old warhorses, I felt, had been with me the longest, I still played them, and so they alone deserved to play me out on the mythical castaway creek. They were:

1. Helen Shapiro, 'Marvellous Lie'
2. Bing Crosby, 'Ain't Got a Dime to My Name'
3. Max Bygraves, 'Underneath the Arches'
4. Dean Martin, 'A Day in the Country'
5. Tommy Steele, 'What a Mouth'
6. Peter Sellers, 'I'm So Ashamed'
7. Cliff Richard, 'The Next Time'
8. Bernard Cribbins, 'I've Grown Accustomed to Her Face'

On reflection, I think that was exactly the right thing to do. Even typing up the names and titles makes me feel as though I'm once again back in the midst of my dearest, oldest friends. On the show, though, I was continually probed as to whether this reduction of my life in and around music to a handful of comforting toddler tunes was in itself psychologically telling. I just as continually assured the expert host Kirsty Young that it was not. It was simply a good angle, I thought, and probably gave airtime to some tunes the show didn't play very often. There were also one or two probes about Mum and Dad which seemed to suggest that, if I wanted to wow the crowd with a wobbly lip and a few tears, now would be a great time. This didn't happen of course, mainly because I could almost see the ghost of the old man standing behind Kirsty, rolling his eyes. Also, as I pointed out in an exchange that was understandably cut from the final broadcast, I was quite happy if need be to change any of my choices because we were, after all, only fooling about in a radio studio and not signing an affidavit. This, I know, goes against the spirit of the long-running sketch but my natural instinct as a broadcaster is to fan away any whiff of the confessional and get on with cheering people up. My cancer got a few questions as well, again quite understandably, but I made it clear that I didn't find it an interesting subject. Besides, it was bad enough living it recently without so swiftly wishing to re-live it.

On the whole, the programme seemed to go over well enough and it's now on the *DID* website – a resource I plunder before any long journeys these days. The picture atop my page there is from pre-illness days and you will note how very like a Halloween pumpkin is the girth of my happy old head.

Shortly after this assumed accolade came a quite literal one. I was told I was to be inducted into the Radio Academy Hall of Fame. Again, without wishing to play down every nice thing that happens to me, I am aware that getting gifted a place in the Radio Academy Hall of Fame, while being several rungs superior to the Lewisham Kwik-Fit Employee of the Month Club, is not recognized by the public as much as, say, a BAFTA Fellowship. However, once I found out that my peers in the RAHOF included both Arthur Askey and Jimmy Clitheroe, I was straight on the phone to my tailor to warn him he might need to top up his stock of high-end cummerbund cloth.

Little did I know that by the time I would eventually be inducted and stand on stage receiving the fulsome applause of my peers, I would barely be in the radio industry at all. This, as we shall see, would not be my choice.

Just One Victory

T he Sony Gold award, *Desert Island Discs* ('one of the most recognizable voices on the airwaves...') and the Radio Academy Hall
of Fame invite all came in quick succession, and these in turn were
followed by another broadcasting institution: the Call to Abolish
BBC Local Radio. Now whenever this hardy annual of the Beeb's
detractors rolls around an equally vociferous gaggle of Protectors of
Local Radio form ranks on the other side of the fence to make faces
at those who want to see an end to Radio Cornwall and the like. My
show, at BBC Radio London, was often held up as one of the shining
lights of local broadcasting that would be lost if such philistinism
prevailed, and so it was in this particular round of the perennial
exchange. I was happy to aid the cause in this way although I hoped
nobody would ever point out that my show was just about the least
local show on the air. Indeed, at times, its content barely belonged
to Planet Earth.

For a start there were the two superlative co-hosts that assisted me
in doling out the daily hoopla, Amy Lamé and Baylen Leonard. Amy
was from Keyport, New Jersey, and Baylen from Bristol, Tennessee,
and while both were now settled in the capital we rarely spoke about
that. Then there was a third contributor who basically only showed
up when he had nothing better to do – his day job was as an international financial advisor – and who was Chinese. David Kuo looks
like the singer John Denver, had John Denver been born a native
of Beijing. From an immensely privileged background – his junior
school uniform was *all white* – his guileless delivery and bulletproof
optimism, coupled with a keen yet apparently unconscious sense of

the absurd, fascinated listeners, who were never quite sure if he was an actor playing a role. He wasn't.

I had inherited David when I took over a show on which he had been the bloke who turns up to tell you, in two minutes, how 'the markets' were looking that day. This naturally held no interest for me and I gently told him so on the very first morning we were thrown together. Instead of taking umbrage, he exploded with laughter and said, 'I know. It's terrible, isn't it! Nobody cares!' Moments before he had come on air I had been performing a semi-regular piece in which, backed by the theme from *Star Trek*, I made a series of urgent noises that suggested that I was experiencing astral projection. David seized the moment:

'You know you were pretending to astral project a few minutes ago?'

'I wasn't pretending, David. I *was* astrally projecting. It is a radio staple – please don't let daylight in upon magic.'

'Well, OK, you know you were having an astral projection a few minutes ago?'

'Of course, I've just got back, hence the towel.'

'Well,' he went on with a chuckling delivery that is his trademark, 'I have done that for real and it's a very unnerving experience.'

'David. What did you just say?'

'I mean, I wasn't looking to leave my body, it just happened.'

Now, ladies and gentlemen, I didn't care if the producer at that moment told me that the Prime Minister had just resigned. David Kuo was plainly not going to be kept to his two minutes that day.

'Well, briefly—'

'Oh please, don't be brief,' I urged him, plumping up a cushion.

'Well, I was in a flat on the fifteenth floor of a block in Hong Kong and I wanted to get a piece of fruit from the bowl that was on the other side of the room but I was quite tired because I had just sat down after a lot of running on the spot.'

I warned him the story better start picking up some momentum.

'It does, it does. Anyway I don't know why, but I tried to mentally cause one of the oranges to levitate over to me.'

It was at this point in what till then had been an unexpected diversion from our financial correspondent that I sensed one of those glorious broadcasting moments when nobody listening could possibly walk away from their radios.

'Had you levitated anything before?' I asked in an awed voice.

'No,' said David, as though I'd simply asked him if he'd ever been to Aberystwyth. 'Well, not successfully anyway. But this time I thought I saw it wobble a little so I went to get a bit closer to it, but as I stood I fell through the floor and plummeted down.'

'You went through the floor?' I gasped.

'Yes, in fact through quite a few until I reached about the fourth floor, whereupon I shot straight back up again.'

There was then a silence as we both regarded each other. Me, dumbfounded and intrigued; he with the satisfied air of someone who knows he's just told you something fresh. In my experience, when you have a piece of solid-gold radio like this in your lap, the last thing you do is respond too hard or, worse, try and top it with a smart remark. I let the dead air reign for about five seconds – something all good presenters know you never try and fill with a clichéd whistle or throat clearance – before pressing him further, my voice close to the microphone and awash with wonder.

'So. Did you see anything on your travels?'

'Oh yes, I was fully aware,' he continued brightly. 'I could see everyone in their apartments going about their business as I dropped through.'

Again, nothing but the clock ticking. Then:

'And did you raise your hat to them as you went through?'

'Oh! No, no, no, no, no . . . ' He found that idea risible. 'They couldn't see me, I don't think, or else they would have thrown stuff at me.'

'Right. And once you catapulted back to your own flat again; what did you think then?'

'Well, I was shocked, obviously, but once I'd stopped shaking I found it most interesting. I had read about such things.'

'I see. And, last thing, why do you think you only went down to the fourth floor? Why didn't you keep going to the centre of the earth?'

'That's a good question. I think it has to do with energy reserves. I only had enough psychic energy to take me down to the fourth.'

'And the levitating orange?'

'I just walked over and got one in the end, though I would often go through the floor after that.'

This extraordinary tale was no one-off. The next day he was back and, somehow, we got on to the subject of what are and aren't acceptable ways to accessorize pets. Recapping a story I'd told about my brother wanting to paint the shell of our tortoise with the Union Jack – he was talked out of it – David revealed that as a young boy he had kept a pet chicken to whose claws each day he would apply a fresh coat of coloured varnish. David was devoted to this chicken and it broke his eight-year-old heart when one day it went missing. His dad even took him round local houses with a photograph of the bird, asking if it had been seen in any of their yards. No luck. After a while his father sat young David down and told him that these things happen, a new chicken would come along one day and that the best policy was always, 'Don't cry for the loss, give thanks that you had him at all.' Kuo Minor consoled himself with this until the next day when at dinner he couldn't help but notice that whatever creature was being served up had vivid blue toenails on the end of its leg. With a scream of outrage he confronted his parents, who put the blame on the family's cook (I said they were loaded). When he steamed into the kitchen to demand answers as to why his beloved pet was now his beloved lunch, the cook assured him that his father had told her it was OK to make a stew of his son's favoured fowl. Incredibly, David calmed down and took a philosophical view of this.

'It was then,' he said ruefully, 'that I realized that our family, who had been chased off the mainland by the Communists, were tightening their belts and I had to do my bit too.'

'So did you finish dinner?' I asked.

'Oh yes, absolutely,' he replied without a shred of emotion. 'Waste not, want not and all that.'

This then was my introduction to David Kuo. And the four of us, along with producer Julia McKenzie, whose zeal at temporarily decorating whatever studios we found ourselves in often reached a state of High Art, created a radio world of which I remain hugely proud. Wherever we found a home on the network, the shows we made remain the best work I have done across my entire career. In 2012, once again, our output did its part in earning BBC local radio a reprieve from the budgetary axe. And this is where I find I must reach for the phrase, thanks a lot, you dirty, lousy, ungrateful bastards.

Right to the end, Amy, Baylen, David and I would arrive with a blank sheet of paper and a boxful of wildly eclectic music and tear a show out of the ether. Instead of yet another interview with whatever deadbeat local politician was looking into the upcoming budget cuts in Barnet, the listeners responded in their droves to such subjects as 'What Have You Used to Dry Yourself with?' 'Poor Prizes You've Won', ' 'Why, as an Adult, Have You Had to Hide?' and 'Improvised Eating Utensils'. During a typical show there would be about ten such topics requesting contributions, and the public never failed to magnificently respond to these seemingly impossible subjects.

For example: Improvised Eating Utensils. After a solid few entries on this, including polishing off a pot of yoghurt by sucking it up through a hollowed-out Biro and eating a curry from a credit card, a chap called in and regaled us with the following tale. It appears he and a few of his circle had been out enjoying a few drinks one Sunday along the Old Kent Road. Eventually emerging from the pub, they found they still had a little time on their hands and upon passing a nearby army surplus store decided to explore its stock. There is little doubt that the alcohol made these otherwise resistible items of kit and clothing suddenly appear essential and the party spent a good deal of their remaining cash on flak jackets, torches, unwieldy boots, itchy balaclavas and camouflage trousers.

Out into the afternoon air once more and the group found

themselves to be quite ravenous, so they made their way towards the Hole in the Wall. At the mention of this long-vanished restaurant, I confess I began salivating like a cartoon cannibal. Well, perhaps the word 'restaurant' is over-aggrandizing the venue. The Hole in the Wall wasn't even a café. It had no tables, chairs or waiters. It was, in actual fact, a hole in the wall. Imagine if someone had taken one of those hamburger vans you see at funfairs or outside football matches and shoved it sideways into the side of a dilapidated building. Even that makes the Hole in the Wall sound more salubrious than it was. It was a ramshackle, single-counter open aperture set at an inconvenient height surrounded by collapsed fencing and which announced its presence via a crudely worded home-made billboard that extended over the pavement and was lashed on to the lamp post outside.

Had the Hole in the Wall simply sold hamburgers, chips and hot pies, as might be the case these days, then it would not be the South London legend that it is for those of us who were fortunate enough to queue 'neath its misspelled menu. For the Hole in the Wall was one of the last outlets that exclusively sold the sort of succulent working-class fare once commonplace but that today has completely vanished. It sold hot steaming saveloys, salt beef, faggots and pease pudding, all ladled out in generous heart-stopping portions and sold at prices that could make the then rising Wimpy Bars look like the choice of the Rothschilds. Until the mid 1980s quite a few of the butcher's shops in the more ragged parts of London retained 'hot counters' selling such manna, but nobody could touch the Hole in the Wall. Those of you who don't know what it is to take in your fingers a hot swollen sav, its fluorescent red skin rippled and bursting, then to dunk it hard into a rich mound of vinegar-drenched pease pudding, next withdrawing it to admire this creamy yellow crown before finally chomping down the over-moist bulging mouthful, *literally haven't lived*. And faggots! Those dark, peaty cannonball-shaped cousins of the haggis, full of meaty punch and slight peppery aftertaste . . . Oh man, I might have to finish this book here to go and forever feast upon this lost ambrosia until a heart attack takes me off to a fat and happy afterlife. I swear, if I found out that death row was the only place on earth where you still could get food like George served up at the Hole in the Wall, I'd start sharpening up an axe and go looking for a particularly venal politician or banking executive. It would be worth it.

Anyway, such was the lure that led our boozy army surplus gang to pass all other vendors and keep their eye on the prize. However, on rounding the corner into Dunton Road, where this inelegant eatery squatted, their hearts sank to see George shutting up shop for the day. Quickening their pace, they were soon waving pound notes at him hoping the sight of hard currency might find a reprieve and spring the desired portions. The proprietor apologized but said that while it was true they could see quite a lot of what they fancied still under glass, his associate had already left with all the cartons, wrappings, knives and forks necessary to carry the food off. (The Hole in the Wall had no premises attached.) There seemed to be no hope for them, until George wondered aloud, 'Unless you've got anything you could take it away in . . . ' It was at this moment my caller said he saw that the company's impromptu stop at the surplus store had been no drunken impulse. It was kismet, pure and simple, with one item in particular, *one that he almost hadn't bought,* that he now saw would, in fact, save the day. It was a pith helmet. Taking the glorious pith from his head, he looked George square in his honest trader's eye and stoutly said, 'Fill 'er up!'

And so it was that this dome-shaped symbol of empire was soon filled deep with the best pease pudding in London then adorned with a coronet of all the remaining saveloys. The gang trooped off happy and triumphant, helping themselves to the communal bounty. 'Never did a meal taste so good,' said the caller, and I can understand that completely.

On air, so enamoured was I with this story that I vowed to call any future autobiography I might write 'A Pith Helmet Full of Saveloys'. Well, that promise was reneged upon, as we know, but at least here I can once again share it with, I trust, a suitably impressed public. Certainly I hope you would rather be reading that than a reminiscence about how it's getting harder to park your car in Catford, which, trust me, is what some BBC executives believe Marconi went to all that trouble for. While I'm sure there'll always be kudos to be earned by endlessly highlighting the problems and 'issues' of living in London, the manic, ridiculous, life-affirming free-for-all that was created in total partnership with our audience each day reflected the spirit of living in one of the greatest cities in the world better than any amount of generic news-based bullshit that was all the university-schooled, media-studies-emboldened vampires who now controlled BBC local radio could come up with.

Are you beginning to sense we fell out with each other? I wouldn't have minded so much had not these same tepid crumbs so recently shanghaied me as poster boy to save their own dreary jobs.

The final incarnation of the show was broadcast from three to five on weekday afternoons. This, I must tell you, is not the most cherished bit of real estate on the radio schedule map. I had worked at the station on and off for many years during which times it seemed to change its name roughly every fortnight: Radio London, Greater London Radio, GLR, BBC LDN, 94.9, BBC London, BBC Radio London – all of these phrases, numbers and acronyms would be desperately juggled, hoping to bring an upswing in its otherwise moribund profile. Along with Baylen, Amy and David, I had worked various shifts, all with considerable success – including the station's breakfast show, though I had given that up when the five o'clock alarm calls, accompanied by the necessary early nights, began to outweigh the job satisfaction.

Eventually, I was asked to return to have a go at their flat-lining afternoons. At first I said no, but when Wendy pointed out to me, 'Well, you'll only be upstairs playing records anyway – you might as well go and get paid for it . . . ' I saw some truth in that. To be honest, and not a little vulgar, the money was hardly a siren call. Local radio means local radio, no matter how vital or teeming the catchment area, and I would be signing on for a fee that, after deductions, was basically £250 a show. Now some may feel that's still a fair exchange for goofing about, but I remind you I had been on the radio for more than two decades and was widely regarded as one of the best in the business, with a show that despite its presumed perimeters was listened to by people all over the world. Across the corridor, my network colleagues would be raking in ten times that. Your jaw may truly hit the floor when I tell you that the trio of wonderful co-hosts who aided me and earned all the accolades and industry awards right alongside me, got a flat fifty quid. That's fifty quid *before deductions*. In London. They would also sometimes be asked to man the station's switchboard too. So why did we do it? Well, corny and homespun as it sounds, it was such breathless, unbounded, terrific fun. God, we enjoyed ourselves, and, while that in itself shouldn't entitle you to employment, so did the audience. True, a good deal of them tuned in for our show then tuned straight back out again, but that wasn't our fault.

The first inkling I had that management resented the tallest poppy on its poster was when some new nerdy little pipsqueak that I had never seen before came into the room where, five minutes before show time, the participants of that day's show would often assemble. We had never had so much as a single note from what people refer to as 'the suits' before, so we thought it must be some sort of meet-and-greet social call. She introduced herself and I believe I was effusive in welcoming her to the Good Ship Tree House. (The show, no matter where it was on the schedules, was always known as The Tree House.) She seemed confused by this and then got down to the real reason she had swung by. It was to tell me how to do a radio show. To add insult to injury, it was specifically to tell me how to do a radio show that featured the Beatles. I mean, honestly! This was like a government official coming round my house to offer me advice on how to watch televised football while nicely pissed on white wine.

The occasion that had sparked the gormless intrusion was the fiftieth anniversary of the Beatles recording 'Love Me Do'. A valid enough reason for celebration, I'll grant you, but it was the utter vacuousness of the approach that astounded me and made me think that, if these were the sort of people gaining control of the place, I would not be figuring in their numbing plans. The conversation went like this:

'Right so, I don't know if you are aware, but we're doing a thing about the Beatles here next week because they recorded their first song fifty years ago.'

'OK. I play the Beatles every day, so maybe we'll mark it by playing nothing but the Monkees.'

Unhelpful I know, but I had meant this as a joke. She looked a bit put out by it.

'No, we want every show to join in, that's the point,' she said frostily.

Sensing an element of dim bulb about the woman, I offered a conciliatory hand. 'OK, I'll come up with a pip of an idea, we shall excel, don't worry.'

This didn't placate her and she carried on with the mission as agreed at whatever terrible meeting had spawned it.

'I mean, you could ask your audience . . .'

My eyes widened.

' . . . I don't know, something like, "Call in and tell us what *your* favourite Beatles record is".'

I promise you, that's what she said. At that moment I knew that my kind of radio was as doomed as the dinosaur. If midget corporate thinking like that was the future, then what chance phone-ins like 'Your Worthless Pop Memorabilia, Please', 'What Famous People Said to You in Dreams' and 'When Your Gift for Imitating Farmyard Animals Came in Handy'.

Nope, the Technicolor age was coming to a close. The era of vanilla was upon me.

A bit later, the station had the dreadful idea of sending its presenters out to broadcast their shows from a specially painted doubledecker bus parked up in a different London borough each day. Why, nobody knows. Not a single soul I have ever met gives two fucks about from where a radio show is broadcast. Just make it good, chum, that'll do the trick. I mean, seriously, has anybody ever said,

'Well, that was a load of shit but at least it was local.' So of course I refused to join the pointless and frankly ignoble cavalcade around the various shopping centres within the M25, and once more I guess the dopes who see such limping stunts as 'being part of the community' duly noted it. I think the bus even had a few branded balloons tied to it, so help me God.

Then one day at around lunchtime I was at home burning the two or three custom CDs I took in each day to freshen up the act when the phone went and I was told that the show was finished, at best being moved to a single spot on Sundays. I won't lie to you, my months of silence while enduring the cancer treatment seemed like a fleeting moment compared to the aeons I spent, dumb and stupefied, staring at the phone receiver after hearing the news. My latest Broadcaster of the Year Award had so recently taken its place on the shelf behind me that not a single speck of dust had so far had a chance to settle upon it. Worse still, the following Wednesday I was scheduled to go to Manchester and be cemented in the Radio Pantheon of Blessed Immortals alongside Jimmy Clitheroe and Arthur Askey! Yet, somehow, between these two noisy top-level hurrahs from my industry I was to be quietly 'let go' from local radio? What?

Well, as Spud himself would have so perfectly put it: 'Fuck. That.'

The journey from my home in Blackheath to the BBC London studios in Portland Place takes about forty minutes. Every second of the journey that day doubled down on my bubbling ire. Look, I had been fired plenty of times before, both on TV and radio, and on most of those occasions I could completely see why the hierarchy had decided to hand me my dinner pail. I mean, Radio 1 for example – what was I even doing on there? Good though those shows were, I think I was all of a hundred and two years old when I first started spooking out the nation's pop kids. At other times it's been me who made the decision to suddenly steam out of a production like the *Scharnhorst* being pursued by the fleet. I impetuously said goodbye to £50,000 once after falling out with the script editor on a show called *Hell's Kitchen* and bolting from the studio I conjured up language so ripe it made Gordon Ramsay stand up and applaud. My good friend Jonathan Ross still isn't sure if it was me or a foul-mouthed version of Halley's Comet that flew past him on the stairs of his production company after another of my dramatic exits.

The thing is, I have never put so much store by any one job that it could make a coward of my self-respect. Equally, I do not brood, plot or complain once a pay cheque and I have been rent asunder. Not for me hissed plotting in corridors, waspish emails or pointed retaliatory think-pieces in the *Guardian*. No, I find the only way to achieve satisfaction and catharsis in a soured workplace is to walk up to the parties involved and let them know exactly where everybody stands. This was uppermost in my thinking as the wheels of the underground train ground to a screeching halt at Bond Street tube and I alighted the carriage with the determined stride of a man on a mission. What happened next made media headlines for weeks afterwards, wound up on the TV's evening news and, I have to say, was rattling good fun.

Churning across Cavendish Square towards Broadcasting House, the dudgeon pulsing through me was now so intense I fancy I was actually making the noise of a steam locomotive as I walked. Into the building I bundled and, not waiting for the lift, took the stairs, bounding up them two steps at a time.

Striding into the large open-plan office, I opened up at full tilt and without support act.

'Anybody else know they were getting rid of us from up here?' I thundered at a volume I was later told shook windows in far-off Krakatoa. Now be aware I had dozens of very good friends in the department, I had no argument with anyone but a specific trio of management and this initial volley was meant to be little more than a bellowed 'all staff' email. A stunned silence naturally followed the kaboom until eventually one of my chums asked what on earth I was talking about. This response could not have been better timed, for at that exact moment out of a meeting room at the far side of the office came the guilty three.

'Oh here we go!' I roared, and felt a keen thrill rising at what they were about to receive, every bit as vital as the recent cancer had been draining. I was back! The sober-suited group looked ashen. 'You weasels!' I began, if anything cranking up the decibels. 'You lousy, no good, slippery weasels!' Despite the fury, I was choosing my words carefully. Though I enjoy swearing enormously in everyday conversation and particularly at inanimate objects, I knew fights with authority were best punctuated with the comic. One of their number attempted to contain the carnage by saying we should conduct the discussion in private.

'Yes, you'd love that, wouldn't you? In one of your suffocating meeting cubicles, I suppose? Well, no! Embarrassing isn't it, being singled out? Well you're not safely minimizing this one, mate – let's let everyone know how you dreary pen-pushers operate. Plus, you seem to forget, I don't fucking work for you no more!' I allowed myself the one f word in alerting them for the first time that I would not be working out a winding-down period to allow safe transference of my programme to their chosen pliant plant.

I think it was about this moment that popcorn sellers began walking the aisles of the open-plan doing a brisk trade. I'd like to say that the following two or three minutes were what might be termed a 'ding-dong' row, but in truth it was simply a monologue, a broadside. As I rolled out a series of ludicrous descriptive slights – 'crumbs', 'dim bulbs' and 'weasels' yet again – such was their disbelief that my ding failed to garner from them even a cursory reciprocal dong. I do remember coming to the end of one flaming outburst after which I shamefully paused in case spontaneous applause might result. It went like this:

'Let me tell you something. If there's one thing that sums up the timid, moribund miasma of grey thinking and rock-bottom morale that is choking local radio in this country, it's the fact that I am going and you three, YOU THREE, are staying!'

I remember thinking, 'Oh that was pretty good, Baker!' even as I said it, but of course it didn't solicit even a single handclap from the onlookers, who were frankly too agog at events. When I write the stage show of this though, it most certainly will get a ripple – and thunderously so – possibly followed by a swift curtain and the interval.

I do remember one of the hapless triumvirate attempting some sort of corporate muscle-flexing toward the end of my spiel, saying something along the lines of, 'Well, you can forget all about the offer of a Sunday show now . . .'

I responded with a piece of theatre that if I saw it in a script I would excise the passage for being too far-fetched. Stunned at the presumption of the piss-poor threat, I let out an agonized groan before turning round and bending over. 'You,' I said, pointing to my right buttock, 'kiss this side, and you,' I indicated his colleague, 'kiss that side.' I promise you, that's exactly what happened. Afterwards, hunkering down in a nearby pub, an awestruck Baylen Leonard told me that though he was aware of such audacious choreography he had never seen it performed in real life before.

And then, guess what? I picked up my headphones and box of records and headed toward the studio. If legions of security guards had blocked my entrance to it, I would have had no complaint. Even as I sat down in my chair at the mic, I fully expected to be asked to leave the building while an emergency reel of soothing tunes was broadcast in my stead. But no. So dense were the various layers of management that plainly such a swift decision could not be arrived at until a meeting room became available and the proposal was agreed then carried forward to the next gathering of a higher quorum, whereupon it might be discussed by the relevant committee who may, at a later date, consider it worth putting before the board.

It was this typical paralysis that allowed me to charge forth and perform the Viking funeral of a show that has, to some extent, now passed into radio lore. It's all there on YouTube if you wish to hear it and, though it is remembered as a show steaming full of *Sturm und Drang*, it is also a very funny two hours, wherein I repeatedly allow the mood to drop and ask Baylen how it's all going. Even in its most bombastic moments I was fully aware that it was, above all, gripping radio, and after just twenty minutes we were trending at number one on Twitter. Not bad for a local radio show in the traditional doldrums spot.

When it was all over and I'd played the 'Candy Man' theme tune for the last time, overlaying it with the appropriate sound of fireworks, I had no idea what was going to happen. Sitting amid the still-smoking wreckage as the news jingle swept in, I looked over at the producer and my co-hosts and, as soon as the smiles had reached their zenith, announced we were going to the pub to get absolutely hammered. Gathering my things for the final exit, including the twenty-three boxes of mini-discs, each crammed with familiar inserts and sound effects, I hauled open the studio door still fully expecting to see a gathering of uniformed heavies waiting to give me the bum's rush. However what I saw was more akin to the final scene of *Goodbye, Mr Chips*. People had come from all over the BBC building and were lining the walls and corridors applauding me out.

I apologize if this seems like the most appalling self-mythologizing, but these are the facts and we're stuck with them. Apparently, the tone of the blow-up had acted as a lightning rod to much of the frustration felt by those at the sharp end of creating programmes and my hand was pumped and my back slapped as never before. Quite where the legions of weasels, poltroons and dim bulbs were at this time or what they made of such a popular revolution, I cannot say. Outside the building there were news camera crews and waiting journalists, all eager for me to continue the harangue. However in this I rather disappointed them. I was now in a terrific mood and the last thing I felt like I had mounted was some sort of personal crusade. The storm had well and truly passed; those who needed to get a soaking had received a thorough drenching and any point I wished to hammer home needed no further blows to secure it to the cathedral doors. Besides, I had not renounced the entire, and I have to say, beloved BBC, just a particular sect of nitwits within one of its more underperforming branches. As far as I was concerned, I would be back in the building seventy-two hours hence to be playing The Sausage Sandwich game on Radio 5 Live with a member of the UK lacrosse team. And so it proved.

It was, however, obvious that the story was not going to go away. I am assured that over the next few days the usual toing and froing went on in print and elsewhere with, at one point, the boss of BBC London having to go on his own station to explain to listeners the jumbled old thinking behind my ejection from the roster. What I understand they settled on was that this was simply the usual procedure at a network when the time had come to 'refresh' the schedules. *Refresh!* What a supreme weasel word, what a disingenuous shifty retreat. As I say, a few weeks previously I had been their human shield against the axe and much-ballyhooed sole award winner. That peculiarly I alone had to be 'refreshed' didn't seem worth addressing, though of course my replacement, whoever that might be, would be only too happy to conduct 'issue-based' phone-ins as directed and leap aboard corny double-decker buses. (Appropriately enough, the last time I heard it, the topic under discussion was what to do about hard skin on the feet.) Some said I had acted with arrogance at a time when several companies had gone to the wall and had laid off hundreds of staff. My reply to that is, when a firm dismisses hundreds it is, of course, a tragedy. But when a management decide to fire just one person – that is personal. And I reserve the right to retaliate personally.

So now we come to the following week and my seemingly totally bizarre induction into the Radio Academy Hall of Fame – an event rammed to the gunnels with every leading mover and shaker in the business and one at which I would be required to address the room with my thoughts on both the accolade and the industry in general. Arriving at the beautiful location for the ceremony, a former church in Manchester, I was aware my entrance caused something of an expectant frisson around the room. I scanned the tables at the rear, trying to determine where the BBC London delegation might be skulking but, wouldn't you know it, they had decided that they couldn't make the event that year after all. Oh, this was now weasellyness of a stratospheric order!

Despite this undoubted body blow, the Academy bravely voted to go on with the show. Good people received various encomiums,

Mick Hucknall sang some songs, Sir Alex Ferguson gave a speech – about what I can't recall – until we arrived at the grand finale. Peter Kay took the stage to introduce me. Peter was a long-time fan of the Treehouse – often turning up unannounced to sit in on it and read the odd email – and even though this entire passage is already swarming the borders of own-trumpet-blowing, I cannot bring myself to put before you what he said in his twenty-minute ad-libbed intro lest you wonder whether my head these days is required to wear one of those 'oversized vehicle' plates. As the room stood to greet my arrival onstage, I knew exactly what I was going to say. I let everyone get settled again and watched them lean ever so slightly forward, ready for me to put match to gunpowder. Here's exactly what I said in full:

> Thank you so much for that, and thank you to Peter for a magnificent introduction that I shall constantly replay in my head in what we can only describe as an orgy of self-congratulation. So. As you are probably aware, I accept this honour in the most peculiar of circumstances. There is so much I could say tonight, but this happy, generous occasion is neither the time nor the place. So just let me say, I appreciate this more than you know and I sincerely thank you all very, very much.

And off I walked, into the flashbulbs. I mean, what? Pow! Nothing like a bit of humility and graciousness to *really* make your enemies look like chumps, eh? BBC London's hierarchy had bottled it for that? For shame! What a bunch of lily-livered goofballs. Sure, everyone in the room felt a little cheated at first, like the crowd at a long-awaited heavyweight bout seeing it decided by the very first punch, but soon they were all coming over and shaking my hand, informing me such restraint was the hallmark of a class act. One or two, though, detected the method at work and said their chuckling 'bravo' with a wink. In subsequent years I have accepted several other broadcasting awards and, I confess, had a little more fun while on the dais. One running gag goes:

I'd like to start my speech by offering a sincere olive branch to my old foes, the management at BBC London, to whom I say, in all honesty, it's high time we buried the— Oh, hang on . . . what am I saying – they're not here tonight, are they? I forgot that. None of their output got nominated. Again.

I know, I know. Cheap, obvious and scratching open an old wound that nobody cares about any more. Except, I do. I will never forgive those dull-eyed twerps for taking away the finest, stupidest, most brilliant and original radio show on the air for no other reason than they didn't get it even if their audience did. Their stupid 'refreshing' was born of an envy of a freedom of spirit and a style of broadcasting that, because it didn't figure in their tedious time at Media and Business Studies, they seek to suppress.

Sadly, as you go around the radio dial these days, you can only surmise that they and their type are winning. My two-hour Saturday show on BBC Radio 5 Live continues to be supported and does very well, thank you. However, I am only too aware that the good people who run that network turn a blind eye to the fact that it doesn't fit in with anything else that might come under their brief as a 'vision' for the station. In fairness, it wouldn't fit in anywhere else either. It is a peculiar pirate ship moored in their waters and they are quite entitled to replace it one day with something more apposite, such as a conventional look forward to that day's sporting highlights. When they do, I will no longer be in radio at all. I will still be in the Radio Hall of Fame – just not actually on the radio. How's that for Wonderland logic? On the day this happens I will take all the glittering prizes down from my shelf and melt them in one of those giant fiery braziers in which you often see tar bubbling away beside roadworks. Then I will take the residue and strain it through a sieve until I have enough liquid to make a broth. I will double-boil this broth and drink deep of its rich golden goodness. What is left I shall keep until the next blood moon rises, whereupon, over an open fire on a ley line, I will turn it into smoke and watch it spiral up to the heavens, inhaling some of its vapour as it passes. Then I shall be satisfied. Then I shall be invincible. Then I shall have entered my own Radio Hall of Fame. Ladies and gentlemen, I thank you.

One last David Kuo story. David's parsimony is only matched by his bizarre tendency to cling to a set of superstitions so odd that listeners often worried about his mental health. A famous example of this is his belief that immersion in water has the ability to change the outcome of sporting events. Thus, should his team, Chelsea – a nauseating choice that still hasn't stopped me calling him a friend – fall behind in a televised match, his first reaction is to run a bath and jump in it. Following a disastrous evening at the roulette wheel, he once startled fellow gamblers in an expensive casino by decamping to the men's room, where he proceeded to remove his shoes and socks, and energetically wash his feet in the handbasin. 'The feet particularly,' he says in all seriousness, 'hold the key to one's luck.' This link between scrubbing one's plates and shortly thereafter coming into £££'s has never successfully been explained to me. He also believes that the number 4, not 666, is the number of the beast.

His meanness with money – given that he is a financial advisor and as rich as Croesus – should also see to it that he is the sort of person that I'd usually give the widest of berths, but the stories of his penny-pinching rarely have the outcomes he wished. My favourite among these is probably the time when, loath to pay for a removals van, he tried to do the job himself in an unending series of shuttles with his own hatchback. Finding the kitchen dishwasher too heavy to manipulate alone, he had the brainwave of fetching his daughter's old skateboard from the garage and wheeling the thing out to the car on that. This worked fine until he momentarily left it while he opened the boot. Now here you must know that David Kuo's house is on a hill. As he 'popped the trunk', he became aware of something gently rolling by him on the kerb behind. Sure enough, away went the weighty white goods on its skateboard down the incline, picking up momentum with every yard. Giving chase, and we can only hear the sound of a furiously picked banjo over this, he never quite caught up with the appliance until it hit a hedge and went flying, under its own steam, grinding and tumbling across the flagstones and finally smashing into the rear door of a parked car. One can only imagine that insurance workers, enjoying an after-work cocktail while swapping tales of incredible claims they have had to deal with over the years, often recount the details of this case and probably respectfully remove their hats as they do.

Today, David Kuo lives and broadcasts worldwide, albeit seriously, in Singapore. Baylen Leonard is a successful and familiar voice on national radio and Amy Lamé works for the Mayor of London, overseeing the capital's nightlife. So, all in all, a nice bit of talent management from our local wireless mandarins. But, dear God I miss that programme. And yes, if asked, I'd go back to it in a heartbeat, though it is probably not advisable to hold my breath until that happens.

Coda

The planet Venus is completely shrouded in swirling clouds of sulphuric acid and its atmosphere of 95 per cent carbon dioxide is permanently ravaged by colossal double-eyed hurricanes whose severity far outstrips anything known on Earth. Venus, scientists agree, is the most hostile climate in our solar system. And yet I, a layman, would ask the experts to hold their horses before rubber-stamping these findings.

It is March 2015 and I am on a hillside in Bolton. I'm sure I have been cold in my life before, but as I stand watching some young actors pretend to play football I realize that what I had taken for low temperatures previously were actually balmy days in the tropics. There are many old sweats in the TV crew, seasoned by decades of outdoor filming in locations ranging from mountain peaks to trawlers off the Iceland coast and yet, by common consent, all agree that these are extraordinary circumstances. It is bitter. Standing at the side of a pitch that didn't exist till we arrived and won't exist after we've gone, my layers – thermals, thick jumper and Puffa jacket – are as warming as wisps of satin against the elements. Inside my usually trusty boots, climate change deniers are citing my feet as proof that we have nothing to worry about. Meanwhile, out on the field, the poor lads taking part in the scripted action have only replica 1970s kits to defend themselves from the knives in every icy gust that roars down the slope. As if this weren't agony enough, the next scene requires it to be raining and so any minute now, Sandy Johnson, the director, will cue the several fire hoses raised on platforms to begin dousing the cast in an artificial storm.

We are filming the fifth episode of *Cradle to Grave*, the eight-part series based on the first of these books. That's right, we have now reached the point where autobiography is commenting upon autobiography. The title *Cradle to Grave* was insisted on by the BBC so it didn't look like we were overly promoting *Cradle to the Grave*, the soundtrack album by Squeeze, even though that's what the expression actually is and what the theme tune clearly said – on top of which, the band had provided all the original music in the shows.

I've known Chris Difford and Glenn Tilbrook – who in effect *are* Squeeze – since the late seventies. Chris and I attended the same school, and originally the pair had wanted to make a stage musical from the material, but I had already entered into a writing partnership with another old friend, Jeff Pope – or to give him his full name these days, Oscar-Nominated Jeff Pope.

On that day in Bolton we were recreating a 1969 West Greenwich first XI fixture from a competition called the Black Cup. In this fictional retelling, we had to weave the various threads and stories from *Going to Sea in a Sieve*, a period that in reality took place over the first fifteen years of my life, into a few months placed in a notional 1974. In the real 1974 I would have been at work in One Stop Records for well over a year and would have been a few years older than my screen self, magnificently realized by Laurie Kynaston, who in turn was actually twenty-one when we filmed *Cradle*. Keeping up with this?

Anyway, on that perishing day in Bolton, everyone's frostbite was prolonged further when one of the cameras broke down – possibly stomped on by a passing polar bear – just as the action required a corner kick to be taken. There were no Winnebagos or heated refuges to assemble in, so the cast did the only thing they could to keep in touch with their blood and continued running about playing football. Despite being lagged like the boiler at a nursing home, I ran on to the pitch to join in. Taking up a position in the penalty box, I waved an arm and bellowed to the actor taking the corner that if he could place the ball anywhere near me I'd show him why I was known as the Alf Wood of SE16. Rather like you are now, the assembled youngsters greeted my invoking of Alf Wood with a tremendous cross-section of puzzled stares. With chattering teeth I informed them, with not a little hauteur, that Alfred Edwin Howson 'Alf' Wood (born 25 October 1945) was Millwall's dynamic centre forward during the period under examination, and that any actor worth their salt ought to have known that from the deep background research necessary to get inside the skin of the character 'freezing non-speaking schoolboy number 6'. Over came the ball and I lashed at it madly, though my ankle-high Timberlands blunted my accuracy and sent the ball spinning crazily upwards. Not to be denied, I next attempted to head it towards the net, but this time the ball struck the peak of my baseball cap, causing the hat to fly off and cross the line instead.

Flailing about, I soon became aware of someone calling me. I no longer had the ball, so how could I be expected to distribute it in the way that once got me compared to Billy Neil (born 10 November 1944)? Then it became several voices and the tone more insistent. Looking toward the crew, I now saw them all waving their hands at me. I waved back. Then, cupping his hands around his mouth, Sandy yelled, 'Dan – get off the fucking pitch! We're still turning over on B camera!' Suddenly I saw all. Where I had believed because one camera had failed the entire unit had stopped for tea, in fact the show had, as it must, gone on. None of what they had shot was useable now though, unless Jeff and I could get together and quickly write a new scene explaining why this portly old boy in a Puffa jacket and sporting a top-of-the-range 21st-century iPod had suddenly gatecrashed a schoolboys' kickabout in 1974.

With apologies, I hastily ran to the sidelines. As I did, a startling truth occurred to me:

'Dear God. Have I just been told to fuck off out of my own life story?'

I most certainly had.

Well, as the old man was so fond of saying, there it is.